THE PHARAOHS'
5 LAWS
OF SUCCESS

FIRST EDITION

TARÍK KARENGA

AMENISM, INC.
Union City, California

The Pharaohs' 5 Laws of Success, First Edition

Published by Amenism, Inc.
1684 Decoto Road, #249
Union City, CA 94587

Copyright © 2022 by Tarík Karenga

All rights reserved. No part of this publication may be reproduced, stored in a retrieval system, or transmitted in any form, or by any means electronic, mechanical, photocopying, recording, or otherwise, without the written permission of the author and the publisher. The trade name "Amenism" is the property of Tarík Karenga.

The term "Amenism" herein refers to Amenism the religion according to the Reemergent Kingdom, which works interdependently with and is an integral part of the Kemetan Mystery System, so for all intents and purposes the religion and the Mystery System are virtually one and the same (Budge, 1923); (James, 1992); (Karenga, in press).

On the cover: Statue of Amenhotep III in the Luxor Museum
Photographer: Simon Hayter

Cover design: Tarík Karenga

ISBN 978-0-9669-7425-6

In honor of my father and mother:
Maulana Karenga, Ph.D.
and B. L. Scott, BA.

Contents

Introduction 1

1. Make Yourself Loved 3
2. Seek Wise Counsel 9
3. Empower Those Who You Influence 27
4. Become A Placemaker 31
5. Express Your Gratitude 39

   Conclusion 57

   Notes 61

   Bibliography 163

   Index 181

INTRODUCTION

"The wise feeds his ba (i.e., soul) with what endures."[1]
—Ptahhotep, Vizier to Pharaoh Isesi

O you who seek philosophy, history and theology, the kings of ancient Egypt were known as the Pharaohs and were among the greatest teachers, educators and instructors in all of human history.[2] Gazed upon as both human and divine, they ruled and directed the actions and affairs of their people;[3] however, their own actions were compliant with Divine Law[4] that was founded upon a divine, universal organizing principle called *Maat* (mah-AHT),[5] which the ancient Egyptians taught was established at the time of creation, and which God joined to a person's heart at birth.[6]

Thus the Pharaohs were charged with establishing, maintaining and, if necessary, reestablishing *Maat* for the well-being of the community[7] and they skillfully undertook this massive responsibility by constantly and systematically engaging *Maat* ". . . in all areas of moral concern"[8] and human activity,[9] which induced the members of the community to assist them in achieving this exacting task.[10] For example, Pharaoh Amenhotep III said that he desired "to make the country flourish as in primeval times by means of the designs of *Maat*."[11] Upon achieving this lofty objective, Pharaoh Sethi I received the following praise: "You have fixed *Maat* in Egypt; it has become united with everyone."[12] From the foregoing statement we may infer that a desired result was produced from specific value-driven action steps executed by the Pharaoh and then constantly role modeled by each person in the community to ensure long term success. Simply put, it became a team effort initiated by the king, and it is one of the primary reasons that ancient Egypt, from its very first emergence as an earthly kingdom to the arrival of the Arabs and to its subsequent conversion to the foreign religion of Islam, endured for more than 7,000 years,[13] while at the same time making important contributions to the world in the Arts and Sciences,[14] testifying to a people's tremendous ". . . capacity for human greatness and progress."[15]

The Pharaohs' 5 Laws of Success is in essence a reintroduction to the philosophy, history, and theology of our ancient Egyptian ancestors who resolved to design and live their lives not based on mere contemporary standards of the day, but on eternal truths that remain just as relevant to our personal, social and professional success today as they were in antiquity. Moreover, by raising up and restoring these three pillars of the Reflective Arts in our daily life, together, we can achieve true and lasting success for ourselves and also for one another.[16] Here, then, begins *The Pharaohs' 5 Laws of Success* and the continuous process of conceiving and actualizing ever-higher levels of our infinite potentiality—together.[17]

CHAPTER 1

MAKE YOURSELF LOVED

To live an exemplary life by striving for excellence in the choices of one's values, intentions, thoughts, desires and actions, understanding that success begins with "the leadership of the Pharaoh" in you.[1]

"I have created love of me on earth and I have increased my praises in my city, for I knew I would find them later."[2]
—Hor, ancient Egyptian priest

In ancient Egypt the quest for excellence (*i.e.*, moral and social worthiness) was a central concern and it is here the central focus of the *Pharaohs' 1st Law of Success, "Make Yourself Loved."*[3] Making oneself loved does not involve attempting to please others in order to gain acceptance, validation, or approval. Nor does it involve deceptively manipulating others in order to have them do things for one's own benefit. Rather, it is the art of living an exemplary life by striving for excellence in the choices of one's values, intentions, thoughts, desires and actions, which places the development of character, *i.e.*, one's "moral disposition," rather than material wealth as one of the highest values in life.[4]

A piece of literature touted by scholars as being the oldest complete wisdom book in the world, and that was written by the ancient Egyptian *Vizier*, or Prime Minister, Ptahhotep is a valuable record of the past from which we gain some insight concerning the values that were practiced in ancient Egyptian culture.[5] Values, of course, are important because they provide the basis for how we prioritize our lives. Inscribed on the outside of Egyptian temples throughout Egypt was the injunction: "know thyself," and admittedly one of the first steps to discovering self-knowledge is to examine our own values on the basis of whether we are ". . . providing a model for those who come after."[6] For example, in the instructions for the _new_ king Merikara his father Kheti writes, "Make yourself loved by all the people. A good character is remembered when the years have passed."[7] Added this Pharaoh, "Make your monument last through love of you."[8]

A close examination of Egypt's countless monuments will reveal to the observer that the Egyptians planned for them to last for eternity. Take for example the Great Pyramid at Giza rising to a breath-taking height of 450 feet, and constructed with nearly two and a half million stone blocks weighing an average of two and one-half tons each.[9] Moreover, of the famed seven wonders of the ancient world, only the Great Pyramid remains. How does this relate? Re-examine the words of Pharaoh Kheti and you will see that the same concept of building for eternity that directed the planning of monuments was also an important factor in the development of one's character through the act of striving for excellence in the choices of one's values, intentions, thoughts, desires and actions that causes one to become loved, not out of a sense of entitlement, but instead, because he or she earned it.[10]

Early emphasis on the importance of developing a good character was right in sync with the value that ancient Egyptians placed on education. This was evident by the fact that heirs to the throne were enlightened with ancient wisdom well in advance of stepping into their role as Pharaoh.[11] Now, the religion of the ancient Egyptians is called "Amenism" and holds that wisdom is the convergence of spiritual knowledge, insight and understanding.[12] Even more, as an ancient Egyptian song of praise proclaims, "I cry, the beginning of wisdom is the way of Amen."[13] Therefore the possession of wisdom implies that one is living his or her life according to the way or Will of God, which the ancient Egyptians also referred to as the "way of life."[14]

That is actually good news if you believe that you have all but ruined your chances for success and you have now become immobilized by past mistakes. Perhaps there are things that you regret having said or done that are troubling the forward flow of your personal history. Nevertheless, these are things from which you can and must recover beginning at this very moment, here and now. Feeling guilt, shame, frustration or a sense of responsibility for past mistakes is perfectly normal, but if you allow those feelings or unresolved conflicts to become personal excuses for failing to develop and exercise skills and abilities for the purpose of contributing in ways that express moral agency, then you will have committed your greatest wrongdoing of all.[15]

The convergence of spiritual knowledge, insight and understanding, which enables you to recognize your faults and correct them accordingly, will be your rite of passage to move ahead; and your actions, which now demonstrate your commitment to the well-being of all those around you as being the pathway to your own well-being will serve as your vindication. Happiness, forgiveness, redemption and reform are within your grasp in that no matter the challenges you face in life, whether preexisting, self-imposed, or thrusted upon you by others, you can effectively prevail by reorienting your life in a bold new direction, equipped with wisdom.

Understanding the important role that values, character, and wisdom play in your quest for excellence will help you to grasp the following statement that was made by the *Vizier* Ptahhotep, namely: "Every man teaches as he acts" and therefore a part of our accountability as leaders by example is to be aware of the impact that our actions are having on the lives of those around us.[16] It is no wonder that Ptahhotep also cautions, "If you are a leader and command many, strive for excellence in all you do so that no fault can be found in your character."[17] Take a moment to think about the impact that your actions are having on the lives of the people around you and resolve from this day forth to strive for excellence in every situation so that the examples that you constantly teach through your own actions are worthy of being emulated by others.[18] Additionally, it is of further benefit for you to know the three styles of leadership. Let us take each in turn.

The first style of leadership is the leadership of the *aggressor*. These are the leaders who impose their will on those who lack sufficient influence, power and authority to protect, defend and promote their own interests. To followers of the religion of Christianity, the *unnamed* Pharaoh of the biblical Exodus is one example of the aggressor style of leadership, and of particular interest is the acknowledgment in the Christian Bible of his not being Egyptian at all through the use of the Greek word *heteros*, meaning "another of a different kind," and although this *unnamed* Pharaoh was not an actual historical figure, the hardening of his heart by the God of the Israelites along with his <u>not</u> being Egyptian helps to explain his utter disregard for traditional Egyptian values, standards of conduct, and his unrelenting efforts to oppress, abuse and take advantage of the Israelites, for had this mythical, non-Egyptian foreign ruler been allowed to observe the famed wisdom of Egypt, surely he would have ascended to a sustainable form of leadership rather than compel men, women, and children against their will.[19]

The second style of leadership is the leadership of the *supremacist*. These are the leaders who self-servingly use a wide range of factors such as socioeconomic status, religious and political affiliations, job titles, gender, race, ethnicity, age and national origin as proxies for superiority.[20] This style of leadership is also a form of control but unlike the aggressor who primarily subscribes to the blatant use of physical force, the supremacist combines aggression with the subtle and overt use of psychological manipulation for self-serving purposes, but ultimately at the expense of developing or reinforcing an existing *delusional sense of superiority* (DSS), the delusional sense that one person or group is superior to another person or group,[21] and as a result sufferers of this *delusional sense of superiority* create and institutionalize systems of oppression that act as a ". . . barrier of (spiritual), social, (educational), political and economic restrictions . . ." that are meant to be imposed on others,[22] demonstrating that ". . . when social reality is involved, phenomena do not have to be real to be real in their consequences."[23]

The third style of leadership and the most conducive to long term success is "the leadership of the Pharaoh."[24] Let us examine *the leadership of the Pharaoh* as described by psychologist Dr. Na'im Akbar who states, "The leadership in our personal, family and community life must be the leadership of the Pharaoh. The leadership of the Pharaoh personifies the aspirations for human excellence. The leadership of the Pharaoh stands as an image of excellence because he (or she) is the person who is working hardest to be the best that we can all be, and all we must do in supporting that leadership is to in fact help them to achieve that excellence. Because once it's achieved in the leadership, it's achieved for the whole community. So if we accept that leadership, then we have a responsibility to support that leadership and enhance it, because their development is our development."[25]

The title *Pharaoh* comes from the two ancient Egyptian words "Per-aa," which Egyptologist E. A. Wallis Budge translates as the *Great House* and adds, "…in which all Egyptians took asylum."[26] This too is the form your leadership must take upon and be received by others as a haven that helps not hinders, inspires not discourages, nurtures not exploits, and makes flourish rather than deprives. Dr. Maulana Karenga, an Egyptologist and an authority on ancient Egyptian ethical philosophy addressed this point well when he stated, "The ancient Egyptians believed that the primary task in the quest for worthiness was not to love others but to make yourself worthy of being loved by others."[27]

Furthermore, it was said of Pharaoh Sesostris I, "He is a master of grace, rich in sweetness, and through love hath he conquered."[28] Pharaoh Sesostris I himself put it in this way: "I excel by acting for my maker, pleasing God with what he gave."[29] A worthwhile objective most readily achieved through the application of the *Pharaohs' 1st Law of Success,* "*Make Yourself Loved,*" meaning to live an exemplary life by striving for excellence in the choices of one's values, intentions, thoughts, desires and actions, understanding that success begins with "the leadership of the Pharaoh" in you.[30]

CHAPTER 2

SEEK WISE COUNSEL

To obtain advice from credible sources whose convergent faculties of spiritual knowledge, insight and understanding will assist you in making good decisions before taking action.[1]

"No king is foolish while he hath courtiers. He is wise already, when he cometh forth from the womb."[2]
—Pharaoh Kheti

Making important decisions concerning matters that impacted the well-being of the kingdom was a necessary function of kingship, and indispensable to that function was the use of advisers, which is in observance of the *Pharaohs' 2nd Law of Success, "Seek Wise Counsel."* To seek wise counsel means to obtain useful, accurate, and targeted information in the form of advice from credible sources whose convergent faculties of spiritual knowledge, insight and understanding (*i.e.*, wisdom) are relevant to your specific needs, and will assist you in making good decisions before taking action.

This law encompasses the fact that we are social by nature and although we form concepts of ourselves as individuals it is not in an isolated sense, for it stems from how we view ourselves in relation to others.[3] So if we want to reinforce concepts of ourselves as *persons-in-community* who are considerate of the rights, needs and concerns of others, naturally we must seek wise counsel, which will assist us in making good decisions, especially when our decisions affect the lives of so many others.[4] Every day we make decisions that impact our lives personally, socially, and professionally, but none are more important than the decisions we make that impact the lives of those around us. Given that, a responsible act is one borne of a decision tempered by wise counsel.

Some of the most common sources of wise counsel that were accessed by the Pharaoh included the Elders, the chief lector priest, and the *Vizier*, the highest official of the state. Of course, a king's ability to make good decisions did not rely solely on the counsel of the living, as he also consulted the organized bodies of knowledge that were taught by the learned men and women of the past. During the process of passing on the kingship, Pharaoh Kheti instructed his son in this manner:

"Follow in the footsteps of your ancestors, for the mind is trained through knowledge. Behold, their words endure in books. Open and read them and follow their wise counsel."[5]

As you discuss matters over with those who serve as your advisers, wise counsel is received by way of interpersonal communication; whereas, in the case of following the wise counsel of the ancestors, knowledge is obtained chiefly from books, which is to say that continuing your journey forward into the future can sometimes mean returning to the past. So if after taking counsel with all of your trusted advisers you still require additional information, remember the words of the ancient Egyptian scribe Duauf, who said, "There's nothing better than books!"[6]

One particular source of wise counsel found throughout ancient Egyptian literature was also central to the culture: prayer. Greek historian Herodotus once said that the Egyptians were the most religious of all peoples.[7] Indeed, spirituality (*i.e.*, the act of engaging the spirit in activity) and religion (*i.e.*, an interdependent spiritual system of socialization for engaging in a personal relationship and spiritual union with God alongside the cultivation of the Arts and Sciences) permeated every aspect of Egyptian life to the extent that there was no separation between temple and state, the sacred and the secular—religion and the Arts and Sciences.[8] Even their writing system, which would later be called hieroglyphs by the Greeks, was by the Egyptians known as Medu Netur (MEH-doo nay-TOOR), meaning "words of God."[9] With this in mind it should come as no surprise that prayer was a primary source of wise counsel, because it served as the means by which the Pharaoh and his people communed with the eternal *source* to whom they owed their very existence, and of whom it is written, "He hears the petitions of him that invokes him."[10]

A series of sacred hymns give a revealing account of this eternal *source* that was known to the ancient Egyptians by the name of Amen (ah-MEN), meaning "the hidden one," who was reverently addressed as "Father," and was worshipped as the "*ever-living one eternal God*," as evidenced by the monotheistic statement: "Amen is one."[11] Hence, all of the other Egyptian Gods are, says Egyptologist E. A. Wallis Budge, "merely (spiritual) forms of him" who the Egyptians also called the Great God.[12] Curiously, however, we also learn that Amen is both spirit and a triune God existing simultaneously in three phases. A papyrus at Leyden says: "All the gods are three, Amen (ah-MEN), Ra (RAH) and Ptah (p-TAH), and there are none like unto them."[13] God, in his name of Amen represents God's spirit in its essential phase of *Spirit* (proper);[14] his name of Ra represents God's spirit in its phase of *Soul*;[15] Ptah, God's spirit in its phase of *Mind*.[16] Elsewhere in Egyptian literature we read that humans (male and female) are created in the image of God, and as early as 2140 B.C.E. Pharaoh Kheti says, "He (God) gave the breath of life for their noses. *They are his images and came from his person*."[17] Combine this universal belief that humans are created in the image of God with the scientific fact that the first man and woman created were black, and it rationally and justifiably follows that so too is God.[18]

Along with a telling account left of Amen as the "*ever-living one eternal God*" were instructions for his petitioning through prayer.[19] The Egyptian scribe Ani wrote,

> "*Noisy, vain repetitions are an abomination to the sanctuary of God. Pray thy prayer with a loving heart in secret. He will do for thee all that is necessary for thy daily needs.*"[20]

When you study these sage words a few things become immediately apparent. First, all counsel, whether received in prayer or from trusted others should be conducted in quiet surroundings that are free from distractions in the interest of concentrating all of your attention on the matter at hand. Doing this communicates to God and to your advisers that your concerns are of major importance to you and at the same time demonstrates that you value *their* time, attention, and input as well. Second, while maintaining a "loving heart," it is a good practice to keep the details of your concerns strictly between you and those from whom you receive wise counsel.

The heart, known in ancient Egypt as the *ib*[21] is, according to the religion of Amenism, representative of a person's conscience[22] and is the part of the *Khat* (body) [23] around which the *Ka* (mind personified) ,[24] the *Ba* (soul) ,[25] and the *Khu* (spirit) , also spelled , , are centered.[26] To investigate why this is so, we first need to learn that Tekhi (**TEK**-ee) , the ibis-headed form of Amen who was called Thoth by the Greeks, was esoterically said to be ". . . the mind residing in the (physical) heart"[27] and was spoken of as the scribe of God, the "maker of Law," the "lord of wisdom," and the "*Heart of Ra*."[28] With this new development, let us turn our attention back to the papyrus at Leyden to examine an important cryptic passage that records a sequence of events describing the process by which God in his names of Amen, Ra and Ptah imparts Divine Law to humans by way of divine revelation. The text thus reads that the cities of Amen, Ra and Ptah:

> "... are established upon the earth for ever, [namely,] Waset (Thebes), Anu (Heliopolis), and Hetkaptah (Memphis). When a message is sent from heaven it is heard in Anu, and is repeated in Memphis to the Beautiful Face (i.e. Ptah). It is done in writing, in the letters of Thoth (i.e. hieroglyphs), and dispatched to the city of Amen (i.e. Thebes), with their things. The matters are answered in Thebes."[29]

If we become aware that the three cities are also metaphors for the three phases of the Triune-Phase Spirit of God, it becomes clear that the soul is the part of us that hears and receives God's divine revelation, which is conceived in our heart,[30] and with our mind it is perceived as spiritual knowledge.[31] It is then repeated by the soul to the mind, which is conceived in our heart, and with our mind it is perceived as spiritual insight.[32] Next, if we remember that Amen in his form of Tekhi is "the mind residing in the heart," the scribe of God, the "maker of Law," and the "*Heart of Ra*," and that the heart, to which *Maat* is joined at birth, is representative of a person's conscience, we may then make the determination at this stage in the sequence of events that God's divine revelation is written in our heart as Divine Law, which is expressed as moral counsel that God imparted to humans for the purpose of instructing them in the practice of the ten cardinal virtues of *Maat* in their daily lives;[33] Divine Law is then perceived with our mind just as it has been alluded to—as our conscience, an important faculty responsible for distinguishing right from wrong based on whether our values, intentions, thoughts, desires and actions are congruent with the Will of God.[34] All matters of the heart are then sent to and answered by the spirit, which is conceived in our heart and perceived with our mind as spiritual understanding. Ultimately though, if it has been found that we have done the Will of God, then spiritual knowledge, insight and understanding converge in the heart as wisdom,[35] which provides us with the means to conceive and actualize ever-higher levels of our infinite potentiality, and the lord of which, as you will recall, is Tekhi.[36]

    We originally wanted to know why the heart is the part of the body <u>around</u> which the mind, soul and spirit are centered. Fortunately, sufficient evidence has been adduced to conclude with the following assertion of Amenist theology that the heart is the gateway to spiritual, social, educational, political, and economic "conditions of opportunity" afforded to all[37] on the grounds of its primacy in its ability to literally transmute the spiritual faculties of the mind, soul and spirit into revelatory-perceptions within the mind that in turn activate appropriate behavioral responses to a divine revelation within us.[38] What is more, apart from the realization that religion enfolds both spirituality and science, we unmistakably have one very clear indication of why, unlike the stomach, intestines, lungs, liver and brain, which were all removed from the body of the departed during the process of mummification, the heart was left in place.[39] Now familiarize yourself with the deeper meaning of these words of Pharaoh Sesostris III which were inscribed on a freestanding stone slab called a *stela* (**STEE**-luh): "That which my heart has conceived, my arm performs."[40]

    So according to the teachings of Amenism, we as humans are not only created in the physical and spiritual image of God, we are also created of his essence.[41] This enables us to be identified and spiritually united with, as well as to receive wise counsel from God at the most intimate level, which is that of the spirit. Yet, we are also able to know and identify with God on a personal level by, as one might expect, having a personal relationship with God, but also by learning from the exemplary life and mystery teachings of the three persons of the Holy Trinity Osir (oh-**SEER**), Iset (ee-**SET**) and Heru (hay-**ROO**).[42] To illustrate, Osir and Iset, husband and wife, yet brother and sister by spirit, came down to earth from heaven to civilize humankind.[43] As the founding father and first king of Egypt at its inception as an earthly kingdom, Osir taught his people agriculture, improved their habits and manners, gave them a code of laws, and instructed them to worship and perform services to God.[44] Osir, ". . . the Great Ancestor-God of all Egypt," whose complexion is black, and who is described here by two of his many titles as the "Great Black One," and "Lord of the Perfect Black,"[45] eventually left Egypt and traveled the world transmitting civilization to all nations.[46] While away, his evil younger brother Seth[47] continually sought to take control of Egypt, but to no avail due to the care with which Egypt's founding mother and first queen Iset administered the kingdom in her husband's absence.[48] The description of Seth that has come down to us from ancient Greek biographer Plutarch is as follows:

> "He was rough and wild, his skin was white and his hair was red—an abomination to the Egyptians, who compared it to the pelt of an ass."[49]

Meanwhile, having civilized all nations, Osir returned to Egypt where Seth, along with a number of conspirators, began to plot his demise. Unbeknownst to Osir, his brother Seth had secretly obtained his bodily measurements, and from them he built an attractive wooden chest to Osir's exact proportions.[50] Seth then invited Osir to a banquet and announced to his guests that he would give the chest to anyone who could fit perfectly inside. One after another the guests tried and failed to fit into the chest. Finally, Osir tried and found that he fit inside of the chest perfectly. Without hesitation the conspirators, who were posing as guests, slid the lid over the chest and secured it in place with spike nails over which they then poured melted lead, and then threw the chest into the Nile River where Osir suffered death by drowning.[51]

When Iset heard about her husband's death she set out at once in search of the wooden chest containing her husband's body, which had in the meantime washed up on the shores of Byblos. Having come to rest there an Erica tree sprang up on that very same spot, growing to such an enormous size that it eventually encompassed the chest within its trunk.[52] Thereafter, the king of Byblos upon seeing the tree had it cut down and used for one of the pillars in his palace. When Iset received word of this, she immediately set out for Byblos to recover the body of her husband. There, she met the queen of Byblos and was appointed nursemaid to her newborn son, enabling Iset to share her story with the queen and ask to be given the pillar encompassing the chest that contained her husband's body. This the queen did, and Iset, cutting free the chest, transported it back to Egypt where it was promptly hidden. Unfortunately, Seth discovered the chest one night while hunting and cut the body of Osir into fourteen pieces, which he scattered and buried throughout Egypt.[53] Upon learning of this, Iset immediately went out in search of the fourteen pieces of which she found but thirteen after they had lain buried for three days.[54] The fourteenth piece, the phallus, "... had been greedily devoured by a Nile crab, the Oxyrhynchid, forever accursed for this crime."[55]

For this reason Tekhi (mentioned above) provided Iset with the secret means for fashioning Osir an artificial phallus, and for rejoining the body of Osir through the process of mummification.[56] Iset then proceeded to perform the astounding feat of projecting her soul in the form of a falcon descending over the body of Osir, whereupon spiritually reviving him their

Seek Wise Counsel

two souls conjoined in spirit.[57] From this conjoining in spirit of two divine souls, Iset <u>spiritually</u> drew from Osir his essence and conceived a divine child.[58] She who declared, "I am the great virgin" on account of her never having consummated her marriage, named their child Heru, meaning "he (or she) who is above," because he was not begotten of flesh, but rather, he was begotten of spirit and conceived of a virgin in order that he may be born of spirit <u>above</u> the flesh, which is to say that after his divine birth (*i.e.*, virgin birth) and first appearance as a newborn babe, Heru is shortly thereafter depicted as a child, but in order to avenge his father's murder he miraculously transforms himself from a child into a man, and then finally into an Elder, being that peak stage of development in which he is depicted with the body of a man and the head of a falcon, symbolizing the newborn soul emerging above the flesh, directly into the realm of spirit, hence the three latter stages of Heru's development corresponding to the three stages of spiritual rebirth in the Mysteries.[59] Regarding the spiritual revival of Osir and the conception of Heru, the sacred and holy text says:

> "She made light [to appear] from her feathers, she made air to come into being by means of her two wings, and she cried out the death cries for her brother. She made to rise up the helpless members of him whose heart was at rest, she drew from him his essence, and she made therefrom an heir."[60]

Thus, by the secret means taught to her by Tekhi, Iset spiritually revived her husband Osir and conceived Heru, but it was not until after the birth of Heru and the subsequent defeat of Seth that, with the assistance of Tekhi, her son Heru (as an Elder), and Anup (ah-**NOOP**), the Jackal-headed form of Amen, Iset resurrected her mummified husband Osir forthwith,[61] whereas her son Heru (as an Elder) awakened him and raised him to his feet.[62] In a Hymn to Osir his son Heru, who after defeating Seth and returning as an Elder, says:

> "Ha, [[Osir]], I have come to thee. I am [[Heru]], and I restore thee unto life upon this day with the funeral offerings and all good things for [[Osir]]. Rise up, then, [[Osir]]. I have stricken down thine enemies for thee; I have delivered thee from them. I am [[Heru]] on this fair day at the beautiful coming forth of thy powers (in his resurrection), who lifteth thee up with himself on this fair day as thine associate God. Ha, [[Osir]], thou hast received thy sceptre, thy pedestal, and thy flight of stairs beneath thee."[63]

Soon after, Osir and his son Heru were confronted with a series of false accusations mounted against them by Osir's younger brother Seth, to which Osir responded and was justified upon being proclaimed by Tekhi to be "true of voice."[64] In the end, Osir ascended back to his kingdom in heaven as ruler and judge of the souls of those who have passed, leaving his son Heru to rule over his kingdom on earth.[65]

As incredible as the religious beliefs of the ancient Egyptians were, the manner in which their religious beliefs materialized in the institution of kingship was even more so. Briefly, every king was said to have had a divine birth, having been begotten of spirit and born of a *Virgin Mother* by whom the king had been divinely conceived when his then virgin mother-to-be was descended upon by God Amen himself.[66] Of his own free will, desire and decision the king accepted God Amen's gift of *true life* through his belief in the life, ". . . divinity, death and resurrection . . ." of Osir, thereby acknowledging Amen as his heavenly Father; and by making his actions compliant with Divine Law that was itself founded upon a divine, universal organizing principle, which the ancient Egyptians called *Maat*, for it was the <u>new</u> king's acceptance of God's gift of *true life* through his belief in Osir, and by acting in accordance with

Maat that enabled him to attain spiritual union with God.⁶⁷ But except in so far as the <u>new</u> king held dominion over his people, his right to the throne descended through the female line by marriage to the royal heiress, ensuring the spiritual revival and resurrection of Osir in the <u>new</u> king when the royal heiress herself became queen and was identified with the second person of the Holy Trinity, Iset, though according to Amenism, she simultaneously reigned in the capacity of "God's wife," meaning the wife of Amen and mother-to-be of the future heir to the throne.⁶⁸

Correspondingly, more than just simply occupying the throne, it was primarily the <u>new</u> king's active role in transmitting civilization to all nations by way of the Egyptian Mystery System and through student Initiates, which was in actuality the transference to earth of the Kingdom of Heaven located within his own spirit, that identified him with the first person of the Holy Trinity Osir;⁶⁹ although, he ruled the kingdom as and recognized himself to be the very person of Heru, the Son of God and third person of the Holy Trinity for whom the day of his divine birth is called the "Day of the Great Coming Forth," that is to say, "*Coming Forth as the (Newborn) Sun*," because according to the Egyptian Calendar the birth of Heru is known to have taken place on the fourth day of the month of Makhiar (mah-kee-**AR**) *i.e.*, December 25th (Gregorian), which corresponds to the ". . . the astronomical event in which the Sun, having appeared to stand still or rise from the same spot for approximately three days in a row during the period of the *winter solstice* and at its apparent maximum distance south of the celestial equator, reverses its movement and begins to *visibly* rise increasingly northward," causing the days to *grow* longer.⁷⁰ The herald of this most momentous event was the brightest star in the sky, Sepdta (**SEP**-tah), which is commonly called Sirius (Sothis in the Greek)⁷¹ and was associated with none other than Iset over whose temple at Sais we read, "The fruit which I have begotten is the sun."[72] Elsewhere we read a passage recording Heru as saying, "May I rise up, a Babe [from between] the knees of Sothis, when they close together."[73] The above salient theme cannot be overlooked, for it has all of the makings of spiritual revival, union, salvation, rebirth, and resurrection wherein most notably the emergence of the king's soul above the flesh, directly into the realm of spirit rendered the sovereign of the country the third person of the Holy Trinity: Heru.[74] Apart from his spiritual rebirth, it is here worth mentioning that the king's ceremonial divine birth was immediately followed by the baptism by water and naming ceremonies; and that the king was <u>also</u> baptized by fire or in priesthood parlance, **born** of spirit in its phase of soul, the officiating priest conferred on him the title "*Son of the Sun*," meaning the Son of Ra; but, because he was **begotten** of spirit proper, the same priest affirmed that his heavenly Father was Amen.[75]

If you are new to Amenist theology couched in terms of ancient Egyptian philosophy then you may as well start getting used to having been divinely conceived and born of a virgin (*e.g.*, your biological mother) in the truest and most philosophical sense that you were begotten of spirit and then came into biological life <u>spiritually</u> and <u>experientially</u> one step removed from the realm of spirit by means of the birth of your physical body that you, the spiritually unborn and immaterial living soul, inhabit.[76] This is your divine birth (*i.e.*, virgin birth) that you may now choose to embrace, or against which you may choose to rebel. But how, then, will you attain spiritual union with the divine if you are at variance with your own nature? As for your pending spiritual rebirth, which simultaneously lifts the soul from its bodily prison in which it lies spiritually unborn, in sleeping repose, and in proximal separation from *true life*,[77] it was traditionally ventured by Initiates of Egypt's Mystery System under the instruction and close supervision of priests[78] along with the aid of an important religious book not surprisingly titled, the *Book of "Coming Forth as the (Newborn) Sun"* that was customarily placed in the tombs of the departed.[79]

We are informed by author George G. M. James that self-development was available to ". . . the surrounding neighbors of Egypt," as well as to every member of Egyptian society through the Egyptian Mystery System by way of education (*e.g.*, through the cultivation of the Arts and Sciences), and the practice of virtue (*e.g.*, by doing *Maat*).[80] Accordingly, the five chief aims of the Egyptian Mystery System are: (1) revival of the spirit, which simultaneously brings about a flourishing of the spirit through philosophical enlightenment in truth;[81] (2) spiritual union with God, which simultaneously liberates the soul ". . . from its bodily fetters;"[82] (3) salvation of the soul, which simultaneously brings one's ". . . life into harmony with God, (humankind and nature);"[83] (4) spiritual rebirth, which is the birth of the soul, and which simultaneously lifts the soul from its bodily prison in which it lies spiritually unborn, in sleeping repose, and in proximal separation from *true life*;[84] and (5) spiritual resurrection of the soul, which simultaneously awakens and raises the soul from a sleeplike state that resembles spiritual death, to renewed activity that enables the transference to earth of the Kingdom of Heaven located within one's own spirit.[85]

While it is true that the staunchest member of the Egyptian Mystery System *i.e.*, the living king, ruled on earth as Heru, he necessarily occupied the throne by virtue of his identification with Osir, understandably signifying Heru as the lawful heir.[86] By all accounts, it was not until the biological death of the king that he was completely assimilated to Osir, but it was only by doing *Maat* while in Egypt on earth that the king obtained immortality,[87] which culminated in his resurrection and ascension into heaven where, as Osir, one of his primary roles was to judge the souls of the departed according to the righteousness of their hearts.[88] But well before this momentous event took place, the Ba (soul) and the Ka (mind personified) of the king which were separated at death, were also slated to be reunited pending a favorable judgment from God according to the righteousness of the king's <u>own</u> heart, which if found lacking, the biological death of the king would be followed by the *second death*, meaning the death and complete annihilation of the king's soul.[89]

From our beginning studies in Amenist theology, we learn that the Spirit of God that in fact dwells within our physical body is triune, consisting of spirit in its essential phase of spirit proper, spirit in its phase of soul, and spirit in its phase of mind.[90] What may peak your interest; however, is the underlying interconnectedness of spirit, soul, mind, heart and body that we find in ancient Egyptian literature time and time again,[91] but be forewarned that the cohesion among the five physical and spiritual parts of man and woman is constantly under the threat of being supplanted by a ". . . barrier of (spiritual), social, (educational), political and economic restrictions imposed on blacks . . ." and other peoples of color with, but not limited to, these devastating results: unmet needs, unaccessed opportunities, unrealized potentiality, and spiritual death.[92] Notwithstanding a barrier of restrictions, we as Amenists are charged with the mastery of the gateway[93] to spiritual, social, educational, political, and economic "conditions of opportunity," which supersedes all such restrictions and thereby provides an effective recourse to the barrier created by them that was meant to prevent us from conceiving and actualizing ever-higher levels of our infinite potentiality.[94] To be sure, when all five physical and spiritual parts of man and woman regain their cohesion they cease, as such, to be individual parts alone and instead become parts of one community by means of spiritual union; hence, the uniting of the human and the divine for which the ancient Egyptians had a particular word.[95]

Seek Wise Counsel

Just by way of introduction, the England-born Egyptologist Gerald Massey was highly instrumental in bringing to the attention of the modern world, ancient Egyptian mystery teachings (miscalled myths), religious narratives, concepts, rituals and even words that were appropriated for the religion of Christianity.[96] Most notably, the ancient Egyptian word ⟨⟩ ◌ that Massey transliterated as *krst*, referring to the mummified Osir raised to his feet[97] and whose raiment, made from white linen wrappings, is outfitted with the "Great Collar" ⏀ that loops around the back of his neck and over his shoulders with the crossed loose ends falling across the front of his upper torso to form an X.[98] Hence, Osir, who was called Osiris by the Greeks, is in actuality the risen Christ for whom X is mysteriously the hieroglyphic monogram.[99] Massey says:

> "Dr. Budge, in his book on the mummy, tells his readers that the Egyptian word for mummy is *ges*, which signifies to wrap up in bandages. But he does not point out that ges or kes, to embalm the corpse or make the mummy, is a reduced or abraded form of an earlier word, karas (whence krst for the mummy). The original word written in hieroglyphics is ⟨⟩ ◌ krst, whence kas, to embalm, to bandage, to knot, to make the mummy or karast (Birch, *Dictionary of the Hieroglyphics*, pp. 415-416; Champollion, *Gram. Egyptienne*, 86). The word krs denotes the embalmment of the mummy, and the krst, as the mummy, was made in the process of preparation by purifying, anointing, and embalming. To karas the dead body was to embalm it, to bandage it, to make the mummy. The mummy was the Osirian *Corpus Christi*, prepared for burial as the laid-out dead, the karast by name. When raised to its feet, it was the risen mummy, or sahu. The place of embalmment was likewise the krs.

Thus the process of making the mummy was to karas, the place in which it was laid is the karas, and the product was the krst, whose image is the upright mummy=the risen Christ. Hence the name of the Christ, Christos in Greek, Chrestus in Latin, for the anointed, was derived, as the present writer previously suggested, from the Egyptian word krst."¹⁰⁰

"Finally, then, the mystery of the mummy is the mystery of the Christ. As Christian, it is allowed to be forever inexplicable. As Osirian, the mystery can be explained."¹⁰¹

In his own words, Massey unapologetically explained in detail the ancient Egyptian origin of the word "Christ" that he transliterated as *krst*, presumably in Greek since the ancient Greek alphabet does not have the letter -*c*-, but that is also <u>transliterated</u> as *crst* both in Latin, the language of the Romans, and in English, which is a Latin based language, now that it has been taken into account the hieroglyphic spelling of Roman Emperor Domitian's name and titles inscribed on an ancient Egyptian obelisk which reads: " 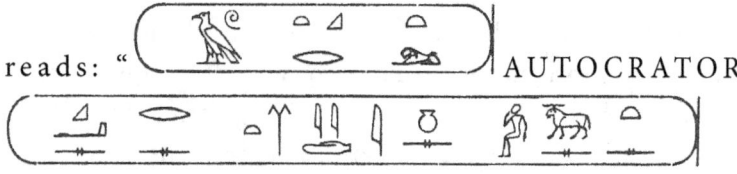 AUTOCRATOR Caesar Domitianus Sebastus."¹⁰²

With respect to the ancient Egyptian meaning of the word "Christ," author D. M. Murdock reports that frankincense and myrrh were two of the spices used in the process of mummification to anoint the body of the departed.¹⁰³ In our case, the great and departed king, who was the mummified Osir and was also, according to research conducted by Murdock, "the anointed."¹⁰⁴ How it was that the term "anointed" became the literal meaning of the word "Christ" in this context is apparent, but in order to derive the deeper esoteric meaning of the word "Christ," we will need to revisit the subject of mummification in conjunction with spiritual union. For example, in order for Iset to physically rejoin the body of Osir we know that the process of mummification called for all of the internal organs, except for the heart, to be removed from the body. We also know that spiritual union, meaning the union of the human and the divine, was not reattained until the precise moment that the two divine souls of Osir and Iset conjoined in spirit, and thereby spiritually fastened together and unified the body, heart, mind, soul and spirit of Osir—therein lies the deeper esoteric meaning of the word "Christ," the hieroglyphic monogram of which was found present across the upper torso of the mummified Osir, and which finds further practical application in ancient Egyptian hieroglyphs where it is represented by two butterfly clamps ⧖ ⧖ crossed to make an X, meaning Christ and signifying conjoined complementary male and female spiritual forces (*e.g.*, infinite spiritual power and infinite spiritual affinity) of the indwelling Triune-Phase Spirit of God through which the Pharaoh attained spiritual union <u>with</u> God.[105] Called an X-fastener,[106] it can be seen auspiciously embedded among the hieroglyphs that form the word community ⊗, which was itself non-coincidentally included as part of the original name of the country that foreigners would later call Egypt, but that its black, native African founding fathers and mothers so aptly named *Kemet* ⧖⧖⊗, meaning the *Black Community of Christ*.[107]

Long since has it been known that it was a common cultural practice between Egyptian husbands and wives to endearingly address one another as brother and sister, which for the Pharaoh, the queen, and members of the Egyptian Mystery System was also in reference to their identification with husband and wife Osir and Iset,[108] who are not in actuality brother and sister by blood, but rather by spirit,[109] denoting one heavenly Father we all have in common,[110] and further corroborating the assertion made by author George G. M. James that one of the chief aims of the Egyptian Mystery System was to attain spiritual union with God. This leads right into the disclosure that the association between spiritual union and seeking wise counsel, which heretofore has been obscure, should now be within the purview of the student of this philosophy; therefore, we shall meet at the point from which we departed in our discussion of prayer as a source of wise counsel, adding to it the attainment of spiritual union with God alongside the cultivation of the Arts and Sciences, whereby we become the counselor as well as the counselee. Simply put, the ultimate goal of seeking wise counsel is to eventually be able to do the same for others when they in turn seek wise counsel of you.[111] This then, is the *Pharaohs' 2nd Law of Success*, wherein spiritual knowledge, insight and understanding converge in the heart as wisdom, and comes forth on the tongue as *Wise Counsel*.

CHAPTER 3

EMPOWER THOSE WHO YOU INFLUENCE

To engage others in cooperation on common goals, questing to achieve as a team collectively, that which cannot be accomplished individually.[1]

> *"Advance your officials so that they will act by your laws."*[2]
> —Pharaoh Kheti

When King Amenemhet I conveyed the essence of his experience in the *Wisdom Teachings* for his son Sesostris I, despite his extreme caution in trusting subordinates he conceded that "no success is achieved without a helper."[3] Therein lies the importance of delegating, the key to applying the *Pharaohs' 3rd Law of Success*, "Empower Those Who You Influence." We previously established that each one of us is a leader, due to the fact that by our actions we either intentionally or inadvertently set examples that in turn influence the actions of others. So beginning with the people who are closest to you, your role is to engage them in cooperation by empowering them with direct involvement in defining, defending, promoting, and achieving common goals. In short, you must learn to delegate. Doing this, moves you from the status of being an individual to that of being part of a team. In reality, the level of success achieved by the Pharaoh was determined in great part by his careful delegation of power and authority to those who served as his deputies, which included members of the royal family, officials, nobles and priests. In this way cooperation was gained, new challenges were met as a shared responsibility, and success became a continuous collective process that produced enhanced results that could not have been possible through the king's effort alone. Here are some simple steps you can take that will help you to delegate more effectively:

1). Remember that delegating, if done correctly, is mutually beneficial to both you and those to whom you delegate. "Make great thy nobles" exclaims one Pharaoh to his son, for no one will invest in achieving goals with others indefinitely without also being able to share in the success and affluence created by everyone's combined efforts.[4]

2). The king offers this suggestion on how to delegate each task to the right member of the team saying thus: "Exalt not the son of an important man above a humble one, but take for thyself a man because of his ability."[5] Additionally, meet with the members of your team and take an assessment of each member's ability to contribute to the success of the team as a whole.* What better way to communicate that each member of the team is equally important and that without each and every one of us the goals of the team could not be achieved?

3). Next, simply delegate tasks by matching each member's ability to the demands of the assignment, and then everyone will have been assigned a task for which he or she is best suited.*

4). Going forward, it is suggested that you do not supervise members too closely, but rather, give members a certain degree of autonomy while staying informed of new developments by meeting regularly with members to check on the progress of assignments.* Ancient records tell us that the Pharaoh met with and received briefings from his highest officials daily.[6] This gives everyone an opportunity and the personal space to take the initiative, which will help them to develop and grow into responsible and dependable members of the team who keep the operation moving even when you are not present. How else could the Pharaoh have mastered the art of being in many places at one time?

Without exception, no other official worked as close to the Pharaoh as the *Vizier*. The tasks assigned to his position were so important that they were delivered orally to each new *Vizier* in person by the king himself.[7] Pharaoh Thutmose III referred to the office of the *Vizier* as "…the established support of the whole land."[8] Take a moment and ask yourself whether you have good support in your own life. In other words, are you routinely surrounded by people who are supportive of your needs, goals and desires? If not, then consider reassessing those areas in your life where a lack of support is causing you to be disadvantaged and resolve to improve your situation immediately!

One of the most powerful ways that you can remedy this problem is to begin placing yourself in the company of people who can help and encourage you to grow in areas that relate to the goals you want to achieve, and that align with the kind of person you are committed to being; your charge, then, is to become a member of a community with a global network so that you and others can evolve beyond what can be termed the vicious cycle of struggle and frustration.[9] Granted that initial struggle is advantageous, because it helps you to gain a greater degree of access to certain mental, physical and spiritual faculties for overcoming challenging situations; however, prolonged struggle without measurable progress runs the risk of becoming an accepted condition; for example, in experiments conducted by psychologist Dr. Martin Seligman it was found that people who experience repeated stressful events that seem to be inescapable may develop a sense of helplessness and hopelessness and, as a consequence, give up trying to improve their situation.[10] Fortunately, there is an empowering alternative. Becoming a member of a community with a global network can be the beginning of your transitioning from a state of struggle and frustration, to one of flourishing and sheer fulfillment.

In the case of the Pharaoh, his "transition from man to king" was made official at the coronation ceremony during which birds were released and arrows were launched in the directions of the four cardinal points.[11] Consider these facts along with the discovery that the Great Pyramid is situated in the center of earth's entire land mass and you may be sure that the Pharaoh was well aware that from where he stood he was truly at the center of the whole world.[12] There, he extended the reach of his influence, power and authority in all directions in part through the process of delegating to members of the royal family and the many builders, artists, and scholars with whom he was surrounded. In a similar manner you too are standing at the center of your own world called *your life*, because in all directions you are surrounded with family, friends, colleagues and coworkers to whom you are now called to delegate with the understanding that by being engaged in cooperation on common goals, together we can meet any challenge, surmount any obstacle, and achieve any goal. A statement of fact which embodies the essence of the *Pharaohs' 3rd Law of Success, "Empower Those Who You Influence."* Therefore, let us quest to achieve as a team collectively, that which cannot be accomplished individually.

CHAPTER 4

BECOME A PLACEMAKER

To create "conditions of opportunity" in which needs can be met, enabling the experience of "... ever-higher levels of human life and achievement."¹

> *"There is no place in the world where I have not come to bestow my beneficence."*²
> —Osir the risen Christ

Egypt, geographically located in the northeastern corner of Africa, was in ancient times the education center of the whole world, benefiting not only the Egyptian, but also the Nubian (*i.e.*, the ancient Sudanese), the Hebrew, the Syrian, the Phoenician and the Greek.³ As a Syrian prince once said to a visiting Egyptian envoy, "For skilled work came forth from it (Egypt) to reach this place where I am, and teaching came from it to reach this place where I am."⁴ Astonishingly, however, the only arable region of Egypt consisted of a fertile strip of land that stretched along the eastern and western banks of the world's longest river, the Nile, which author Stephanie Fitzgerald says, "…accounted for only about 3 percent of the country's total land area."⁵ The same land had gradually been built up by the black life-giving topsoil carried down from Ethiopia during its annual rainy season that also caused the annual inundation of the Nile; the remaining 97 percent of Egypt's total land area was barren desert.⁶ Nevertheless, foreigners regularly ventured into Egypt and even though many of them had obvious differences in physical appearance from the native Egyptians, in the main, they were still given an opportunity to learn a full array of disciplines such as mathematics, geometry, engineering, physics, medicine, astronomy, architecture, law, art, literature, religion, philosophy, and ethics without regard to color or race.[7] Such gesture was of monumental importance, for in providing useful service to humanity the ancient Egyptians, under the leadership of the Pharaohs, have been indelibly written upon the pages of history as one of the foremost contributors to the spiritual, moral and intellectual development of humankind. It is within this context that you will comprehend the full significance of the *Pharaohs' 4th Law of Success*, *"Become a Placemaker."*[8]

The *Pharaohs' 4th Law of Success* says that we have all been endowed with infinite potentiality to succeed personally, socially and professionally. However, one's potentiality often remains largely unrealized as long as self-development stifles beneath daily conditions of unmet spiritual, emotional, intellectual, volitional, and physical needs.[9] A *Placemaker* is therefore one who creates "conditions of opportunity" in which needs can be met, and so helps those in need realize more and more of their infinite potentiality.[10] An ancient Egyptian priest once wrote: "There is no good deed except a good deed which you have done for him who has need of it," and nowhere was the ancient Egyptians' dedication to helping those in need more strikingly demonstrated than in their sovereign's manner of treating the most vulnerable among them.[11] Pharaoh Amenemhet I, founder of ancient Egypt's 12th Dynasty once said, "I gave to the beggar, I nourished the orphan; I admitted the insignificant as well as him who was great of account."[12] Not surprisingly, Egyptian queens were known to care for the needy after the fashion of their kingly husbands. An alabaster statue of Queen Amenirdis, the loving wife of Pharaoh Piankhi, bears the following inscription: "I was the wife of the divine one, a benefactress to her city (Thebes), a bounteous giver for her land. I gave food to the hungry, drink to the thirsty, clothes to the naked."[13]

That an Egyptian queen's beneficence could equal or exceed that of her male consort provides an indication of an Egyptian woman's high status relative to that of women from most other ancient cultures. A closer examination by Egyptologist, historian, linguist and philosopher Dr. Theophile Obenga enabled him to say, "In antiquity, Egypt stood out as the only civilization to have truly guaranteed women a status equal to that of men."[14] For example, women could own property, enter into marriage, initiate divorce and conduct business.[15] Women could also choose from an unrestricted range of professions such as musician, scribe, doctor, priestess, judge, prime minister and even the sovereign of Egypt, as historical records of female Pharaohs such as Nitocris, Sobekneferu, Hatshepsut and Tawesret will attest.[16] Intent on protecting the rights of women, Pharaoh Rameses III said, "The foot of an Egyptian woman may walk where it pleases her and no one may deny her."[17] These nurturing and protective qualities of the Pharaoh were expressed through the institution of kingship as the ability to respond to life's challenges with a course of action conducive to collective adaptation and can be summed up in the phrase *social responsibility*.[18] The premise is that to fulfill the role of *Placemaker* we must not only exercise our authority to lead, but we must also act upon our social responsibility to nurture and protect.

As if to metaphorically convey this enduring wisdom, certain ancient references to the Pharaoh were designated by the terms "Good Herdsman" and "Good Shepherd," while statues, carvings and paintings frequently depicted the king emulating Osir by holding two ceremonial tools: the herdsman's and shepherd's crook ↑ and flail ⚒ , perpetuating the concept of the perfect ruler who responsibly seeks the well-being of his people as a herdsman tends his herd, and as a shepherd tends his flock.[19] Of God in his name of Ra, who incarnates himself as Osir, and both with whom the king is identified, "It is said: he is the herdsman of mankind. No evil is in his heart. When his herds are few, he passes the day to gather them together."[20] Pharaoh Kheti said as much when he wrote, "Well-cared for is humankind who are the flocks of God."[21]

In the preceding chapter we saw that all authority was delegated by the king, but it was with the understanding that if authority was not balanced with social responsibility, then individual liberties would be diminished and leadership by coercion or force would eventually obtain. Authority, therefore, was not simply "the power or right to give commands, enforce obedience, take action, or make final decisions," but was in essence a form of socialization, here defined by educator, psychologist and historian Dr. Asa Grant Hilliard as, "pulling your people together in a value system we share, with a mission and a purpose."[22] Interestingly, modern scholars have identified the ten cardinal virtues of truth, justice, harmony, balance, reciprocity, order, righteousness, wisdom, temperance, and courage as constituting a core value system inherent in a divine, universal organizing principle that the ancient Egyptians called *Maat*; and, just as natural law is an expression of *Maat* throughout the cosmos, Divine Law, referred to elsewhere in Egyptian literature as the "laws of *Maat*," is expressed as moral counsel that God imparted to humans by way of divine revelation, and for the purpose of instructing them in the practice of the ten cardinal virtues of *Maat* in their daily lives.[23] According to the teachings of Amenism *Maat* is joined to our hearts at birth, which innately predisposes us to increase good in the world; however, in no way does this moral innate predisposition with which we come into the world relieve us of the responsibility and duty to embrace and, as previously stated, systematically engage *Maat* ". . . in all areas of moral concern" and human activity.[24]

Become a Placemaker

Treasury scribe of the temple of Sethi I, Huyshery addresses future generations thus:

> *"I say to you, future people coming after me:*
> *I was one worthy, cool -------*
> *who had put Maat in his heart*
> *without neglecting her occasion.*
> *Since I left the womb she was joined to my heart."*[25]

Far from being merely an assumption, then, "... human nature is endowed by the creator and is essentially good, for it is ... rooted in Maat."[26] Notwithstanding, humans have been given free will to choose in their hearts either to do *Maat*, meaning to practice the ten cardinal virtues of *Maat* in one's daily life and in compliance with Divine Law, or its antithesis, to do *isfet*, a phrase which means to render up oneself to the "ten bodily fetters" of falsehood, injustice, discord, imbalance, exploitation, disorder, unrighteousness, folly, greed, and cowardice in one's daily life and in defiance of Divine Law.[27] Evil is therefore the offspring of doing *isfet*; however, free will, which can be utilized to do *isfet*, "... is not responsible for the existence of evil in being," because evil as well as good "... is in the structure and process of being."[28] Nevertheless, doing *isfet* increases evil and lessens good, while doing *Maat* increases good and lessens evil.[29] Additionally, humankind is said to have propitiated God by doing his will, and God's Will is for humankind to do *Maat*.[30]

To be sure, at issue is the salvation of the soul and its ultimate destination in the hereafter, about which we are taught by high priest Petosiris:

> *"No one reaches the salutary West (i.e., heaven) unless their heart is righteous by doing Maat"* and *"none is exempt from being reckoned."*[31]

There is an ancient Egyptian sacred text titled the *Book of Gates*, in which God informs the souls of the departed who did *Maat* while on earth: "*Maat* is yours that you may live."[32] And of those justified souls who have been welcomed into heaven and who now subsist on *Maat* it is said: "They are masters of their refreshment, which is fiery water to the sinful and the evil ones."[33] So it is that according to what we accept in our hearts, which subsequently gives rise to the good or ill works that stand as expressions of our values, intentions, thoughts, desires and actions, we are the agents of our own salvation or damnation. That is to say that the monotheistic religion called "Amenism" of which in antiquity ". . . there were at least *half a billion followers* . . . ." is not a cult, nor is it a religious belief system that is based on doing good works to earn salvation, but rather, it is an interdependent spiritual system of socialization inherent in the original Mystery System for cultivating the Arts and Sciences in conjunction with being engaged in a personal relationship and spiritual union with God, based on the acceptance of God's gift of *true life* through Christ and as founded on doing *Maat*, which ensures salvation and from which good works spring.[34]

In keeping with these facts, it is of capital importance to note that certain ancient Egyptian texts depict *Maat* as a winged Goddess and identify her as the daughter of Ra, who along with her Father preexisted the establishment of her attributes of truth, justice, harmony, balance, reciprocity, order, righteousness, wisdom, temperance, and courage throughout the cosmos at the time of creation, and as a consequence prevailing wisdom held that if *Maat* were to be abandoned society (*i.e.*, the spiritual, social, educational, political, and economic organization of the community) along with the entire universe would collapse into chaos.[35] For this reason it was only natural that the primary **mission of life** was to establish, maintain and, if necessary, reestablish *Maat*, which was accomplished by constantly and systematically engaging *Maat*

". . . in all areas of moral concern" and human activity, from law and economics to education, entertainment, history, labor, politics, religion, sex and even war.[36] And it is through this act of exercising personal control over our destinies and daily lives that doing *Maat* compels cooperative human effort essential to its maintenance, and creates situations and circumstances wherein we are more apt to do what is right, which thereby enhances our innate predisposition to increase good in the world; after all, to increase good in the world is the **purpose of life**, for it is written in Amenist Scriptures that at the time of creation God created ". . . every good thing," but that God ". . . laid the foundation [of things] by *Maat*."[37] What, then, is "good?" Good is the offspring of values, intentions, thoughts, desires and actions conceived in the heart of one who nurtures himself or herself daily by doing *Maat*.[38] It is no wonder that Pharaoh Queen Hatshepsut affirmed, "I know that he (God) lives by it; It (*Maat*) is my bread too."[39]

In his book, *Maat: The Moral Ideal in Ancient Egypt*, Dr. Maulana Karenga sheds new light on an Amenist account of creation by identifying God in his name of Ptah as being the original *Placemaker*, who "in the unboundedness of pre-creation infinity" pulled himself together into a primordial mound that instantaneously became the ground on which he stood up, and from which he "designed and brought into being the whole universe."[40] All of creation, then, is in some respect an extension of the Creator. Although, clearly, creation in and of itself is not the Creator—a glimpse of insight which in turn raises the question: What is the equivalent of an extension of a human being, even if only in a relative sense? The answer to this question invariably includes family members, friends, coworkers, colleagues, and acquaintances by way of our relationships, but according to some psychologists it also and more subtly includes those with whom we share certain personal similarities, namely, our values.[41] It is the case that pulling people together around shared values, especially those that are inherent in the divine, universal organizing principle known in ancient Egypt as *Maat*, is in a very real sense an act of pulling together extensions of one's own self and therefore serves as a fundamental basis for organizing progress.

Symbolically it represents the primordial mound in that it is firm ground on which to stand up, design and bring into being a place not only for ourselves, but also for others; and though initially you will begin by investing in the well-being of those nearest you, the ultimate aim of the *Placemaker* is to work together with your community to extend the reach of a shared beneficence beyond the local level by building institutions such as schools, businesses, banks, hospitals, courts of law, temples, and charitable organizations to gradually help more and more people in need, whomever and wherever they may be. Ever the true *Placemaker*, Pharaoh Rameses III made it a point to reinforce this view when he said, "I sustained alive the whole land, whether foreigners, (common) folk, citizens, or people, male or female."[42] Recall now Egyptologist E. A. Wallis Budge's translation of the title "Pharaoh" as, the *Great House* "…in which all Egyptians took asylum" and you will realize that helping those in need begins with making a place for them within one's own self; then, from *this place* you will be able to create the right "conditions of opportunity" in which their needs can be met, and in turn enable them to experience ". . . ever-higher levels of human life and achievement."[43] These, then, are the teachings of the *Pharaohs' 4th Law of Success, "Become a Placemaker."*

CHAPTER 5

Express Your Gratitude

To outwardly demonstrate our heartfelt appreciation to those who helped make our success possible.¹

> "Be content with Maat daily, it is food that does not sate, the lord god of Abydos lives on it daily!"²
> —Baki, ancient Egyptian granary chief

Some of the first humans that migrated from ". . . the birthplace of humanity in East Africa's Great Lakes region, around the Omo Valley" of Ethiopia, made their way northward to a region in the Nile River Valley that in the present day is modern Sudan, and it is here, specifically in the northern part of the country in an area known by the relatively modern term "Nubia," that important archaeological discoveries were made from which researchers have concluded that approximately 500 years preceding the inception of Egypt's 1st Dynasty of mortals when Pharaoh Mena united ". . . Egypt into a unified kingdom," the ancient Sudanese had already developed a pharaonic system of their own, were engaged in the practice of Amenism, and ruled their own kingdom that the ancient Egyptians called (1) *Kash*, from which we derive the term "Kush," and (2) *Ta-Seti*, meaning "Land of the Bow," because of the highly skilled Ta-Setian archers, and also because according to archaeologist Dr. Bruce Williams, Ta-Seti is the very name that was used by the ancient Sudanese themselves.³ Notwithstanding, the ancient Greeks miscalled this region "Ethiopia," meaning "the country of burnt faced men;" however, they did not apply the same term to the country that was lying directly to the north of Ta-Seti, viz. Egypt, for although ancient Greek and Latin writers such as Herodotus, Aristotle, Lucian, Apollodorus, Aeschylus, Achilles Tatius of Alexandria, Strabo, Diodorus of Sicily, Diogenes Laertius and Ammianus Marcellinus knew very well that like the ancient Ta-Setians the ancient Egyptians were black, we are told by author Anthony Browder that ". . . (t)he first Greek visitors to Egypt . . . were (so) greatly impressed by the Temple of Ptah" in the city of Memphis that they subsequently began to use a Grecian form of the sacred name of that city for the whole country; thus, *Het-Ka-Ptah*, meaning "the temple of the Ka of Ptah," is the sacred name of the aforementioned city called in Greek, "Aiguptos," from which we later derive the term "Egypt."[4] Furthermore, author George G. M. James informs us that Egypt's climate of profound spiritual, religious and scientific knowledge

> ". . . filled the Greeks with awe, and . . . that the staunch faith of the Egyptians, together with their mysterious forms of worship, led to the universal conviction among the Ancients, that Egypt was not only the Holy Land but the Holiest of lands or countries, and that indeed, the Gods dwelt there."[5]

Ironically, the ancient Egyptians maintained that their civilization came from the south (*i.e.*, inner-Africa), and when in the Nile Valley we trace backwards the pattern of migration, we proceed from Egypt to Ta-Seti, and then on even farther south to the actual country of Ethiopia (formerly Abyssinia) where humanity began and where, according to Greek historian Diodorus Siculus,

> ". . . the Ethiopians, as historians relate, were the first of

all men, and the proofs of this statement, they say, are manifest. For that they did not come into their land as immigrants from abroad, but were the natives of it, and so justly bear the name of autochthones (sprung from the soil itself), is, they maintain, conceded by practically all men ... They say also that the Egyptians are colonists sent out by the Ethiopians, Osiris having been the leader of the colony. For, speaking generally, what is now Egypt, they maintain, was not land but sea, when in the beginning the universe was being formed. Afterwards, however, as the Nile during the time of its inundation carried down the mud from Ethiopia, land was gradually built up from the deposit."[6]

As corroborating evidence, Egyptologist Gaston Maspero said: "By almost unanimous testimony of the ancient historians, they [the Egyptians] belonged to an African race which first settled in Ethiopia, on the Middle Nile; following the course of the river, they gradually reached the sea."[7] Not only do these remarkable statements speak volumes about the African origin of the ancient Egyptians and the religion of Amenism, but when we revert to using the same proper names for countries that our African ancestors themselves used, the above statements also intimate that according to the teachings of the Kemetan Mystery System as well as the religion of Amenism, Kemet (*i.e.*, the *Black Community of Christ*) began in ancient Abyssinia (*i.e.*, ancient Ethiopia) as a secret order comprising native African votaries of Christ (Osir), who after making their way to the northeastern corner of Africa established Kemet as the Kingdom of God on earth, and from there transmitted civilization to the rest of the ancient world.[8] Let us therefore, unless it is warranted, dispense with substituting the terms Ethiopia, Nubia (or Kush) and Egypt for the proper names Abyssinia, Ta-Seti and Kemet in a coordinated effort to express our gratitude toward the Fathers and Mothers of civilization from whom we have descended.[9]

    Highly esteemed among the ancient Kemetans was the virtue of gratitude that was expressed toward God, the king, and also toward one another, so it is fitting to go into some detail concerning the standards of conduct that were expected of the Kemetan in his or her daily personal, social and professional life by examining Divine Law, the observance of which, along with doing God's Will, are two of the highest expressions of gratitude.[10] In this case, the crucial question is: What other extant documents besides the papyrus at Leyden support our understanding that the ancient Kemetans received Divine Law? In response to this question, our first text of interest comes from an unexpected source. Discovered on the inside walls of coffins, mortuary inscriptions now known as the *Ancient Egyptian Coffin Texts* quote God in his name of Ra as saying,

> "I have made *every man like his brother*, and I have forbidden that they do [[*isfet*]], (but) it was their hearts which undid that which I had said."[11]

    While there was no other mention in the text pertaining to what God actually said, the text does; however, establish the principle of human equality, and it also alludes to God having imparted moral counsel to humans for the purpose of instructing them in the practice of the ten cardinal virtues of *Maat* in their daily lives, which suggests Divine Law.[12] Special emphasis is again given to the innate predisposition of humans to increase good in the world, but it is acknowledged that humans have been created with free will to choose in "their hearts" to do *Maat*, or to do *isfet*, which is referred to in the Mysteries as the "Two Paths."[13] With this in mind, we shall now turn our attention to an important religious book concerning the belief in the afterlife and immortality that was customarily placed in the tombs of the departed titled, the *Book of "Coming Forth as the (Newborn) Sun."*[14] The section of the book that adds significantly to our understanding of Divine Law in ancient Kemet is Chapter 125, wherein after the resurrection of the departed in a spiritual body called the *sahu*, and ascension into the afterlife, the soul of the departed humbly enters the "Hall of Judgment called the Great Hall of Maati (The Two Truths)" and is admitted into the presence of Osir and his forty-two divine judges.[15] There, the departed advances and delivers the Opening Address of his *Declaration of Maat* in which he affirms his righteousness and also his self-correction of past offenses against God, humankind and nature saying:[16]

> "Hail to you, ye lords of truth! Hail to thee, great one, [[Osir]], lord of truth! I come unto thee, my lord! I draw nigh unto thee to behold thee! I have learned and I know thy name! I know the names of the forty and two who are with thee, who live and watch the wicked who come before the justified one. Hail, I know ye, O lords of truth! I bring unto you truth (i.e., Maat)! I have destroyed the evil within me!"[17]

Immediately after the Opening Address of the *Declaration of Maat* were forty-two Declarations of Innocence that were made by the departed from the standpoint of being innocent of neglecting to cease from knowingly and willingly transgressing Divine Law (*i.e.*, the "laws of *Maat*") while on earth, and of ever having committed certain other transgressions of Divine Law as well.[18] Furthermore, the particular Declaration of Innocence of not transgressing says Dr. Maulana Karenga, ". . . suggests and requires rules one can observe or transgress" (*e.g.*, Divine Law).[19] The objective of the departed, of course, was to have done away with all of his transgressions while on earth and prior to being admitted into the presence of God in the afterlife, so that what he spoke with his mouth and presented with his hands as he stood before the Lord of judgment, was solely "an offering of *Maat*."[20]

Thus, it is through the examination of the following Declarations of Innocence as well as of the *Ancient Egyptian Coffin Texts,* and the papyrus at Leyden that present-day Amenists can affirm with certainty that God imparted Divine Law to humans by way of divine revelation, and for the purpose of instructing them in the practice of the ten cardinal virtues of *Maat* in their daily lives.[21]

The Forty-Two Declarations of Innocence from the Papyrus of the Scribe Nebseni:

1. [hieroglyphs][22]

I am not one who does *isfet* (*i.e.*, I am not one who renders himself up to falsehood, injustice, discord, imbalance, exploitation, disorder, unrighteousness, folly, greed, and cowardice).[23] Commentary: *Isfet* is the universal chaos principle and by rendering up oneself to its "ten bodily fetters" in one's daily life and in defiance of Divine Law, evil is increased in the world.[24] Furthermore, according to Webster's New World Dictionary, "Chaos implies total and apparently irremediable lack of organization" (*i.e.*, the opposite of *Maat*).[25]

Corresponding Divine Law: To do *isfet* is contrary to doing *Maat*.

2. [hieroglyphs][26]

I am not one who robs.[27]

Corresponding Divine Law: To rob is contrary to doing *Maat*.

Express Your Gratitude

3.  [28]

I am not one who covets.[29]

Corresponding Divine Law: To covet is contrary to doing *Maat*.

4. [30]

I am not one who steals.[31]

Corresponding Divine Law: To steal is contrary to doing *Maat*.

5. [32]

I am not one who kills people.[33]

Corresponding Divine Law: To kill is contrary to doing *Maat*.

6. [34]

I am not one who damages grain measures.[35] For example, in order "(t)o falsify its fractions."[36]

Corresponding Divine Law: To falsify is contrary to doing *Maat*.

7. [37]

I am not one who does fraud.[38]

Corresponding Divine Law: To defraud is contrary to doing *Maat*.

8. [39]

I am not one who steals God's property.[40]

Corresponding Divine Law: To steal God's property is contrary to doing *Maat*.

THE PHARAOHS' 5 LAWS OF SUCCESS

9. 〰 [hieroglyphs] [41]

I am not one who speaks lies.[42]

Corresponding Divine Law: To lie is contrary to doing *Maat*.

10. 〰 [hieroglyphs] [43]

I am not one who takes away food (*i.e.*, I am not one who deprives others of food).[44]

Corresponding Divine Law: To deprive is contrary to doing *Maat*.

11. 〰 [hieroglyphs] [45]

I am not one who is contentious.[46] Commentary: "contention most frequently applies to heated verbal strife, or dispute."[47]

Corresponding Divine Law: To be contentious is contrary to doing *Maat*.

12. 〰 [hieroglyphs] [48]

I am not one who transgresses (*i.e.*, I am not one who transgresses Divine Law).[49]

Corresponding Divine Law: To transgress is contrary to doing *Maat*.

13. 〰 [hieroglyphs] [50]

I am not one who kills a sacred bull.[51]

Corresponding Divine Law: To disregard the sacrosanct is contrary to doing *Maat*.

14. 〰 [hieroglyphs] [52]

I am not one who does [acts of] deceit.⁵³

Corresponding Divine Law: To deceive is contrary to doing *Maat*.

15. [hieroglyphs]⁵⁴
I am not one who robs bread rations.⁵⁵

Corresponding Divine Law: To impoverish is contrary to doing *Maat*.

16. [hieroglyphs]⁵⁶
I am not one who eavesdrops.⁵⁷

Corresponding Divine Law: To eavesdrop is contrary to doing *Maat*.

17. [hieroglyphs]⁵⁸
I am not one who babbles.⁵⁹

Corresponding Divine Law: To babble is contrary to doing *Maat*.

18. [hieroglyphs]⁶⁰
I am not one who is disputatious "... except concerning my own property."⁶¹ Commentary: "dispute implies argument in which there is a clash of opposing opinions, often presented in an angry or heated manner."⁶²

Corresponding Divine Law: To be disputatious is contrary to doing *Maat*.

19. [hieroglyphs]⁶³
I am not one who copulates [with] "... the wife of a man" (*i.e.*, I

am not one who commits adultery).⁶⁴

Corresponding Divine Law: To commit adultery is contrary to doing *Maat*.

20. 〰️ 𓂀𓅡𓂋𓅡𓌟𓀀 ⁶⁵
I am not one who fornicates.⁶⁶

Corresponding Divine Law: To fornicate is contrary to doing *Maat*.

21. 〰️ 𓂀𓀀 𓏺𓆳𓊃𓀀 ⁶⁷
I am not one who does [the causing of] fear.⁶⁸

Corresponding Divine Law: To cause fear is contrary to doing *Maat*.

22. 〰️ 𓉐𓅡𓊃𓈖𓀀 ⁶⁹
I am not one who trespasses (*i.e.*, I am not one who encroaches or intrudes upon the rights and/or property of others).⁷⁰

Corresponding Divine Law: To trespass is contrary to doing *Maat*.

23. 〰️ 𓊃𓅡𓎡𓀀 ⁷¹
I am not one who is hot-tempered.⁷²

Corresponding Divine Law: To be hot-tempered is contrary to doing *Maat*.

24. 〰️ 𓀀𓏺𓌃𓂋𓏛 〰️ 𓂋𓏤𓈖 ⁷³
I am not one who is deaf to the words of Truth.⁷⁴

Corresponding Divine Law: To be deaf to the words of Truth is

Express Your Gratitude

contrary to doing *Maat*.

25. I am not one who stirs up strife.[76]

Corresponding Divine Law: To stir up strife is contrary to doing *Maat*.

26. I am not one who winks [at wrongdoing].[78]

Corresponding Divine Law: To connive is contrary to doing *Maat*.

27. I am not one who engages in abnormal sexual intercourse; I am not one who sodomizes.[80]

Corresponding Divine Law: To engage in abnormal sexual intercourse is contrary to doing *Maat*.

28. I am not one who swallows his heart (*i.e.*, I am not one who silences his conscience).[82]

Corresponding Divine Law: To silence the conscience is contrary to doing *Maat*.

29. I am not one who [utters] curses (*i.e.*, I am not one who invokes evil, sickness or misfortune on others).[84]

Corresponding Divine Law: To utter curses is contrary to doing *Maat*.

30. 𓈖𓏤 𓎛𓈖 𓂝𓂋 𓀀 [85]

I am not one whose arm goes forth [excessively] (*i.e.*, I am not one who overworks).[86]

Corresponding Divine Law: To overwork is contrary to doing *Maat*.

31. 𓈖𓏤 𓄿𓇋𓂋 𓂝 𓀀 [87]

I am not one whose heart hurries (*i.e.*, I am not one who is impatient).[88]

Corresponding Divine Law: To be impatient is contrary to doing *Maat*.

32. 𓈖𓏤 𓉐𓂋𓂻𓀀 𓇋𓐝𓀀 𓈖 𓇋𓈗𓀀 𓇋𓏏𓀀 [89]

I am not one who transgresses his color; I am not one who [white] washes [the image of] God (*i.e.*, I am not one who commits moral offenses against his nature; I am not one who bleaches out the melanin in his skin).[90] Commentary: In the religion of Amenism the ancient Kemetan term *Flesh of Ra* refers to the brown to black pigment known as melanin which is responsible for giving the skin its color, and according to author and psychiatrist Dr. Richard King, the study of melanin began in ancient Kemet.[91] Furthermore, since it is taught in Amenist Scripture that humans are created in the image of God, it is a sin *i.e.*, moral offense, to knowingly and willingly misrepresent God by diminishing his most fundamentally important, manifest visual trait in humans that speaks to the hidden mysteries of his divine spiritual nature; namely, one's skin pigmentation.[92]

Corresponding Divine Law: To commit moral offenses against one's nature or to misrepresent God is contrary to doing *Maat*.

Express Your Gratitude

33. [hieroglyphs][93]

I am not one who multiplies his voice on account of his words (*i.e.*, I am not one who gossips).[94] Commentary: Gossiping causes others to repeat the verbal indiscretions that one has said and therefore multiplies one's voice in the mouths of others accordingly.

Corresponding Divine Law: To gossip is contrary to doing *Maat*.

34. [hieroglyphs][95]

I am not one who commits sins; I am not one who does evil.[96]

Corresponding Divine Law: To commit sins (*i.e.*, moral offenses) or to do evil, is contrary to doing *Maat*.

35. [hieroglyphs][97]

I am not one who does [the uttering of] "curses [on the king]."[98] Commentary: The king is identified with God.

Corresponding Divine Law: To utter curses on the king is contrary to doing *Maat*.

36. [hieroglyphs][99]

I am not one who wades in water (*i.e.*, I am not one who fouls water).[100]

Corresponding Divine Law: To foul water is contrary to doing *Maat*.

37. [hieroglyphs][101]

I am not one who is loud-voiced (*i.e.*, I am not one who speaks in a haughty voice).[102]

Corresponding Divine Law: To speak with a haughty voice is contrary to doing *Maat*.

38. [hieroglyphs]¹⁰³

I am not one who curses God.¹⁰⁴

Corresponding Divine Law: To curse God is contrary to doing *Maat*.

39. [hieroglyphs]¹⁰⁵

I am not one who makes "puffings-up" (*i.e.*, I am not one who puffs himself or herself up with self-importance).¹⁰⁶

Corresponding Divine Law: To be pompous is contrary to doing *Maat*.

40. [hieroglyphs]¹⁰⁷

I am not one who makes self-distinctions (*i.e.*, I am not one who makes distinctions of himself or herself from others for honor, praise, special recognition, or to create the perception of superiority).¹⁰⁸

Corresponding Divine Law: To make self-distinctions is contrary to doing *Maat*.

41. [hieroglyphs]¹⁰⁹

I am not one whose possessions are great, "... *not even* [[with]] my (own) property" (*i.e.*, I am not one who has acquired more than he or she needs).¹¹⁰

Corresponding Divine Law: To be greedy is contrary to doing *Maat*.

Express Your Gratitude

42. [hieroglyphs][111]

I am not one who scorns [the presiding form of] God in my [municipal] *Community of Christ* (*i.e.*, city).[112] Commentary: According to the teachings of Amenism, every municipal *Community of Christ* (*i.e.*, district or city) had its own presiding spiritual form of God Amen.[113]

Corresponding Divine Law: To scorn the forms of God is contrary to doing *Maat*.

 Notice that Divine Law is by no means a collection of commandments; but rather and as previously stated, Divine Law is expressed as moral counsel that God imparted to humans by way of divine revelation, and for the purpose of instructing them in the practice of the ten cardinal virtues of *Maat* in their daily lives; therefore, Divine Law has inherent free will at its very core.[114] Any and all subsequent commands given by God, then, reach their fullest fruition when compliance with Divine Law of one's own free will, desire and decision precedes them, and when the catalyzing agent is gratitude. Amenist Scripture says, "Command was given for them to hear. Counsel was given for them to learn."[115]

 Finally, the departed delivers the Closing Address of his *Declaration of Maat* in which he reaffirms his life of doing *Maat* while on earth for which he afterwards humbly requests a welcomed entrance into Amenta (heaven), but whether he was rewarded with immortality and an afterlife in heaven, or whether he was punished with the prevention of his Ba from reuniting with his Ka, and an eventual *second death* in which his soul was completely annihilated, the departed needed first to be judged of the righteousness of his heart.[116] Here, in the Great Hall of Maati and on the Day of Judgment called "the Day of Assessing Characters" and the "Day of Great Reckoning," the heart of the departed was weighed in a balance against an ostrich feather ⁅, the hieroglyphic symbol for *Maat*; and provided that the weight of his heart was equal to that of the feather of *Maat*, the departed was proclaimed *maa-kheru* (mah-**AH** ker-**ROO**), meaning "true of voice" and was henceforth justified.[117] Assimilation to Osir was now accorded to the departed along with having the name of Osir prefixed to his own, and the monogram of Christ, which was formed by the crossed loose ends of his "Great Collar," placed directly over the middle of his upper torso.[118]

Having thus become one with Osir, <u>in him</u> the departed received the reward of immortality and a welcomed entrance into Amenta (heaven) where the Ba of the departed joined his Ka, and where his Khu was transfigured into an Akhu (**AH**-koo), spelled 𓇋𓐍𓅱𓀭, 𓇋𓅱𓀭, meaning a glorified spirit (*previously interchangeably spelled* 𓐍𓅱𓀭, 𓅱𓀭, 𓅱).[119] The *Book of "Coming Forth as the (Newborn) Sun"* says: "From assimilation with him (*i.e.*, Osir) comes the perfection of being," and with that, the transfigured, justified souls of the departed took up their abode in the Duat (**DOO**-aht) *i.e.*, the Kingdom of Heaven, where they received *Maat* (*i.e.*, "Truth") as bread upon which to subsist, and were granted the ability to "assume whatever (spiritual) form" they wanted "in whatever place" their spirit wished to be.[120]

Another important expression of gratitude in ancient Kemet was that of gift-giving on special occasions such as ". . . the birth of a child" or the arrival of the New Year, which according to the Kemetan calendar is on the first day of the year, and of the first month, which is Mesut Ra (**MAY-SOOT RAH**), meaning the "birth of Ra" and corresponds to the Gregorian calendar date of June 25th.[121] Gifts were called añew (uh-**NYOO**) 𓇋𓈖𓏤𓅱, and the various añew that were either

Express Your Gratitude

given or exchanged on New Year's Day ranged from "... small quantities of food," articles of clothing, and "objects in daily use" to scarabs, New Year's flasks and wish seals upon which were inscribed, "May Ra grant you a happy New Year ... May your name be established in the House of [[Osir]]," and many other New Year's wishes.[122] The aforementioned New Year, which was also a national festival, was celebrated with family, friends, and members of one's community by offering a customary New Year's greeting, for example, "May [your] year open happily," or, "Happy New Year," and by preparing an offering table (*e.g.*, "Table of the Sun" called also "Table of Ra") "... on the last day of the year, and of the last month," as <u>early</u> Christian biblical scholar Jerome writes, "... filled with food of various kinds, and a cup containing wine and honey mixed together ... either as an expression of thankfulness for the fertility of the past year, or invoking fertility for the coming year."[123] Also, a chapter of The *Book of "Coming Forth as the (Newborn) Sun"* says of the soul of the justified departed that "... he takes his place **on the day of the New Year** with those who are under Osiris (*i.e.*, Osir)," and that after a trial of knowing this chapter "... he has given to him cakes and drink ... , and a quantity of meat off the table of the Sun (*i.e.*, the Table of Ra)."[124] In what present-day Amenists recognize as Kemet's Reemergent Kingdom that began in the year 52580 Z.T.E. according to the Kemetan calendar or 2020 C.E. according to the Gregorian calendar, the offering cup containing the mixture of wine and honey called "oimellas" is placed in the center of the *Table of the Sun* and (1) is used to pour libation for our ancestors; and (2) the remaining portion of its contents is poured into individual cups belonging to attendees of the Feast of the New Year, and is drank together as a gesture of solidarity following a brief praise of thanksgiving using or modeled after the here presented extract from a 19th Dynasty Amenist hymn:[125]

> *"Hail to thee, Ra, lord of truth . . . lord of mercy most loving . . . to whom the sixth and the seventh days are sacred ; sovereign of life, health, and strength—whose name is hidden from his creatures ; in his name which is Amen (hidden). Hail to thee, who art in tranquility. . . Amen, sustainer of all things—We who thou hast made (thank thee) that thou hast given us birth ; we give thee praises on account of thy mercy to us.—Beloved of Aptu (Thebes) ; high crowned in the house of the obelisk (Heliopolis). The ONE alone without peer—living in truth forever."*[126]
>
> *Amen-Ra*[127]

At this point, a final show of gratitude by wishing all who attended the New Year's Day Feast an additional "Happy New Year" is in order, but one should be keenly mindful that in Kemet the living were not the only ones toward whom gratitude was expressed. To cite an instance, after the passing of Pharaoh Sethi I, his son and successor Rameses II undertook the massive project of restoring his father's mortuary temple, adding to it an inscription recounting his good deeds to him.[128] From beyond his tomb Sethi I is made to reply: "See, every day I am full of joy, because I come back to life."[129] Rameses II understood what the message meant. His father was telling him that to pronounce his father's name and to commemorate his life and legacy was in a very real sense to cause him to live again, for in doing so the king lives on in you.[130] Go one step further by realizing that it is in outwardly demonstrating our heartfelt appreciation to those who helped make our success possible, that like the kings of ancient Kemet, we too engage the *Pharaohs' 5th Law of Success*, "Express Your Gratitude."

Conclusion

> *"The tongue of a man is the rudder of a boat,
> (but) the Universal Lord is its pilot."*[1]
> —Amenemaopet, ancient Kemetan high official

In the Mysteries it is taught that ancient Kemet was the Kingdom of God on earth, which was said by the ancient Kemetans to have been transferred from heaven to the very location chosen by God for transmitting civilization to all nations.[2] Yet, owing to a complex series of historical events and cultural shifts, ancient Kemet eventually fell in a state of ruin, and its people suffered the devastating loss of cohesion.[3] It is known that all civilizations eventually decline and fall, so in that regard ancient Kemet was no different, but the wider reality is that the *fall* of Kemet was largely attributable to the supplanting of Amenism and over 1,000 years of all the successive invasions launched by the Persians, Greeks, Romans, and Arabs, during the course of which we are told by Senegalese historian Aboubacry Lam, six migratory waves fleeing these foreign invasions left Kemet and eventually reached West Africa.[4] Some centuries later millions of our ancestors, primarily from Central and West Africa, were forcibly transferred to foreign lands while having the greatest immoral and atrocious injury inflicted upon them in the form of a "Holocaust of Enslavement, which claimed an estimated

50 to 100 million lives" and as a result, we as their descendants have heretofore almost entirely lacked written records that identify our respective African countries of origin, much less that reconnect the rest of Africa with the history of ancient Kemet.[5] So out of the need to claim and protect the above account of our migration from Kemet to West Africa, and also in solidarity with the West African nation of Ghana whose twelfth president since its independence from Great Britain, Nana Akufo-Addo, declared the year 2019 C.E. or 52579 Z.T.E. the "Year of Return," not to mention out of being inspired by Amen himself, this extraordinary episode in African history that was once preserved solely as Senegalese oral tradition is now officially recognized as Scripture in the religion of Amenism, making possible its intergenerational cultural transmission to all people of African descent, whether on the continent of Africa or in the Diaspora.[6]

To that end, multidisciplinary scholar and preeminent Egyptologist Dr. Cheikh Anta Diop firmly stated that all blacks ". . . can legitimately trace their culture to ancient Egypt (*i.e.*, ancient Kemet) and build a modern culture on that foundation."[7] That being the case, having a common cultural heritage as well as some common ancestry means also being of the same ethnicity—Kemetan—as ethnicity *is* "the part of a person's self-concept related to his or her identification with a particular group of people, based on having a common cultural heritage, ancestry, country of origin, or nationality."[8] Let us not forget, however, that Kemet, meaning the "Black Community of Christ," is inclusive of all humanity, since all humans have a common black ancestry which invariably includes non-blacks who carry mutated versions of particular genes, resulting in diminished human skin pigmentation.[9] The decision of our ancient Kemetan ancestors to designate their country by the name *Kemet* is therefore not only in reference to the historical Osir the Christ and to the corresponding <u>exclusive</u> agency called "Christ" that are both said to be located ". . . in the bosom of the

Conclusion

spirit" of God that dwells within us all, but also to the divine, perfect black image with which all humans were endowed by God at the time that God first created them in his own image.[10]

All this despite repeated attempts by the followers of Seth to completely and permanently sever us from our cultural heritage of ancient Kemet, where wall paintings in tombs and temples frequently depict Kemetan men and women seemingly with ocherous red and yellow skin respectively, but which was based wholly on an acute consciousness of themselves in relation to God. In this case, an African consciousness of self that stemmed from a long held religious belief made known in an Amenist account of creation in which Amen in his ram-headed form and in his name of Khnum (kuh-**NOOM**) formed man and woman on his potter's wheel on the Island of Elephantine from ocherous red and yellow Kemetan *clays* respectively.[11] What an incredibly humble gesture of paying homage to the Creator through the color symbolism of Amenism by depicting themselves as being formed from ocherous red and yellow Kemetan clays, which speaks directly to the **meaning of life** that was revealed in the teachings of the ancient Kemetan scribe Ani who wrote: "He who magnifies him (*i.e.*, God) is magnified."[12] Thus our own magnification like that of our ancient Kemetan ancestors will be witnessed in all of the opulence and splendor that comes with spiritual revival, union, salvation, rebirth and resurrection here beginning anew. Welcome to the Reemergent Kingdom and 34th Dynasty of Kemet, a modern continuation of the tremendous legacy of excellence and achievement left by our ancient Kemetan ancestors, who, by cultivating the Arts and Sciences in conjunction with being engaged in a personal relationship and spiritual union with God, made the mastery of the gateway to spiritual, social, educational, political, and economic "conditions of opportunity" attainable for all, and so earned the designation *Seba-ur* (say-bah-**OOR**), meaning teacher, educator, instructor.[13]

THE PHARAOHS' 5 LAWS OF SUCCESS

Pharaoh Sesostris I taught:

> *"The king dies not, who is mentioned by reason of his achievements. It is my name which is mentioned in reality, which passes not away because of eternal things."*[14]

These things of eternity are none other than truth, justice, harmony, balance, reciprocity, order, righteousness, wisdom, temperance, and courage embodied in the divine, universal organizing principle called *Maat*, according to which the ancient Kemetans designed and lived their lives, and which has now become the foundation of this, *The Pharaohs' 5 Laws of Success*. In addressing present-day Kemetans regarding our most ancient philosophy, history, and theology, it is therefore sufficient to say that whosoever among us <u>collectively</u> raises up and restores these three pillars of the Reflective Arts in their daily lives will achieve true and lasting success for themselves and also for one another, which has been revealed in the Kemetan Mystery System and in *the leadership of the Pharaoh* as the continuous process of conceiving and actualizing ever-higher levels of our infinite potentiality (*e.g.*, our Christhood)—together.[15] "Live in truth!"[16]

NOTES

INTRODUCTION

1. Miriam Lichtheim, *Ancient Egyptian Literature*, Volume I, (Los Angeles: University of California Press, 1973), 73. Mine in parentheses. Italics mine.

2. **Rationale: First**, One of the greatest achievements of the Ancient Egyptians was that they were teachers, educators and instructors to the entire ancient world. *See* Theophile Obenga, *African Origin of So-Called Greek Philosophy and Education* [Video Presentation]. *IAS Film Night - 3 November 2016.* Retrieved from https://www.youtube.com/watch?v=vJgd0D3sDzE. Accessed 27 June 2021. Theophile Obenga, *L'Egypte, la Grece et l'ecole d'Alexandrie: Histoire interculturelle dans l'antiquite – Aux sources egyptiennes de la philosophie grecque*, (Paris: L'Harmattan, 2005), 5ff. ". . . Egypt was the greatest education centre of the ancient world . . ." and when the Greeks came in contact with Egypt, it ". . . resulted in the genesis of their enlightenment." George G. M. James, *Stolen Legacy*, (Trenton: African World Press, 1992), 41-42. **Second**, Historian and philosopher Will Durant has defined education ". . . as the technique of transmitting civilization." Will Durant, *The Story of Civilization, Part 1: Our Oriental Heritage*, (New York: Simon and Schuster, 1954), 4. **Third**, Osir, the first person of the Holy Trinity, and with whom the Pharaoh was identified came down from heaven to transmit civilization to all nations. E. A. Wallis Budge, *Osiris and the Egyptian Resurrection*, Volume I, (New York: G. P. Putnam's Sons, 1911), 2, 16. Note: The three persons of the Holy Trinity in the religion of Christianity is a plagiarized,

adapted and reconfigured version of the three persons of the Holy Trinity of Osir, Iset and Heru in the religion of Amenism. Anthony T. Browder, *Nile Valley Contributions to Civilization: Exploding the Myths*, Volume 1, (Washington: The Institute of Karmic Guidance, 1992), 68. E. A. Wallis Budge, *From Fetish to God in Ancient Egypt*, (New York: Dover Publications, Inc., 1988), 18. D. M. Murdock, *Christ in Egypt: The Horus-Jesus Connection*, (Ashland: Stellar House Publishing, 2009), 53-54, 67. According to the teachings of Amenism, the king is both Osir and Heru but with one caveat. The living king is literally Heru who rules on earth, while his active role in transmitting civilization to all nations, which is the transference to earth of the Kingdom of Heaven located within his own spirit, identifies him with Osir, until at death when the king is completely assimilated to him. *See* Margaret A. Murray, *Egyptian Religious Poetry*, (London: John Murray, 1949), 37-38. *See* also Margaret A. Murray, *The Osireion at Abydos*, (London: Bernard Quaritch, 1904), 32-34. *See* also Charles Loring Brace, *The Unknown God: Or, Inspiration Among Pre-Christian Races*, (New York: A. C. Armstrong and Son, 1890), 27. D. M. Murdock, *Christ in Egypt: The Horus-Jesus Connection*, (Ashland: Stellar House Publishing, 2009), 49-51. *See* also Maulana Karenga, *Maat: The Moral Ideal in Ancient Egypt*, (Los Angeles: University of Sankore Press, 2006), 164-165. Tarík Karenga, *Review of the Kemetan Mystery System*, First Edition, (Union City: Amenism, Inc., in press). **Fourth**, one of the hereditary positions held by the Pharaoh was that of high priest. *See* Bob Brier and Hoyt Hobbs, *Daily Life of the Ancient Egyptians*, Second Edition, (Westport: Greenwood Press, 2008), 41, 74-75. **Fifth**, based on a dialog titled "Statesman" and written by Greek philosopher and former slave Plato, in Egypt one was not permitted to be king unless he himself was a priest. *See* Benjamin Jowett, *The Dialogs of Plato*, Volume 3, (London: Clarendon Press, 1871), 611. **Sixth**, ancient Egyptian priests, which included the Pharaoh, were also members of a "Secret Order" and Mystery System in which Pharaoh Amasis once served as Grand Master and whose purpose included the ". . . creation, preservation and transmission . . ." of the Arts and Sciences. *See* George G. M. James, *Stolen Legacy*, (Trenton: African World Press, 1992), 1, 27-28, 35ff; the

Notes

humanities (*i.e.*, the Arts) is defined as "The study of how a culture expresses its values through the creation, preservation and transmission of ideas and works of art." See Michael A. Babcock, *The Humanities: A Christian Approach*, Sixth Edition, (Lynchburg: HPS Publishing, 2003), 1. **Seventh**, some of the most well-known "wisdom teachings" and instructions that have come down to us from ancient Egypt were written by Pharaohs. See "The Instruction Addressed to King Merikare," in Miriam Lichtheim, *Ancient Egyptian Literature*, Volume I, (Los Angeles: University of California Press, 1973), 97-109. See also "The Instruction of King Amenemhet I for His Son Sesostris I," *ibid.*, 135-139.

3. Margaret A. Murray, *Egyptian Religious Poetry*, (London: John Murray, 1949), 40-41.

4. *See* the chapters, "Seek Wise Counsel" and "Express Your Gratitude."

5. The ten virtues of the Egyptian Mystery System are as follows: truth, justice, harmony, balance, reciprocity, order, righteousness, wisdom, temperance, and courage (*i.e.*, the ten cardinal virtues of *Maat*). Asa G. Hillard, III, *SBA: The Reawakening of the African Mind*, (Gainesville, Makare Publishing Company, 1998), 2, 16. George G. M. James, *Stolen Legacy*, (Trenton: African World Press, 1992), 3-4, 30-31, 104-106. Philosopher and Egyptologist Gregoire Biyogo writes that *Maat* is ". . . the universal principle of Truth . . ." Gregoire Biyogo, *Aux Sources Egyptiennes Du Savoir: Volume 1, Genealogie Et Enjeux De La Pensee De Cheikh Anta Diop*, (Yaounde: Editions Menaibuc, 2000), 7n4. Author Jeremy Naydler makes reference to *Maat* as ". . . the divine organizing principle." Jeremy Naydler, *Temple of the Cosmos: The Ancient Egyptian Experience of the Sacred*, (Rochester: Inner Traditions International, 1996), 104. Egyptologist John A. Wilson says of *Maat*: "It was the cosmic force of harmony, order, stability, and security, coming down from the first creation as the organizing quality of created phenomena . . ." See John A. Wilson, *The Culture of Ancient Egypt*, (Chicago: The University of Chicago Press, 1957), 48. Professor of African American Studies Molefi Kete Asante wrote: "When you speak of it as the organizing principle of human society, the creative spirit of phenomena, and the

eternal order of the universe, you come close to understanding what the ancient Kemetic civilization understood." Molefi Kete Asante, *Kemet, Afrocentricity and Knowledge*, (Trenton: African World Press, 1990), 89. The ancient Egyptians depicted *Maat* as the daughter of God and held that maintaining the principle of *Maat* keeps society along with the entire universe from collapsing into chaos; hence the term *divine, universal organizing principle*. Christine El Mahdy, *Tutankhamen: The Life and Death of the Boy-King*, (New York: St. Martin's, 1999), 183. "Adherence to Maat created the good order of society, while abandoning Maat plunged society into chaos." Miriam Lichtheim, *Maat in Egyptian Autobiographies and Related Studies*, (Freiburg, Schweiz: Universitatsverlag; Gottingen: Vandenhoeck und Ruprecht, 1992), "English Summary." *See* also Emily Teeter, "Maat," in *The Oxford Encyclopedia of Ancient Egypt*, Volume 2, ed. Donald B. Redford, (New York: Oxford University Press, 2001), 319-321. According to Webster's New World Dictionary, "chaos implies total and apparently irremediable lack of organization." This is the opposite of *Maat*. *See* "chaos" under synonyms for "confusion" in Webster's New World Dictionary & Thesaurus, Version 2.0, Build #25, Accent Software International, Macmillan Publishers, 1998. *See* also the chapter, "Become a Placemaker."

6. *Maat* is joined to our hearts at birth and it is there that it is firmly established by doing *Maat*. Miriam Lichtheim, *Maat in Egyptian Autobiographies and Related Studies*, (Freiburg, Schweiz: Universitatsverlag; Gottingen: Vandenhoeck und Ruprecht, 1992), 67. Henri Frankfort, *Ancient Egyptian Religion*, (New York: Harper Torchbooks, 1961), 54, 63.

7. Siegfried Morenz, *Egyptian Religion*, (Ithaca: Cornell University Press, 1973), 114ff.

8. Maulana Karenga, *Maat: The Moral Ideal in Ancient Egypt*, (Los Angeles: University of Sankore Press, 2006), 264.

9. The opposite of *Maat* is *isfet* and, like *Maat*, *isfet* can be engaged in all areas of moral concern and human activity, but instead with adverse effects to society. Racism is one form of *isfet* that author Neely Fuller contends adversely affects people in nine major

Notes

areas of people activities. Fuller refers to the opposite of racism as justice and correctness, which is in fact *Maat*. *See* Neely Fuller, Jr., *The United Independent Compensatory Code/System/Concept: A Textbook/Workbook for Thought, Speech and/or Action for Victims of Racism (White Supremacy)*, Revised, (1984), 20-21. *See* also the chapter, "Become a Placemaker."

    10.   Using ancient Egyptian texts, author Siegfried Morenz points out that to live in an environment where *Maat* is prevalent is to be "imbued with" or influenced by *Maat*. *See* Siegfried Morenz, *Egyptian Religion*, (Ithaca: Cornell University Press, 1973), 121.

    11.   Henri Frankfort, *Ancient Egyptian Religion*, (New York: Harper Torchbooks, 1961), 55. Italics mine.

    12.   Maulana Karenga, *Maat: The Moral Ideal in Ancient Egypt*, (Los Angeles: University of Sankore Press, 2006), 32. Italics mine.

    13.   Present-day Amenists calculate the duration of Egypt's first emergence as an earthly kingdom from the time that Egypt was founded on earth by Osir and Iset in circa 43561 Z.T.E. or circa 7000 B.C.E., to the arrival of the Arabs in Egypt and the subsequent conversion of the ancient Egyptians to the foreign religion of Islam in 51201 Z.T.E. or 640 C.E. *See* Tarík Karenga, *Kemetan Calendar and Zodiac*, First Edition, (Union City: Amenism, Inc., 2022), 32-35. *See* also Listervelt Middleton and Asa G. Hilliard, *Master Keys to Ancient Kemet (Egypt)* [Video Presentation], Waset Educational Productions, 1990.

    14.   Maulana Karenga, *Introduction to Black Studies*, Second Edition, (Los Angeles: University of Sankore Press, 1993), 84-90. *See* also Cheikh Anta Diop, *The African Origin of Civilization: Myth or Reality*, (Chicago: Lawrence Hill Books, 1974), 230-235. *See* also George G. M. James, *Stolen Legacy*, (Trenton: African World Press, 1992), 7-154.

    15.   Author, Maulana Karenga teaches that the images that are raise above the earth are meant to reflect a people's ". . . capacity for human greatness and progress." Therefore, if images reflect—achievements testify. *See* Maulana Karenga, *The African American Holiday of Kwanzaa: A Celebration of Family, Community & Culture*, (Los Angeles: University of Sankore Press, 1988), 52.

THE PHARAOHS' 5 LAWS OF SUCCESS

16.   This teaching comes to us from Pharaoh Queen Hatshepsut who said that she restored what had been ruined and raised up what had been dismembered by the foreign invaders called Hyksos. See Maulana Karenga, *Maat: The Moral Ideal in Ancient Egypt*, (Los Angeles: University of Sankore Press, 2006), 80, 398.

17.   In his essay, "The Fully Functioning Person," psychologist Carl Rogers sums up what he calls, "the good life" as a process of "...stretching and growing of becoming more and more of one's potentialities." John Shaw, *The Self in Social Work*, (London: Routledge & Kegan Paul, 1974), 27. While Rogers posits that in order to achieve the "good life" one must (with the help of others) become "more and more" of what he or she <u>can be</u>, the ancient Egyptians taught that the "good life" is achieved through education (*e.g.*, through the cultivation of the Arts and Sciences) and by doing *Maat* (*e.g.*, by practicing virtue), because it is only within this context that one can (with the help of others and most importantly, with the help of God) "... recognize one's true nature and act accordingly, ... " so that ever-higher levels of one's infinite potentiality may be conceived and actualized. Maulana Karenga, *Maat: The Moral Ideal in Ancient Egypt*, (Los Angeles: University of Sankore Press, 2006), 231, 235-236, 253. George G. M. James, *Stolen Legacy*, (Trenton: African World Press, 1992), 28, 72-73, 104-105, 164. This concept is reflected in the words of Pharaoh Sesostris III who said, "That which my heart has conceived, my arm performs." See Pierre Montet, *Lives of the Pharaohs*, (Cleveland: World Publishing Company, 1968), 59. *See* also the chapter, "Seek Wise Counsel." Thus, conceiving and actualizing are the mechanics of becoming. This model provides for the process of uniting our human, finite self with our divine, infinite self, as opposed to being at variance with it, and this, within the context of the African communitarian culture of ancient Egypt from which the very concept of one's infinite potentiality originated. Note: In ancient Egypt the requirements for achieving the "good life" are essentially the same as for achieving salvation of the soul; namely, education (*e.g.*, the cultivation of the Arts and Sciences), and the practice of virtue (*e.g.*, doing *Maat*). George G. M. James, *Stolen Legacy*, (Trenton: African World Press, 1992), 28, 72-73, 104-105, 164. *See* also

Notes

the terms *spiritual union* and *spiritual salvation*, in Tarík Karenga, *Review of the Kemetan Mystery System*, First Edition, (Union City: Amenism, Inc., in press).

Chapter 1

1. Maulana Karenga, *Maat: The Moral Ideal in Ancient Egypt*, (Los Angeles: University of Sankore Press, 2006), 128, 279, 282-288. In the words of the *Vizier* Ptahhotep: "...strive for excellence in all you do so that no fault can be found in your character." Maulana Karenga, *Selections from the Husia*, (Los Angeles: University Of Sankore Press, 1984), 41. For a description of "the leadership of the Pharaoh" see Na'im Akbar, *Restoration of African Consciousness* [Audio Presentation], Institute of Karmic Guidance, 1990.

2. Maulana Karenga, *Maat: The Moral Ideal in Ancient Egypt*, (Los Angeles: University of Sankore Press, 2006), 286. Italics mine.

3. See Maulana Karenga, *Maat: The Moral Ideal in Ancient Egypt*, (Los Angeles: University of Sankore Press, 2006), 128, 279, 282-288. See also E. A. Wallis Budge, *The Literature of the Ancient Egyptians*, (London: J. M. Dent & Sons Limited, 1914), vi.

4. Maulana Karenga, *Maat: The Moral Ideal in Ancient Egypt*, (Los Angeles: University of Sankore Press, 2006), 377.

5. Asa G. Hilliard, Larry Williams and Nia Damali, *The Teachings of Ptahhotep: The Oldest Book in the World*, (Atlanta: Blackwood Press, 1987), 13.

6. George G. M. James, *Stolen Legacy*, (Trenton: African World Press, 1992), 3. cf. J. G. Frazer, *Pausanias's Description of Greece*, Volume V, (London: Macmillan and Co., Limited, 1913), 348-349. Maulana Karenga, *The African American Holiday of Kwanzaa: A Celebration of Family, Community & Culture*, (Los Angeles: University of Sankore Press, 1988), 21.

7. Maulana Karenga, *Maat: The Moral Ideal in Ancient Egypt*, (Los Angeles: University of Sankore Press, 2006), 282.

8. *Ibid.*, 283.

9. Janey Levy, *Great Pyramid of Giza: Measuring Length, Area, Volume, and Angles*, (New York: The Rosen Publishing Group,

2006), 6-13.

10.   Maulana Karenga, *Maat: The Moral Ideal in Ancient Egypt*, (Los Angeles: University of Sankore Press, 2006), 285.

11.   See "The Instruction for King Merikere," in Adolf Erman, *The Literature of the Ancient Egyptians*, (London: Methuen & Co. LTD, 1927), 75-84. *See* also "The Instruction of King Amenemhet I for his Son Sesostris I," in Miriam Lichtheim, *Ancient Egyptian Literature*, Volume I, (Los Angeles: University of California Press, 1973), 135-139. The implication is that these ancient wisdom teachings began as oral instructions and then were later committed to writing.

12.   *See* E. A. Wallis Budge, *Tutankhamen: Amenism, Atenism and Egyptian Monotheism*, (London: Martin Hopkinson, 1923), 1ff. *See* also the chapter, "Seek Wise Counsel." Note: The term "Amenism" herein refers to Amenism the religion according to the Reemergent Kingdom, which works interdependently with and is an integral part of the Kemetan Mystery System, so for all intents and purposes the religion and the Mystery System are virtually one and the same. George G. M. James, *Stolen Legacy*, (Trenton: African World Press, 1992), 1ff. *See* Table 7: Chronological Table, in Tarík Karenga, *Kemetan Calendar and Zodiac*, First Edition, (Union City: Amenism, Inc., 2022), 33, 37. *See* also the terms *Amenism*, *Kemetan Mystery System*, and *religion*, in Tarík Karenga, *Review of the Kemetan Mystery System*, First Edition, (Union City: Amenism, Inc., in press).

13.   The way of Amen is the Will of Amen, and God's Will is for humankind to do *Maat*. *See* Epiphanius Wilson, *Egyptian Literature: Comprising Egyptian Tales, Hymns, Litanies, Invocations, the Book of the Dead, and Cuneiform Writings*, Revised Edition, (New York: Colonial Press, 1901), 344, note 3. A plagiarized, adapted and reconfigured version of this Amenist teaching is in the religion of Christianity. *See* The Holy Bible: *Comprising the Old and New Testaments*, The King James Version, (New York: American Bible Society, 1972), [(OT) Proverbs 9:10], 595.

14.   To live by the divine, universal organizing principle that the ancient Egyptians called *Maat* was referred to as *the path of life, the way of life* and *the way of God*. Maulana Karenga, *Maat: The Moral*

Notes

Ideal in Ancient Egypt, (Los Angeles: University of Sankore Press, 2006), 266-269. *See* also the chapter, "Become a Placemaker."

15. Sins *i.e.*, moral offenses, are to be destroyed while on earth and prior to being admitted into God's Kingdom, and also into God's presence. The deceased says: "I have done away with my sins, I have put away mine offenses, and I have destroyed the evil which appertained unto my members upon earth. Hail, ye divine beings who guard the doors, make ye for me a way, for, behold, I am like unto you." E. A. Wallis Budge, *The Book of the Dead: An English Translation of the Chapters, Hymns, Etc. of the Theban Recension, with Introduction, Notes, Etc.*, Second Edition, Revised and Enlarged, Books on Egypt and Chaldaea, (New York: E. P. Dutton & Co., 1938), 276. Egypt is the Kingdom of God on earth and it is there that *Maat* is to be established, maintained and, if necessary, reestablished, and thus ". . . the deceased declares her virtues saying that she did *Maat* in Egypt, and lives on *Maat*." Maulana Karenga, *Maat: The Moral Ideal in Ancient Egypt*, (Los Angeles: University of Sankore Press, 2006), 139. Italics mine. This means that when a person turns away from doing *isfet* (*i.e.*, returns to righteousness) and commits himself to living by *Maat*, he is in effect entering the Kingdom of God on earth.

16. Asa G. Hilliard, Larry Williams and Nia Damali, *The Teachings of Ptahhotep: The Oldest Book in the World*, (Atlanta: Blackwood Press, 1987), 34.

17. Maulana Karenga, *Selections from the Husia*, (Los Angeles: University Of Sankore Press, 1984), 41.

18. Maulana Karenga, *Maat: The Moral Ideal in Ancient Egypt*, (Los Angeles: University of Sankore Press, 2006), 211-212.

19. Author and biblical authority Chuck Missler points out that in verse 7:18 of the book of Acts in the Christian Bible, "'another' in Greek is *heteros*, meaning 'another' of a different kind." Isaiah 52:4 was also cited as a comparative verse; *see* Chuck Missler, "A Most Remarkable Book: The Book of Jude," *Personal Update News Journal*, (June 2000). Retrieved from http://www.khouse.org/articles/2000/259. Accessed 24 January 2010. The Greek word *allos*, which is also used in the Christian Bible, "means another of exactly the same kind!" *see* John MacArthur,

Found: God's Will, (Colorado Springs: David C. Cook, 1977), 26. *See* also The Holy Bible: *Comprising the Old and New Testaments*, The King James Version, (New York: American Bible Society, 1972), [(OT) Isaiah 52:4], 664; [Exodus 7: 3-4], 59; [Genesis 15:13], 13; [1 Kings 6:1], 339; [(NT) Acts 7:18], 128; [John 14:16], 112. Maulana Karenga, *Maat: The Moral Ideal in Ancient Egypt*, (Los Angeles: University of Sankore Press, 2006), 38-39. Note: The dire events that unfolded in the admonitions of an 18th Dynasty Egyptian sage by the name of Ipuwer are thought by some scholars to be extrabiblical proof of the historicity of the Exodus story, but on the contrary, not only is the story of the Exodus myth, the foreign rulers of the 17th Dynasty called Hyksos were expelled from Egypt at the commencement of the 18th Dynasty during which Ipuwer was said to have lived, and based on the sheer volume of other Amenist teachings that are found in the religion of Christianity, it has been determined that the biblical Exodus is a plagiarized, adapted and reconfigured (as well as mythicized) version of the Admonitions of Ipuwer that was opportunistically meant to bolster up the religion of Christianity by undermining Amenism and defaming Egypt. *See* Alan H. Gardiner, *The Admonitions of an Egyptian Sage*, (Hildesheim: Georg Olms Verlag, 1969), 1ff.

20. Theory of *Delusional Sense of Superiority* (DSS).

21. Writers, psychiatrists and psychologists alike contend that racism is in fact a mental disorder in which the racist acts out aggressively based on a delusional perception and premise about others racially different from himself. Walter V. Collier, *Why Racism Persists: An Uncomfortable Truth*, (Indianapolis: Dog Ear Publishing, 2017), 65. It is this acting out or resultant behavior that initially develops or reinforces an existing delusional sense of superiority (DSS), the delusional sense that one person or group is superior to another person or group. In this case, the racist holds the delusional sense that he or the group to which he belongs is racially superior to another person or group with a different racial identity. *Ibid.*, 65, 68-84. Educational psychologist Dr. Asa G. Hilliard explained how Europeans developed the mental disorder of racism through a series of processes he called the Dynamics

of Domination: "In order for one group of people, in this case Europeans, to control an African population it was necessary first, to erase African memory. Secondly, to suppress the practice of African culture. Third, to teach white-supremacy. Fourth, to control the institution of socialization to prevent African people from educating their own children–from sending their own messages and so forth through media and what have you, the control of wealth, and finally physical segregation." Dr. Hilliard goes on to say, "If you operate a system of domination (a formal system of domination) by those rules that I talk about, you have to confront the truth and the only way that you can be consistent in applying those rules is ultimately to bend the truth and after awhile it results in an adaptive process that we call racism, which is really a mental disorder. It's a disorder in the mental sense because it follows the rules of mental disorder. For example, manifestations of racist behavior as a result of domination are–the denial of reality, perceptual distortion, delusions of grandeur, phobias in the face of differences and projecting blame." *See* Asa G. Hilliard and Listervelt Middleton, *Free Your Mind: Return to the Source African Origins* [Video Presentation], Wa'set Educational Productions, 1998. A delusional sense of superiority was unintentionally produced in elementary school children in a highly controversial classroom experiment conducted in 1968 by Jane Elliott, a third grade teacher in Riceville, Iowa. *See* Jane Elliott, "An Unforgettable Lesson," in *New Scientist* 192, no. 2581 (Dec 9-Dec 15, 2006): 52. Note: The opposite of "delusional sense of superiority" is here referred to as "delusional sense of inferiority" (DSI), the delusional sense that one person or group is inferior to another person or group. As a final note and as previously stated, the factors used as proxies for superiority are wide ranging (*e.g.*, socioeconomic status, religious and political affiliations, job titles, gender, race, ethnicity, age, national origin, etc.) and therefore any resultant behavior that involves any one of these factors may initially develop or reinforce a delusional sense of superiority (DSS).

   22. The modern term *color line* is the antithesis of the heart, known in ancient Egypt as the *ib*. *See* the modern term *color line* in Webster's New World Dictionary & Thesaurus, Version 2.0, Build #25,

Accent Software International, Macmillan Publishers, 1998. Mine in parentheses. Important note: The definition of the *color line* has here been expanded to include spiritual and educational restrictions. *See* the term *ib*, in Tarík Karenga, *Review of the Kemetan Mystery System*, First Edition, (Union City: Amenism, Inc., in press). *See* also the chapter, "Seek Wise Counsel."

23. Editors Maria Wallis and Augie Fleras enumerate the lessons that can be learned from the highly controversial classroom experiment conducted in 1968 by third grade teacher Jane Elliott (cited above). *See* Augie Fleras, "An Optical Delusion: 'Racializing Eye Colour,'" in *The Politics of Race in Canada*, eds. Maria Wallis and Augie Fleras, (Ontario: Oxford University Press, 2009), 179.

24. For a description of "the leadership of the Pharaoh" *see* Na'im Akbar, *Restoration of African Consciousness* [Audio Presentation], Institute of Karmic Guidance, 1990.

25. *Ibid*. Mine in parentheses. Leaders who do not subscribe to *the leadership of the Pharaoh* usually display a combination of leadership styles one and two.

26. Pierre Montet, *Eternal Egypt*, (New York: The New American Library of World Literature, Inc., 1964), 32. E. A. Wallis Budge, *The Dwellers on the Nile: The Life, History, Religion and Literature of the Ancient Egyptians*, (New York: Dover Publications Inc., 1977), 34.

27. Maulana Karenga, *Kawaida: An African Way of Being Man in the World* [Audio Presentation], University of Sankore Press, 1995. *See* also Maulana Karenga, *Maat: The Moral Ideal in Ancient Egypt*, (Los Angeles: University of Sankore Press, 2006), 282-283.

28. Adolf Erman, *The Literature of the Ancient Egyptians*, (London: Methuen & Co. LTD, 1927), 19.

29. Maulana Karenga, *Maat: The Moral Ideal in Ancient Egypt*, (Los Angeles: University of Sankore Press, 2006), 228.

30. We are accountable for how we impact the lives of the people around us.

Notes

CHAPTER 2

1. Maulana Karenga, *Selections from the Husia*, (Los Angeles: University Of Sankore Press, 1984), 50. *See* also the term *wisdom*, in Tarík Karenga, *Review of the Kemetan Mystery System*, First Edition, (Union City: Amenism, Inc., in press).

2. Adolf Erman, *The Literature of the Ancient Egyptians*, (London: Methuen & Co. LTD, 1927), 82. Italics mine.

3. Maulana Karenga, *Kwanzaa: A Celebration of Family Community and Culture*, Commemorative Edition, (Los Angeles: University of Sankore Press, 1998), 38-42. *See* also James M. Henslin, *Sociology: A Down-To-Earth Approach*, Tenth Edition, (Boston: Allyn & Bacon, 2010), 68.

4. Maulana Karenga, *Kwanzaa: A Celebration of Family Community and Culture*, Commemorative Edition, (Los Angeles: University of Sankore Press, 1998), 38.

5. Maulana Karenga, *Selections from the Husia*, (Los Angeles: University Of Sankore Press, 1984), 50. Italics mine.

6. Miriam Lichtheim, *Ancient Egyptian Literature*, Volume I, (Los Angeles: University of California Press, 1973), 185.

7. Herodotus, *The History of Herodotus*, Book II, Translated by George Rawlinson, ed. Manuel Komroff, (New York: Tudor Publishing Company, 1934), 93.

8. George G. M. James, *Stolen Legacy*, (Trenton: African World Press, 1992), 1ff. Theophile Obenga, *African Philosophy: The Pharaonic Period: 2780-330 BC*, (Paris: Per Ankh, 2004), 125-126. *See* also the terms *Amenism*, *Kemetan Mystery System*, and *religion*, in Tarík Karenga, *Review of the Kemetan Mystery System*, First Edition, (Union City: Amenism, Inc., in press).

9. Anthony T. Browder, *Nile Valley Contributions to Civilization: Exploding the Myths*, Volume 1, (Washington: The Institute of Karmic Guidance, 1992), 85. According to Amenism, Medit (**MEH**-deet), word; Medu (**MEH**-doo), words. Also: Netur (nay-**TOOR**), meaning God. E. A. Wallis Budge, *An Egyptian Hieroglyphic Dictionary: In*

Two Volumes, Volume I, (London: John Murray, 1920), 335a; 401a. See also E. A. Wallis Budge, *Tutankhamen: Amenism, Atenism and Egyptian Monotheism*, (London: Martin Hopkinson, 1923), 4.

   10. E. A. Wallis Budge, *Tutankhamen: Amenism, Atenism and Egyptian Monotheism*, (London: Martin Hopkinson, 1923), 41.

   11. E. A. Wallis Budge, *The Book of the Dead: The Papyrus of Ani in the British Museum*, (London: Kegan Paul, Trench, Trubner & Co., 1895), cxxvi. Heinrich Brugsch-Bey, *Egypt Under the Pharaohs: A History Derived Entirely From the Monuments*, A New Edition, (London: John Murray, 1891), 154ff. Albert Churchward, *The Origin and Evolution of Religion*, (George Allen & Unwin LTD., 1924), 255. E. A. Wallis Budge, *From Fetish to God in Ancient Egypt*, (New York: Dover Publications, Inc., 1988), 18, 138. cf. E. A. Wallis Budge, *Tutankhamen: Amenism, Atenism and Egyptian Monotheism*, (London: Martin Hopkinson, 1923), 42. See also, Theophile Obenga, *African Philosophy: The Pharaonic Period: 2780-330 BC*, (Paris: Per Ankh, 2004), 544. Maulana Karenga, "Restoration of the Husia: Reviving a Sacred Legacy," in *Kemet and the African Worldview*, eds. Maulana Karenga and Jacob Carruthers, (Los Angeles: University of Sankore Press, 1986), 87. It is significant to note that in the book, *The Popular Encyclopedia of Apologetics*, authors Ed Hindson and Ergun Caner write, "In Deuteronomy 6:4, Moses said, 'Hear, O Israel! The Lord is our God, the Lord is one!' This statement became Judaism's basic statement of faith (known as the *Shema*). It is a statement that grounds Judaism as monotheistic (belief in one God)." Ed Hindson and Ergun Caner, *The Popular Encyclopedia of Apologetics: Surveying the Evidence for the Truth of Christianity*, (Eugene: Harvest House Publishers, 2008), 474. See also E. A. Wallis Budge, *Egyptian Religion*, (Secaucus: Citadel Press, 1987), 131-133.

   12. E. A. Wallis Budge, *Tutankhamen: Amenism, Atenism and Egyptian Monotheism*, (London: Martin Hopkinson, 1923), 42. Mine in parentheses. The ancient Egyptians also used the epithet "Great God" when addressing Amen in spirit, while at the same time representing him in one of his manifold spiritual forms, or as Ra in one of the three persons of the Holy Trinity. Note: The three persons of the Holy Trinity in the

Notes

religion of Christianity is a plagiarized, adapted and reconfigured version of the three persons of the Holy Trinity of Osir, Iset and Heru in the religion of Amenism. Anthony T. Browder, *Nile Valley Contributions to Civilization: Exploding the Myths*, Volume 1, (Washington: The Institute of Karmic Guidance, 1992), 68. E. A. Wallis Budge, *From Fetish to God in Ancient Egypt*, (New York: Dover Publications, Inc., 1988), 18. D. M. Murdock, *Christ in Egypt: The Horus-Jesus Connection*, (Ashland: Stellar House Publishing, 2009), 53-54, 67. Upon entering the Duat (**DOO**-aht) *i.e.*, the Kingdom of Heaven, the souls of the departed are granted the ability to "assume whatever (spiritual) form" they want "in whatever place" their spirit wishes to be. Maulana Karenga, *Maat: The Moral Ideal in Ancient Egypt*, (Los Angeles: University of Sankore Press, 2006), 160. Mine in parentheses.

    13.   Priests of ancient Egypt described Amen as "The concealed spirit..." and "omnipresent." See Charles Loring Brace, *The Unknown God: Or, Inspiration Among Pre-Christian Races*, (New York: A. C. Armstrong and Son, 1890), 13, 19. From a papyrus at Leyden: "He was a Trinity, i.e. he had three persons or characters." E. A. Wallis Budge, *From Fetish to God in Ancient Egypt*, (New York: Dover Publications, 1988), 18. See also E. A. Wallis Budge, *The Book of the Dead: The Papyrus of Ani*, In Two Volumes, Volume I, (London: The Medici Society, Ltd., 1913), 106-107. E. A. Wallis Budge, *The Literature of the Ancient Egyptians*, (London: J. M. Dent & Sons Limited, 1914), 219. Mine in parentheses. An ancient Egyptian hymn to Amen-Ra makes known that Amen "hides himself in the sundisk" (Ra). See John L. Foster and Susan T. Hollis, *Hymns, Prayers, and Songs: An Anthology of Ancient Egyptian Lyric Poetry*, (Atlanta: Scholars Press, 1995), 67. In an Amenist account of creation Ptah is said to be one of the names of Amen. See Byron E. Shafer, John Baines, Leonard H. Lesko, and David P. Silverman, *Religion in Ancient Egypt: Gods, Myths, and Personal Practice*, (Ithaca: Cornell University Press, 1991), 105.

    14.   Charles Loring Brace, *The Unknown God: Or, Inspiration Among Pre-Christian Races*, (New York: A. C. Armstrong and Son, 1890), 13, 19. *See* also the term *Khu*, in Tarík Karenga, *Review of the*

Kemetan Mystery System, First Edition, (Union City: Amenism, Inc., in press).

15.   It is a well known fact that in ancient Egypt the heart was always closely associated with the soul. Furthermore, Tekhi, the ibis-headed form of Amen, was said to be the "Heart of Ra." *See* E. A. Wallis Budge, *The Book of the Dead: The Papyrus of Ani*, In Two Volumes, Volume II, (London: The Medici Society, Ltd., 1913), 343. *See* also Patrick Boylan, *Thoth, the Hermes of Egypt: A Study of Some Aspects of Theological Thought in Ancient Egypt*, (London: Oxford University Press, 1922), 114. For the hieroglyphic spelling of "Tekhi" *see* E. A. Wallis Budge, *An Egyptian Hieroglyphic Dictionary: In Two Volumes*, Volume II, (London: John Murray, 1920), 842b. Ra is said to be "the living flame, which came forth from Nūn . . ." and the "Venerable ba who came forth from Nun." Jan Assman, *Egyptian Solar Religion in the New Kingdom: Re, Amun and the Crisis of Polytheism*, (New York: Routledge, 2009), 106, 131. From these known facts we may now conclude that Ra, indeed, represents spirit in its phase of soul. *See* also the term *Ba*, in Tarík Karenga, *Review of the Kemetan Mystery System*, First Edition, (Union City: Amenism, Inc., in press).

16.   Ptah is both mind and spirit. E. A. Wallis Budge, *From Fetish to God in Ancient Egypt*, (New York: Dover Publications, 1988), vi-vii, 13-17, 22, 44. Ptah is the "God of order and form in creation;" also, Ptah is said to exercise ". . . Thought, Logos and Creative Power . . ." Ptah conceives in his heart and create by speaking with the use of his tongue. George G. M. James, *Stolen Legacy*, (Trenton: African World Press, 1992), (69), (145), 139-151. *See* also Henri Frankfort, H. A. Frankfort, John A. Wilson, Thorkild Jacobsen and William A. Irwin, *The Intellectual Adventure of Ancient Man: An Essay on Speculative Thought in the Ancient Near East*, (Chicago: University of Chicago Press, 1977), 57-59. *See* also Kwasi Wiredu, ed., *A Companion to African Philosophy*, (Malden: Blackwell Publishing, 2004), 44. For the meaning of the ancient Egyptian expression to "conceive in the heart" *see* the chapter, "Seek Wise Counsel." Amenism holds that the mind is spirit. E. A. Wallis Budge, *An Egyptian Hieroglyphic Dictionary: In Two Volumes*, Volume II, (London:

Notes

John Murray, 1920), 782b. *See* the term *Ka*, in Tarík Karenga, *Review of the Kemetan Mystery System*, First Edition, (Union City: Amenism, Inc., in press).

17. Maulana Karenga, *Maat: The Moral Ideal in Ancient Egypt*, (Los Angeles: University of Sankore Press, 2006), 226, 318. Mine in parentheses. The verse that teaches that humans are created in the image of God refers to God's divine image, in both the physical and spiritual senses. What is more, that we as humans came from God's very person, means that we were created of his essence: spirit. *See* the chapter, "Seek Wise Counsel."

18. Cheikh Anta Diop, *Civilization or Barbarism: An Authentic Anthropology*, (Brooklyn: Lawrence Hill Books, 1991), 11-14. *See* also Maulana Karenga, *Introduction to Black Studies*, Second Edition, (Los Angeles: University of Sankore Press, 1993), 77-79. *See* also William A. Haviland, Harald E. L. Prins, Dana Walrath and Bunny McBride, *Anthropology: The Human Challenge*, 13th Edition, (Belmont: Wadsworth, Cengage Learning, 2010), 153-154.

19. Albert Churchward, *The Origin and Evolution of Religion*, (George Allen & Unwin LTD., 1924), 255.

20. E. A. Wallis Budge, *The Dwellers on the Nile: The Life, History, Religion and Literature of the Ancient Egyptians*, (New York: Dover Publications Inc., 1977), 209. Italics mine.

21. Also "ab;" *see* E. A. Wallis Budge, *Osiris and the Egyptian Resurrection*, Volume II, (New York: G. P. Putnam's Sons, 1911), 130. *See* the term *ib*, in Tarík Karenga, *Review of the Kemetan Mystery System*, First Edition, (Union City: Amenism, Inc., in press).

22. E. A. Wallis Budge, *The Book of the Dead: The Papyrus of Ani*, In Two Volumes, Volume I, (London: The Medici Society, Ltd., 1913), 73, 234.

23. E. A. Wallis Budge, *Osiris and the Egyptian Resurrection*, Volume II, (New York: G. P. Putnam's Sons, 1911), 117, 134.

24. "(P)ossessing the form and attributes of a man," the Ka is symbolized as a pair of upraised arms in Egyptian hieroglyphs, and is sometimes seen positioned over the head of the person to whom the

THE PHARAOHS' 5 LAWS OF SUCCESS

Ka belongs. George G. M. James, *Stolen Legacy*, (Trenton: African World Press, 1992), 1992, 123. Educated in ancient Egypt, Greek philosopher and scientist Aristotle equated the ancient Egyptian concept of the Ka with the intellect. Cheikh Anta Diop, *Civilization or Barbarism: An Authentic Anthropology*, (Brooklyn: Lawrence Hill Books, 1991), 358. See also Theophile Obenga, *A Lost Tradition: African Philosophy in World History*, (Philadelphia: The Source Editions, 1995), 41-55. E. A. Wallis Budge, *An Egyptian Hieroglyphic Dictionary: In Two Volumes*, Volume II, (London: John Murray, 1920), 782b. *See* the term *Ka*, in Tarík Karenga, *Review of the Kemetan Mystery System*, First Edition, (Union City: Amenism, Inc., in press).

    25.   The Ba is symbolized as a bird with a human head.

    26.   The Khu is symbolized as a crested ibis. Richard King, "The Symbolism of the Crown in Ancient Egypt," in Ivan Van Sertima, ed., *Egypt: Child of Africa*, (New Brunswick: Transaction Publishers, 1994), 363-365. *See* also E. A. Wallis Budge, *Osiris and the Egyptian Resurrection*, Volume II, (New York: G. P. Putnam's Sons, 1911), 116-135, 132-134. E. A. Wallis Budge, *The Book of the Dead: The Papyrus of Ani*, In Two Volumes, Volume I, (London: The Medici Society, Ltd., 1913), 80. E. A. Wallis Budge, *An Egyptian Hieroglyphic Dictionary: In Two Volumes*, Volume I, (London: John Murray, 1920), 23b, 24a, 197a. cf. Cheikh Anta Diop, *Civilization or Barbarism: An Authentic Anthropology*, (Brooklyn: Lawrence Hill Books, 1991), 358. cf. John A. Wilson, *The Culture of Ancient Egypt*, (Chicago: The University of Chicago Press, 1957), 119. cf. Jeremy Naydler, *Temple of the Cosmos: The Ancient Egyptian Experience of the Sacred*, (Rochester: Inner Traditions International, 1996), 213-215. In the Reemergent Kingdom, the plural form of the word "Khu" is "Khuu" (KOO-oo). Heretofore the two terms *Khu* and *Akhu* have been conflated by Egyptologists and scholars alike; however, Amenists in the Reemergent Kingdom differentiate the term Khu from the term Akhu. They teach that when in ancient texts either of the foregoing terms was written without a reed leaf, context is the principal method used to draw out which of the two terms the scribe meant. *See* the chapter, "Express Your Gratitude." *See* also the terms *Khu and Akhu*, in Tarík Karenga, *Review of*

Notes

the Kemetan Mystery System, First Edition, (Union City: Amenism, Inc., in press).

27. Karel Van Der Toorn, Bob Becking and Pieter W. Van Der Horst, *Dictionary of Deities and Demons in the Bible*, Second Edition, Extensively Revised (Grand Rapids: William B. Eerdmans Publishing, 1999), 861. Mine in parentheses. For the hieroglyphic spelling of "Tekhi" see E. A. Wallis Budge, *An Egyptian Hieroglyphic Dictionary: In Two Volumes*, Volume II, (London: John Murray, 1920), 842b. Tekhi is also known by the names Tehuti and Djehuti. *Ibid.*, 886b.

28. See E. A. Wallis Budge, *The Book of the Dead: The Papyrus of Ani*, In Two Volumes, Volume II, (London: The Medici Society, Ltd., 1913), 343. Italics mine. See also Patrick Boylan, *Thoth, the Hermes of Egypt: A Study of Some Aspects of Theological Thought in Ancient Egypt*, (London: Oxford University Press, 1922), 44, 114, 149.

29. See E. A. Wallis Budge, *The Literature of the Ancient Egyptians*, (London: J. M. Dent & Sons Limited, 1914), 219-220. Italics mine. "Waset" and first parentheses mine.

30. Tekhi is ". . . the mind residing in the (physical) heart." Karel Van Der Toorn, Bob Becking and Pieter W. Van Der Horst, *Dictionary of Deities and Demons in the Bible*, Second Edition, Extensively Revised (Grand Rapids: William B. Eerdmans Publishing, 1999), 861. Mine in parentheses. In an ancient Egyptian "theological treatise" referred to as the Memphite Theology, it was written that "Sight, hearing, breathing–they report to the heart, and it makes every understanding come forth." Miriam Lichtheim, *Ancient Egyptian Literature*, Volume I, (Los Angeles: University of California Press, 1973), 54. You are now learning that to the heart is also reported what can be perceived through revelation. Note: Amenist theology operates on multiple levels.

31. Writings ascribed to Tekhi (in Greek, Hermes) called the *Hermetica* state: "Knowledge differs greatly from sense-perception. Sense-perception…uses the body as its organ…But knowledge [ ] is incorporeal; the organ which it uses is the mind itself; and the mind is contrary to the body." Walter Scott, *Hermetica*, (Boston: Shambhala Publications Inc., 1993), 193.

32.   These first two events translate into illumination.

33.   Tekhi is said to be "... the mind residing in the (physical) heart," the scribe of God and the "maker of Law." Hence the statement above that God's divine revelation is written in our heart as Divine Law. Karel Van Der Toorn, Bob Becking and Pieter W. Van Der Horst, *Dictionary of Deities and Demons in the Bible*, Second Edition, Extensively Revised (Grand Rapids: William B. Eerdmans Publishing, 1999), 861. Mine in parentheses. E. A. Wallis Budge, *The Book of the Dead: The Papyrus of Ani*, In Two Volumes, Volume II, (London: The Medici Society, Ltd., 1913), 343. Patrick Boylan, *Thoth, the Hermes of Egypt: A Study of Some Aspects of Theological Thought in Ancient Egypt*, (London: Oxford University Press, 1922), 44, 114, 149. In Amenist theology *Maat* is not only joined to a person's heart at birth, but *Maat* is also married to Tekhi. E. A. Wallis Budge, *The Book of the Dead: The Papyrus of Ani in the British Museum*, (London: Kegan Paul, Trench, Trubner & Co., 1895), cxix. "Command was given for them to hear. Counsel was given for them to learn." Maulana Karenga, *Maat: The Moral Ideal in Ancient Egypt*, (Los Angeles: University of Sankore Press, 2006), 290. *See* the term *Divine Law*, in Tarík Karenga, *Review of the Kemetan Mystery System*, First Edition, (Union City: Amenism, Inc., in press).

34.   The writing palette of Tekhi "is called Seeing and Hearing." Karel Van Der Toorn, Bob Becking and Pieter W. Van Der Horst, *Dictionary of Deities and Demons in the Bible*, Second Edition, Extensively Revised (Grand Rapids: William B. Eerdmans Publishing, 1999), 861. Quoting Alasdair MacIntyre, Dr. Maulana Karenga writes, "As MacIntyre (1981, 140) says, 'virtues are dispositions not only to act in particular ways, but also to feel in particular ways.'" Maulana Karenga, *Maat: The Moral Ideal in Ancient Egypt*, (Los Angeles: University of Sankore Press, 2006), 372. The revered ancient Egyptian peasant Khuwenanpu delivered a brilliant discourse on *Maat* in which he stated that ". . . doing *Maat* is not only doing good, it is *increasing* good and *lessening* evil in the world." *Ibid.*, (184), 233. Italics mine. Additionally, Amenism teaches that *Maat*, which embodies a core value system comprising the ten cardinal virtues of truth, justice, harmony, balance, reciprocity, or-

Notes

der, righteousness, wisdom, temperance, and courage, has been joined to our hearts at birth and that through their practice (*i.e.*, by doing *Maat*) in our daily lives and in compliance with Divine Law, good is increased in the world. *See* Miriam Lichtheim, *Maat in Egyptian Autobiographies and Related Studies*, (Freiburg, Schweiz: Universitatsverlag; Gottingen: Vandenhoeck und Ruprecht, 1992), 67. Thus, we have an innate predisposition to increase good in the world. *See* also the chapter, "Become a Placemaker." A plagiarized, adapted and reconfigured version of these Amenist teachings is in the religion of Christianity. *See* The Holy Bible: *Comprising the Old and New Testaments*, The King James Version, (New York: American Bible Society, 1972), [(OT) Jeremiah 31:33], 706; [(NT) Romans 2:15], 157; [(NT) Hebrews 8:10], 225; [10:16], 227. "Ra has spoken, [[Tekhi]] has written" reads an ancient text. Felix Guirand, *Larousse Encyclopedia of Mythology*, (New York: Prometheus Press, 1960), 27. [[ ]] Double brackets indicate word or term substitution made by the author. Here, the spelling of the name "Tekhi," which is consistent with the teachings of Amenism, has been substituted for the name "Thoth," which is Greek.

35. God's Will is for humankind to do *Maat*; *see* the chapter, "Become a Placemaker." *Maat* is said to be married to Tekhi. *See* E. A. Wallis Budge, *The Book of the Dead: The Papyrus of Ani in the British Museum*, (London: Kegan Paul, Trench, Trubner & Co., 1895), cxix. "… the beginning of wisdom is the way (or Will) of Amen." *See* the chapter, "Make Yourself Loved." Mine in parentheses.

36. Egyptologist E. A. Wallis Budge wrote that Tekhi, otherwise known as Thoth to the Greeks, provided Iset with the secret means to conceive a divine child as well as to spiritually revive and resurrect her husband. E. A. Wallis Budge, *Legends of Our Lady Mary the Perpetual Virgin and Her Mother Hanna*, (London: The Medici Society, 1922), lii. *See* also the chapter, "Seek Wise Counsel."

37. In mortuary texts discovered inscribed on wooden coffins, now known as the *Ancient Egyptian Coffin Texts*, Amen in his name of Ra states that he created everyone equal in opportunity, and equal in the sense of human equality. *See* James B. Pritchard, *Ancient Near*

Eastern Texts Relating to the Old Testament, (London: Princeton University Press, 1950), 7-8. *See* also Maulana Karenga, *Maat: The Moral Ideal in Ancient Egypt*, (Los Angeles: University of Sankore Press, 2006), 247. The modern term *color line* is the antithesis of the heart, known in ancient Egypt as the *ib*. *See* the modern term *color line* in Webster's New World Dictionary & Thesaurus, Version 2.0, Build #25, Accent Software International, Macmillan Publishers, 1998. *See* the term *ib*, in Tarík Karenga, *Review of the Kemetan Mystery System*, First Edition, (Union City: Amenism, Inc., in press). The religion of Amenism clearly teaches that humankind is meant to live and interact as a world community and in this way an appropriate amount of resources can be sent from areas of abundance to those of deficiency for the purpose of creating "conditions of opportunity" throughout the entire world community. *See* excerpt from the *Ancient Egyptian Coffin Texts* in Pritchard, *op. cit.*, 1950, pp. 7-8. The principle of reciprocity applies here also; *see* Robert B. Cialdini, *The Power of Persuasion* [Video Presentation], Stanford University, 2001. According to Dr. Tony Iton, senior vice president of healthy communities, The California Endowment, creating "conditions of opportunity" that do not already exist in one's immediate surroundings, then, speaks to investing in social benefits (which are preventative) and social services (which are responsive); Tony Iton, *Tony Iton on How to Fix California's Health Care Gap* [Audio File], NPR: KQED Forum With Michael Krasny, Aired July 5, 2018. Note: One may be taught about opportunity or, without knowing, be taught away from opportunity, which will impact one's prosperity accordingly.

   38. Sense-perception has been defined as, "awareness of the elements of environment through physical sensation," and therefore activates appropriate behavioral responses to the world <u>around us</u>. Revelatory-perception; however, means "awareness of the faculties of spirit through divine revelation," and is therefore the incorporeal awareness that exists above sense-perception. "The faculties of spirit (*i.e.*, the faculties of the soul, mind and spirit) are spiritual knowledge, spiritual insight, and spiritual understanding respectively." Revelatory-perception and sense-perception were written about in the Shabaka text, also known

Notes

as the Memphite Theology of ancient Egypt. Bruce H. Lipton, *The Biology of Belief: Unleashing the Power of Consciousness, Matter and Miracles*, (Santa Rosa: Mountain of Love / Elite Books, 2005), 15, 87. Maulana Karenga, *Maat: The Moral Ideal in Ancient Egypt*, (Los Angeles: University of Sankore Press, 2006), 188. *See* the term *revelatory-perception*, in Tarík Karenga, *Review of the Kemetan Mystery System*, First Edition, (Union City: Amenism, Inc., in press). Also, wisdom is the convergence of spiritual knowledge, insight and understanding. *See* the chapter, "Make Yourself Loved."

39. John F. Nunn, *Ancient Egyptian Medicine*, (Norman: University of Oklahoma Press, 2002), 54.

40. Pierre Montet, *Lives of the Pharaohs*, (Cleveland: World Publishing Company, 1968), 59.

41. Maulana Karenga, *Maat: The Moral Ideal in Ancient Egypt*, (Los Angeles: University of Sankore Press, 2006), 216-222. Tarík Karenga, *Review of the Kemetan Mystery System*, First Edition, (Union City: Amenism, Inc., in press).

42. Their names in Greek: Osiris, Isis and Horus. *See* Felix Guirand, *Larousse Encyclopedia of Mythology*, (New York: Prometheus Press, 1960), 16, 17, 21. D. M. Murdock, *Christ in Egypt: The Horus-Jesus Connection*, (Ashland: Stellar House Publishing, 2009), 130. E. A. Wallis Budge, *The Gods of the Egyptians: Or, Studies in Egyptian Mythology*, Volume I, (London: Methuen & Company, 1904), 466. Note: The three persons of the Holy Trinity in the religion of Christianity is a plagiarized, adapted and reconfigured version of the three persons of the Holy Trinity of Osir, Iset and Heru in the religion of Amenism. Anthony T. Browder, *Nile Valley Contributions to Civilization: Exploding the Myths*, Volume 1, (Washington: The Institute of Karmic Guidance, 1992), 68. E. A. Wallis Budge, *From Fetish to God in Ancient Egypt*, (New York: Dover Publications, Inc., 1988), 18. Murdock, *op. cit.*, 2009, pp. 53-54, 67. Spellings of the above names are according to Amenism in the Reemergent Kingdom.

43. E. A. Wallis Budge, *Osiris and the Egyptian Resurrection*, Volume I, (New York: G. P. Putnam's Sons, 1911), 2.

44. E. A. Wallis Budge, *Osiris and the Egyptian Resurrec-*

tion, Volume I, (New York: G. P. Putnam's Sons, 1911), 2, 19. According to the teaching of Amenism, the inception of Egypt as an earthly kingdom began at the precise moment that Osir and Iset established Kemet as the Kingdom of God on earth. *See* the term *Kemet*, in Tarík Karenga, *Review of the Kemetan Mystery System*, First Edition, (Union City: Amenism, Inc., in press).

45. "the Great Ancestor-God;" *see* E. A. Wallis Budge, *Osiris and the Egyptian Resurrection*, Volume I, (New York: G. P. Putnam's Sons, 1911), 300. Capitalization mine. *See* also Margaret A. Murray, *The Osireion at Abydos*, (London: Bernard Quaritch, 1904), 29. (Emphasis mine). *See* also Cheikh Anta Diop, "Origin of the Ancient Egyptians," in *Journal of African Civilizations* 4, no. 2 (November 1982): 21. Cheikh Anta Diop, *The African Origin of Civilization: Myth or Reality*, (Chicago: Lawrence Hill Books, 1974), 89. Anthony T. Browder, *From the Browder File: 22 Essays on the African American Experience*, Revised and Expanded, (Washington: The Institute of Karmic Guidance, 2000), 12. *See* also, Felix Guirand, *Larousse Encyclopedia of Mythology*, (New York: Prometheus Press, 1960), 16.

46. Osir himself came down from heaven to transmit civilization to all nations, which was in actuality the transference to earth of the Kingdom of Heaven located within his own spirit. E. A. Wallis Budge, *Osiris and the Egyptian Resurrection*, Volume I, (New York: G. P. Putnam's Sons, 1911), 2, 16. *See* also, Felix Guirand, *Larousse Encyclopedia of Mythology*, (New York: Prometheus Press, 1960), 16. On a pillar in Egypt attributed to Osir, it was reported to have been written: "There is no place in the world where I have not come to bestow my beneficence." *See* Helen Diner, *Mothers and Amazons: The First Feminine History of Culture*, (Garden City: Anchor Press, 1973), 169. Adolf Erman, *A Handbook of Egyptian Religion*, (London: Archibald Constable & Co. Ltd., 1907), 245. Additionally, Historian and philosopher Will Durant has defined education ". . . as the technique of transmitting civilization." Will Durant, *The Story of Civilization, Part 1: Our Oriental Heritage*, (New York: Simon and Schuster, 1954), 4. In everyday practice, civilization was transmitted by way of the Egyptian Mystery System whose central figure (*e.g.*,

Notes

the Pharaoh) was not only identified with Osir, but was also the very person of Heru; furthermore, "... ancient wisdom, and knowledge, religious, philosophical and scientific spread to other lands through student Initiates." George G. M. James, *Stolen Legacy*, (Trenton: African World Press, 1992), 1, 9-10, (12), 69, 154. Mine in parentheses. A plagiarized, adapted and reconfigured version of this Amenist teaching is in the religion of Christianity. *See* The Holy Bible: *Comprising the Old and New Testaments*, The King James Version, (New York: American Bible Society, 1972), [(NT) Matthew 28:16-20], 34. According to author Elmer Towns, in the so-called "Great Commission" of the mythical Christian God Jesus, there are exactly two imperatives; namely, evangelism and education carried out by disciples. Elmer Towns, *Core Christianity: What is Christianity All About?* (Chattanooga: AMG Publishers, 2007), 139.

47. Also referred to as Set and Typhon by the Greeks.

48. E. A. Wallis Budge, *Osiris and the Egyptian Resurrection*, Volume I, (New York: G. P. Putnam's Sons, 1911), 2.

49. Felix Guirand, *Larousse Encyclopedia of Mythology*, (New York: Prometheus Press, 1960), 19. Italics mine.

50. E. A. Wallis Budge, *Osiris and the Egyptian Resurrection*, Volume I, (New York: G. P. Putnam's Sons, 1911), 2-3.

51. E. A. Wallis Budge, *From Fetish to God in Ancient Egypt*, (New York: Dover Publications, 1988), 21, 191-192, 264, 273. James Henry Breasted, "The Philosophy of a Memphite Priest: Hierzu Tafel I und II," in *Zeitschrift Fur Agyptische Sprache Und Altertumskunde*, Volume 39, eds. A. Erman and G. Steindorff, (Leipzig: J. C. Hinrichs'sche Buchhandlung, 1901), 43-44, 50. E. A. Wallis Budge writes: "Plutarch states that Set Induced Osiris to lie down in a box, and when he had done so, Set and his allies fastened down the cover of the box, and threw it into the river, Osiris, of course, being drowned." E. A. Wallis Budge, *A Short History of the Egyptian People: With Chapters on Their Religion, Daily Life, Etc.*, (London: J. M. Dent & Sons Limited, 1914), 172. E. A. Wallis Budge, *Osiris and the Egyptian Resurrection*, Volume I, (New York: G. P. Putnam's Sons, 1911), 3-4. Harold P. Cooke, Osiris: A Study in Myths, Mysteries and Religion, (Boston: Bruce Humphries, Inc. Publishers, 1931), 9-10.

Margaret A. Murray, "Statue of Nefer-Sma-Āa," in *Ancient Egypt*, Part 4, ed. Flinders Petrie, (New York: Macmillan and CO., 1917), 148.

   52. E. A. Wallis Budge, *Osiris and the Egyptian Resurrection*, Volume I, (New York: G. P. Putnam's Sons, 1911), 3-4.

   53. *Ibid.*, 5-7. Felix Guirand, *Larousse Encyclopedia of Mythology*, (New York: Prometheus Press, 1960), 18. Greek biographer Plutarch states: "The dismemberment of Osiris into fourteen parts they refer allegorically to the days of the waning of that satellite from the time of the full moon to the new moon . . ." Plutarch also states that the fragments of Osir's body had not only been scattered, but that they had also been buried. D. M. Murdock, *Christ in Egypt: The Horus-Jesus Connection*, (Ashland: Stellar House Publishing, 2009), 70, 379.

   54. Tarík Karenga, *Kemetan Calendar and Zodiac*, First Edition, (Union City: Amenism, Inc., 2022), 14-15, 49.

   55. Felix Guirand, *Larousse Encyclopedia of Mythology*, (New York: Prometheus Press, 1960), 18. E. A. Wallis Budge, *Osiris and the Egyptian Resurrection*, Volume I, (New York: G. P. Putnam's Sons, 1911), 7. The Greeks would later replace the zodiacal sign Kheper *i.e.*, a scarab beetle, with Cancer, a Nile crab. Tarík Karenga, *Kemetan Calendar and Zodiac*, First Edition, (Union City: Amenism, Inc., 2022), 15, 21.

   56. See E. A. Wallis Budge, *Legends of Our Lady Mary the Perpetual Virgin and Her Mother Hanna*, (London: The Medici Society, 1922), lii. *See* also Pat Remler, *Egyptian Mythology A to Z*, Third Edition, (New York: Chelsea House Publishers, 2010), 98. Osir becomes the first person ever to be mummified.

   57. E. A. Wallis Budge, *Osiris and the Egyptian Resurrection*, Volume I, (New York: G. P. Putnam's Sons, 1911), 280. E. A. Wallis Budge, *Osiris and the Egyptian Resurrection*, Volume II, (New York: G. P. Putnam's Sons, 1911), 42. *See* the terms *spiritual revival* and *spiritual union*, in Tarík Karenga, *Review of the Kemetan Mystery System*, First Edition, (Union City: Amenism, Inc., in press).

   58. E. A. Wallis Budge, *Legends of Our Lady Mary the Perpetual Virgin and Her Mother Hanna*, (London: The Medici Society, 1922), lii. E. A. Wallis Budge, *Osiris and the Egyptian Resurrection*,

Notes

Volume I, (New York: G. P. Putnam's Sons, 1911), 94. *See* also the term *spiritual salvation*, in Tarík Karenga, *Review of the Kemetan Mystery System*, First Edition, (Union City: Amenism, Inc., in press). Essence, here, means spirit. That is to say, Heru was <u>begotten</u> of spirit and <u>conceived</u> of a virgin.

    59.   D. M. Murdock, *Christ in Egypt: The Horus-Jesus Connection*, (Ashland: Stellar House Publishing, 2009), 79, 120-197, 152, 380. John G. Jackson, "Egypt and Christianity," in *Journal of African Civilizations* 4, no. 2 (November 1982): 68-69. E. A. Wallis Budge, *British Museum: A Guide to the Third and Fourth Egyptian Rooms*, (London: British Museum, 1904), 127. Mine in parentheses. E. A. Wallis Budge, *Osiris and the Egyptian Resurrection*, Volume I, (New York: G. P. Putnam's Sons, 1911), 92-94. Heru as a child, Heru as a man, and Heru as an Elder are all one and the same person, but at three different stages of development. *See* Tarík Karenga, *Kemetan Calendar and Zodiac*, First Edition, (Union City: Amenism, Inc., 2022), 22-23, Plate 4. *See* also the term *spiritual rebirth*, in Tarík Karenga, *Review of the Kemetan Mystery System*, First Edition, (Union City: Amenism, Inc., in press).

    60.   E. A. Wallis Budge, *Osiris and the Egyptian Resurrection*, Volume I, (New York: G. P. Putnam's Sons, 1911), 94. Italics mine.

    61.   "By means of them Isis drew seed into herself from Osiris after his death, and conceived Horus . . . By these spells she, assisted by her son Horus (as an Elder) and by Anubis, the divine physician, reconstituted and revivified the body of Osiris, and thus she created her son Horus, and recreated Osiris." E. A. Wallis Budge, *Legends of Our Lady Mary the Perpetual Virgin and Her Mother Hanna*, (London: The Medici Society, 1922), lii. Mine in parentheses. E. A. Wallis Budge, *The Gods of the Egyptians: Or, Studies in Egyptian Mythology*, Volume I, (London: Methuen & Company, 1904), 487. D. M. Murdock, *Christ in Egypt: The Horus-Jesus Connection*, (Ashland: Stellar House Publishing, 2009), 236-237. Anup in Greek: Anubis. The missing lapse of time between Heru's divine birth and his becoming an Elder is explained in Tarík Karenga, *Kemetan Calendar and Zodiac*, First Edition, (Union City: Amenism, Inc., 2022), 22-23. In a completely different text the soul is seen descend-

ing on the body of Osir at the time of his resurrection. *See* Erik Hornung, *The Valley of the Kings: Horizon of Eternity*, (New York: Timken Publishers, 1990), 120. A plagiarized, adapted and reconfigured version of this Amenist teaching is in the religion of Christianity. *See* The Holy Bible: *Comprising the Old and New Testaments*, The King James Version, (New York: American Bible Society, 1972), [(NT) Matthew 12:40, 26:61], 13, 31; [Mark 8:31], 44; [John 2:19], 96. Iset recounts in her own words the birth of her divine child Heru. E. A. Wallis Budge, *Legends of the Egyptian Gods*, (London: Kegan Paul, Trench, Trubner & Co., Ltd., 1912), 179.

62. Strictly speaking, after Iset spiritually revived her husband Osir and during the subsequent process of resurrecting him, Heru (as an Elder) viewed his father as being asleep rather than deceased, and forthwith awakened him and raised him to his feet. *See* Gerald Massey, *Ancient Egypt: The Light of the World*, Volume II, (London: T. Fisher Unwin, 1907), 787, 844-847. That Heru (as an Elder) provided assistance to his mother Iset during the resurrection of his father Osir by awakening him and raising him to his feet indicates that spiritual resurrection simultaneously awakens and raises the soul from a sleeplike state that resembles spiritual death, to renewed activity that enables the transference to earth of the Kingdom of Heaven located within one's own spirit. *See* the terms *proximal separation, spiritual slumber, spiritual rebirth, spiritual death* and *spiritual resurrection*, in Tarík Karenga, *Review of the Kemetan Mystery System*, First Edition, (Union City: Amenism, Inc., in press). A plagiarized, adapted and reconfigured version of this Amenist teaching (*e.g*, revival followed by resurrection) is in the religion of Christianity. "After two days he will revive us; in the third day he will raise us up; and we shall live in his sight." *See* The Holy Bible: *Comprising the Old and New Testaments*, The King James Version, (New York: American Bible Society, 1972), [(OT) Hosea 6:2], 808. *See* also D. M. Murdock, *Christ in Egypt: The Horus-Jesus Connection*, (Ashland: Stellar House Publishing, 2009), 383. Greek biographer Plutarch states: "During this period when Isis was said to be in search of Osiris, the god was claimed to be dead and buried for three days . . . and, on the fourth, he is called out by his son, Horus." D. M. Murdock, *Christ in Egypt: The Horus-Jesus Connec-*

Notes

tion, (Ashland: Stellar House Publishing, 2009), 379. The mystery of the transformation of Heru (as a child) into Heru (as an Elder) is explained in Tarík Karenga, *Kemetan Calendar and Zodiac*, First Edition, (Union City: Amenism, Inc., 2022), 22-23.

63. Gerald Massey, *Ancient Egypt: The Light of the World*, Volume II, (London: T. Fisher Unwin, 1907), 844. [[ ]] Double brackets indicate word or term substitution made by the author. Here, the spellings of the names "Osir" and "Heru," which refer to the first and third persons of God, are consistent with the teachings of Amenism and have therefore been substituted for the names "Osiris" and "Horus," which are Greek. Italics mine. cf. E. A. Wallis Budge, *The Gods of the Egyptians: Or, Studies in Egyptian Mythology*, Volume II, (London: Methuen & Company, 1904), 156.

64. Heru's divine *i.e.*, virgin birth provided Seth with an opportunity to falsely accuse Heru of being illegitimate. E. A. Wallis Budge, *Osiris and the Egyptian Resurrection*, Volume I, (New York: G. P. Putnam's Sons, 1911), 90-91. This answers the question: "How are we justified?"

65. *Ibid.*, 309, 311-312.

66. D. M. Murdock, *Christ in Egypt: The Horus-Jesus Connection*, (Ashland: Stellar House Publishing, 2009), 167-191. *See also* A. H. Sayce, *The Religions of Ancient Egypt and Babylonia*, (Edinburgh: T. & T. Clark, 1902), 249-250.

67. The ten virtues of the Egyptian Mystery System are as follows: truth, justice, harmony, balance, reciprocity, order, righteousness, wisdom, temperance, and courage (*i.e.*, the ten cardinal virtues of *Maat*). Asa G. Hillard, *SBA: The Reawakening of the African Mind*, (Gainesville, Makare Publishing Company, 1998), 2, 16. George G. M. James, *Stolen Legacy*, (Trenton: African World Press, 1992), 3-4, 30-31, 104-106. Philosopher and Egyptologist Gregoire Biyogo writes that *Maat* is ". . . the universal principle of Truth . . ." Gregoire Biyogo, *Aux Sources Egyptiennes Du Savoir: Volume 1, Genealogie Et Enjeux De La Pensee De Cheikh Anta Diop*, (Yaounde: Editions Menaibuc, 2000), 7n4. Author Jeremy Naydler makes reference to *Maat* as ". . . the divine organizing principle." Jeremy Naydler, *Temple of the Cosmos: The Ancient Egyptian*

THE PHARAOHS' 5 LAWS OF SUCCESS

Experience of the Sacred, (Rochester: Inner Traditions International, 1996), 104. Egyptologist John A. Wilson says of *Maat*: "It was the cosmic force of harmony, order, stability, and security, coming down from the first creation as the organizing quality of created phenomena…" See John A. Wilson, *The Culture of Ancient Egypt*, (Chicago: The University of Chicago Press, 1957), 48. Professor of African American Studies Molefi Kete Asante wrote: "When you speak of it as the organizing principle of human society, the creative spirit of phenomena, and the eternal order of the universe, you come close to understanding what the ancient Kemetic civilization understood." Molefi Kete Asante, *Kemet, Afrocentricity and Knowledge*, (Trenton: African World Press, 1990), 89. The ancient Egyptians depicted *Maat* as the daughter of God and held that maintaining the principle of *Maat* keeps society along with the entire universe from collapsing into chaos; hence the term *divine, universal organizing principle*. Christine El Mahdy, *Tutankhamen: The Life and Death of the Boy-King*, (New York: St. Martin's, 1999), 183. "Adherence to Maat created the good order of society, while abandoning Maat plunged society into chaos." Miriam Lichtheim, *Maat in Egyptian Autobiographies and Related Studies*, (Freiburg, Schweiz: Universitatsverlag; Gottingen: Vandenhoeck und Ruprecht, 1992), "English Summary." *See* also Emily Teeter, "Maat," in *The Oxford Encyclopedia of Ancient Egypt*, Volume 2, ed. Donald B. Redford, (New York: Oxford University Press, 2001), 319-321. According to Webster's New World Dictionary, "chaos implies total and apparently irremediable lack of organization." This is the opposite of *Maat*. *See* "chaos" under synonyms for "confusion" in Webster's New World Dictionary & Thesaurus, Version 2.0, Build #25, Accent Software International, Macmillan Publishers, 1998. *See* also the chapter, "Become a Placemaker." Amenism states that spiritual union with God is possible only upon the acceptance of God's gift of *true life* through Christ and as founded on doing *Maat*. The phrase "through Christ" denotes two levels of acceptance: 1) through Osir the Christ and first person of the Holy Trinity by believing in his life, "… divinity, death and resurrection, and absolute control of the destinies of the bodies and souls of men. The central point of each Osirian's Religion was his hope of resurrection in a

Notes

transformed body and of immortality, which could only be realized by him through the (life,) death and resurrection of [[Osir]]." *See* E. A. Wallis Budge, *Osiris and the Egyptian Resurrection*, Volume I, (New York: G. P. Putnam's Sons, 1911), a2. Mine in parentheses. [[ ]] Double brackets indicate word or term substitution made by the author. Here, the spelling of the name "Osir," which refers to the first person of God, is consistent with the teachings of Amenism and has therefore been substituted for the name "Osiris," which is Greek.; 2) through Christ, the <u>exclusive</u> agency of the indwelling Triune-Phase Spirit of God that spiritually fastens together and unifies the five physical and spiritual parts of man and woman to form the *Black Community of Christ*. Note well that Osir the Christ and belief in his life, ". . . divinity, death and resurrection, and absolute control of the destinies of the bodies and souls of men" correspond to and access Christ the <u>exclusive</u> agency located in ". . . the bosom of the spirit" of God that dwells within us all; of Osir it is said, "Osiris is thy name in the bosom of the spirit." *See* Charles Loring Brace, *The Unknown God: Or, Inspiration Among Pre-Christian Races*, (New York: A. C. Armstrong and Son, 1890), 20. Mine in parentheses. *See also* Budge, *op. cit.*, Volume I, 1911, p. a2. *See* the terms *spiritual union* and *Christ*, in Tarík Karenga, *Review of the Kemetan Mystery System*, First Edition, (Union City: Amenism, Inc., in press). According to the teachings of Amenism, spiritual union with God means union (through Christ) of the Spirit of God that dwells within us all, with our heavenly Father Amen from whom our own spirit was begotten. One attains spiritual union with God whenever he or she is "living in truth" *i.e.*, whenever his or her values, intentions, thoughts, desires and actions are congruent with the Will of God, and God's Will is for humankind to do *Maat*. An Amenist hymn that combines God's name of "Amen" with God's name of "Ra" (*e.g.*, Amen-Ra) reads: "We worship thee because thou dwell'st in us!" *See* Francis Ellingwood Abbot, William James Potter and Benjamin Franklin Underwood, eds., "Hymn to Amun-Ra," in *The Index*, (Boston: Index Association, 1879), 161. Amenism is monotheistic as evidenced by the monotheistic statement: "Amen is one." E. A. Wallis Budge, *From Fetish to God in Ancient Egypt*, (New York: Dover Publications, 1988), 18. cf. E. A.

THE PHARAOHS' 5 LAWS OF SUCCESS

Wallis Budge, *Tutankhamen: Amenism, Atenism and Egyptian Monotheism*, (London: Martin Hopkinson, 1923), 42. *See* also, Theophile Obenga, *African Philosophy: The Pharaonic Period: 2780-330 BC*, (Paris: Per Ankh, 2004), 544. Maulana Karenga, "Restoration of the Husia: Reviving a Sacred Legacy," in *Kemet and the African Worldview*, eds. Maulana Karenga and Jacob Carruthers, (Los Angeles: University of Sankore Press, 1986), 87. It is significant to note that in the book, *The Popular Encyclopedia of Apologetics*, authors Ed Hindson and Ergun Caner write, "In Deuteronomy 6:4, Moses said, 'Hear, O Israel! The Lord is our God, the Lord is one!' This statement became Judaism's basic statement of faith (known as the *Shema*). It is a statement that grounds Judaism as monotheistic (belief in one God)." Ed Hindson and Ergun Caner, *The Popular Encyclopedia of Apologetics: Surveying the Evidence for the Truth of Christianity*, (Eugene: Harvest House Publishers, 2008), 474. *See* also E. A. Wallis Budge, *Egyptian Religion*, (Secaucus: Citadel Press, 1987), 131-133. *See* also the chapter, "Express Your Gratitude."

68.   (1). Egyptian society was matrilineal. *See* Margaret A. Murray, *Egyptian Religious Poetry*, (London: John Murray, 1949), 33, 39. (2). According to the teaching of Amenism, the spiritual revival of Osir by Iset takes place before the resurrection of Osir. The queen of Egypt, then, is identified with Iset not just simply by being seated on the throne; *see* the chapter, "Seek Wise Counsel." *See* Murray, *op. cit.*, 1949, p. 33. *See* the term *spiritual revival*, in Tarík Karenga, *Review of the Kemetan Mystery System*, First Edition, (Union City: Amenism, Inc., in press). (3) According to the teachings of Amenism, the queen must be married both to the king and to God Amen who is spirit, in order to ensure the divine birth of the future heir to the throne. That is because like the king, the queen is both human and divine. As Iset, the queen is married to the king, who is identified with Osir; as the mortal queen, she is married to God Amen, who is said to descend upon her in order for her to conceive a divine child. *See* Serinity Young, ed., *Encyclopedia of Women and World Religion*, Volume 1, (New York: Macmillan Reference USA, 1999), 34. *See* also Ivan Van Sertima, ed., *Black Women in Antiquity*, (New Brunswick: Transaction Publishers, 1984), 37. (4). The Pharaoh

Notes

is the Son of God on earth; *see* Gay Robins, *The Art of Ancient Egypt*, Revised Edition, (Cambridge: Harvard University Press, 2008), 37. *See* also Murray, *op. cit.*, 1949, p. 37-39.

      69.   According to the teachings of Amenism, the king is both Osir and Heru but with one caveat. The living king is literally Heru who rules on earth, while his active role in transmitting civilization to all nations, which is the transference to earth of the Kingdom of Heaven located within his own spirit, identifies him with Osir, until at death when the king is completely assimilated to him. *See* Margaret A. Murray, *Egyptian Religious Poetry*, (London: John Murray, 1949), 37-38. *See* also Margaret A. Murray, *The Osireion at Abydos*, (London: Bernard Quaritch, 1904), 32-34. *See* also Charles Loring Brace, *The Unknown God: Or, Inspiration Among Pre-Christian Races*, (New York: A. C. Armstrong and Son, 1890), 27. *See* also D. M. Murdock, *Christ in Egypt: The Horus-Jesus Connection*, (Ashland: Stellar House Publishing, 2009), 49-51. *See* also Maulana Karenga, *Maat: The Moral Ideal in Ancient Egypt*, (Los Angeles: University of Sankore Press, 2006), 164-165. Osir himself came down from heaven to transmit civilization to all nations, which was in actuality the transference to earth of the Kingdom of Heaven located within his own spirit. E. A. Wallis Budge, *Osiris and the Egyptian Resurrection*, Volume I, (New York: G. P. Putnam's Sons, 1911), 2, 16. *See* also, Felix Guirand, *Larousse Encyclopedia of Mythology*, (New York: Prometheus Press, 1960), 16. On a pillar in Egypt attributed to Osir, it was reported to have been written: "There is no place in the world where I have not come to bestow my beneficence." *See* Helen Diner, *Mothers and Amazons: The First Feminine History of Culture*, (Garden City: Anchor Press, 1973), 169. Adolf Erman, *A Handbook of Egyptian Religion*, (London: Archibald Constable & Co. Ltd., 1907), 245. Additionally, Historian and philosopher Will Durant has defined education ". . . as the technique of transmitting civilization." Will Durant, *The Story of Civilization, Part 1: Our Oriental Heritage*, (New York: Simon and Schuster, 1954), 4. In everyday practice, civilization was transmitted by way of the Egyptian Mystery System whose central figure (*e.g.*, the Pharaoh) was not only identified with Osir, but was also the very person of Heru; furthermore, by way of

the Egyptian Mystery System, "... ancient wisdom, and knowledge, religious, philosophical and scientific spread to other lands through student Initiates." George G. M. James, *Stolen Legacy*, (Trenton: African World Press, 1992), 1, 9-10, (12), 69, 154. Mine in parentheses. Plagiarized, adapted and reconfigured versions of these Amenist teachings are in the religion of Christianity. *See* The Holy Bible: *Comprising the Old and New Testaments*, The King James Version, (New York: American Bible Society, 1972), [(NT) Matthew 28:16-20], 34. According to author Elmer Towns, in the so-called "Great Commission" of the mythical Christian God Jesus, there are exactly two imperatives; namely, evangelism and education carried out by disciples. Elmer Towns, *Core Christianity: What is Christianity All About?* (Chattanooga: AMG Publishers, 2007), 139. Additional plagiarism is in the fact that whatsoever *works of his father* that the mythical Christian God Jesus was said to have been engaged in was all tantamount to building the Kingdom of Heaven on earth. *See* The Holy Bible: *Comprising the Old and New Testaments*, The King James Version, (New York: American Bible Society, 1972), [(NT) Matthew 12:28], 12; [(NT) Luke 10:9-11], 72; [11:20], 74; [17:81], 82. The mystery is explained in Tarík Karenga, *Kemetan Calendar and Zodiac*, First Edition, (Union City: Amenism, Inc., 2022), 25. *See* also the terms *spiritual resurrection, Kingdom of Heaven, Kingdom of God on Earth, Kemet,* and *works of his father,* in Tarík Karenga, *Review of the Kemetan Mystery System*, First Edition, (Union City: Amenism, Inc., in press).

      70.   A title of an important religious book that was placed in the tombs of the departed has been translated: "Coming forth as the (newborn) Sun," although many Egyptologists refer to the book as the *Book of the Dead*, because it had reportedly been found buried with the dead. *See* C. C. J. Baron Bunsen and Samuel Birch, *Egypt's Place in Universal History*, Volume 5, (London: Longmans, Green, and Co., 1867), 156, 164. Mine in parentheses. *See* also Maulana Karenga, *The Book of Coming Forth by Day: The Ethics of the Declarations of Innocence*, (Los Angeles: University of Sankore Press, 1990), 19-20. Additionally, the ancient Egyptian word for *day* transliterated as hru (*i.e.*, Heru) and followed by the hieroglyph for the word *sun* written with a determinative

mark conceptually means newborn sun, and theologically refers to the newborn soul. This interpretation is corroborated first by the fact that ancient Egyptian priests taught that the sun was reborn daily. William J. Darby, Paul Ghalioungui and Louis Grivetti, *Food: The Gift of Osiris*, Volume 2, (London: Academic Press, 1976), 620-621. Additional evidence: E. A. Wallis Budge, *An Egyptian Hieroglyphic Dictionary: In Two Volumes*, Volume I, (London: John Murray, 1920), 450a. Gerald Massey, *Ancient Egypt: The Light of the World*, Volume I, (London: T. Fisher Unwin, 1907), 449-450. *See* also D. M. Murdock, *Christ in Egypt: The Horus-Jesus Connection*, (Ashland: Stellar House Publishing, 2009), 83, 95, 79-116, 377, 388, 417-419. The birth of Heru is associated with the end of the three-day period of the winter solstice, which was called the "Day of the Great Coming Forth." *Ibid.*, 104-106. Osir and Heru were both symbolically represented as a "baby sun." *Ibid.*, 110. The Holy Virgin Mother Iset was quoted as saying, "The fruit which I have begotten is the sun." *Ibid.*, 111. Heru ". . . represented the new Sun which was born daily, and which was the successor of Heru-khuti or of Ra, and he was also the offspring of the dead man-god Osiris and his lawful successor." E. A. Wallis Budge, *The Gods of the Egyptians: Or, Studies in Egyptian Mythology*, Volume I, (London: Methuen & Company, 1904), 486. Author, Margaret Murray also noted the identification of Heru with the newly-born sun. *See* Margaret A. Murray, *Egyptian Religious Poetry*, (London: John Murray, 1949), 37. The Sun is also said to be "(a) child in the morning, an old man in the evening . . ." *See* Jan Zandee, "Hymnical Sayings, Addressed to the Sun-God by the High-Priest of Amun Nebwenenef, from His Tomb in Thebes," in *Jaarbericht: Van Het Vooraziatisch-Egyptisch Genootschap, Ex Oriente Lux*, no. 18, (Leiden: Ex Oriente Lux, 1964), 265. A title of the Pharaoh is "*Son of the Sun.*" E. A. Wallis Budge, *The Nile: Notes for Travellers in Egypt*, Eighth Edition, (London: Thos. Cook & Son (Egypt), LTD., 1902), 2. Italics mine. Tarík Karenga, *Kemetan Calendar and Zodiac*, First Edition, (Union City: Amenism, Inc., 2022), 15-17.

     71.   D. M. Murdock, *Christ in Egypt: The Horus-Jesus Connection*, (Ashland: Stellar House Publishing, 2009), 98, 200. Tarík Karenga, *Kemetan Calendar and Zodiac*, First Edition, (Union City: Amenism,

Inc., 2022), 13.

72. D. M. Murdock, *Christ in Egypt: The Horus-Jesus Connection*, (Ashland: Stellar House Publishing, 2009), 111-112.

73. Sir P. Le Page Renouf and Prof. E. Naville, *The Egyptian Book of the Dead: Translation and Commentary*, (London: The Society of Biblical Archaeology, 1904), 127-128. See also D. M. Murdock, *Christ in Egypt: The Horus-Jesus Connection*, (Ashland: Stellar House Publishing, 2009), 202-203.

74. A plagiarized, adapted and reconfigured version of this Amenist teaching is in the religion of Christianity. *See The Holy Bible: Comprising the Old and New Testaments*, The King James Version, (New York: American Bible Society, 1972), [(NT) John 3:3], 96. As Heru, one may see God, "attain the beatific vision" and "hold communion with the immortals." *See* George G. M. James, *Stolen Legacy*, (Trenton: African World Press, 1992), 27. *See* also the term *spiritual rebirth*, in Tarík Karenga, *Review of the Kemetan Mystery System*, First Edition, (Union City: Amenism, Inc., in press).

75. Margaret A. Murray, *Egyptian Religious Poetry*, (London: John Murray, 1949), 39, 41. According to the teachings of Amenism, the ceremonial birth that preceeds but includes the baptism by water and naming ceremonies is in reference to one's divine birth. *See* the term *divine birth*, in Tarík Karenga, *Review of the Kemetan Mystery System*, First Edition, (Union City: Amenism, Inc., in press). Baptism by water and baptism by fire were part of the Egyptian Mystery System of which the Pharaoh was a member. *See* George G. M. James, *Stolen Legacy*, (Trenton: African World Press, 1992), 91. Amenist Theology. *See* D. M. Murdock, *Christ in Egypt: The Horus-Jesus Connection*, (Ashland: Stellar House Publishing, 2009), 49-51. *See* also E. A. Wallis Budge, *The Nile: Notes for Travellers in Egypt*, Eighth Edition, (London: Thos. Cook & Son (Egypt), LTD., 1902), 2. Italics mine. *See* also Pat Remler, *Egyptian Mythology A to Z*, Third Edition, (New York: Chelsea House Publishers, 2010), 105-106. In Amenist theology the phrase "begotten of spirit" refers to the descent of Amen upon one's then virgin mother-to-be; the phrase "born of spirit" refers to one's spiritual rebirth. *See* the terms *be-*

gotten of spirit and *born of spirit*, in Tarík Karenga, *Review of the Kemetan Mystery System*, First Edition, (Union City: Amenism, Inc., in press).

    76.   The rigorous scholarship of not only Dr. George G. M. James, but also that of Dr. Theophile Obenga has established that the ancient Egyptians gave birth to Greek intellectual life starting with Thales, the first Greek to become a philosopher after being taught by the priests of Egypt. *See* Theophile Obenga, *A Lost Tradition: African Philosophy in World History*, (Philadelphia: The Source Editions, 1995), 29-34. Thales would later urge Pythagoras of Samos to go to Egypt for his education as well. *Ibid.*, 34-36. Philosophical teachings formerly ascribed to Ancient Greek philosophers have now been traced back to the ancient Egyptians from whom the ancient Greeks acquired the finest education. For example, one of the doctrines formerly ascribed to the Greek philosopher Socrates states that "There is a realm of true reality, which is above the world of sense." The ancient Egyptians were the authors of this doctrine, not Socrates. *See* George G. M. James, *Stolen Legacy*, (Trenton: African World Press, 1992), (88)-96. Furthermore, one of the doctrines (The Theory of Ideas) formerly ascribed to the Greek philosopher and former slave Plato states: "The ideas (*i.e.*, those things that are spirit and that are located in the heavenly realm) are real and perfect, but the phenomena (*i.e.*, the manifestations of those things that are spirit and that are located in the earthly realm) are unreal and imperfect; and it is the function of philosophy to enable the mind to rise above the contemplation of the visible copies of Ideas, and advance to a knowledge of the Ideas themselves." The ancient Egyptians were the authors of this doctrine, not Plato. *See* James, *op. cit.*, 1992, pp. 97-112. Mine in parentheses. The phenomena that Plato wrote about are commonly spoken of as being one step removed from the Ideal realm. Spirit begets spirit, soul gives birth to soul, and flesh gives birth to flesh; *see* above; also, one's true self is identified with the soul rather than with the body, which is why it is said in the Mysteries that prior to, during, and after one's divine birth, one's biological mother was, is, and remains a virgin, because the same loving act that produced your physical body (*e.g.*, sexual intercourse) did not create you, the soul that inhabits it, for it was Amen who begot your spirit

when he descended upon your virgin mother-to-be, and it was Ra who brought forth and gave birth to your soul. *See* the terms *spiritual salvation, divine birth, spiritual rebirth, begotten of spirit,* and *born of spirit,* in Tarík Karenga, *Review of the Kemetan Mystery System,* First Edition, (Union City: Amenism, Inc., in press). A plagiarized, adapted and reconfigured version of these Amenist teachings (*e.g.,* the Mysteries of the Virgin Birth) is in the religion of Christianity. *See* The Holy Bible: *Comprising the Old and New Testaments,* The King James Version, (New York: American Bible Society, 1972), [(NT) John 3:1-7], 96; [(NT) Matthew 1:18-25], 1; [(NT) Luke 1:27-44], 57, 58.

   77. *See* George G. M. James, *Stolen Legacy,* (Trenton: African World Press, 1992), 27-28. In the Mysteries one's spiritual rebirth is the first advent or *coming forth* of Heru, which occurs at the precise moment in which the Initiate is baptized by fire (*i.e.,* baptized by spirit), which simultaneously lifts the soul from its bodily prison in which it lies spiritually unborn, in sleeping repose, and in proximal separation from *true life.* Baptism by water and baptism by fire were part of the Egyptian Mystery System of which the Pharaoh was a member. *See* James, *op. cit.,* 1992, p. 91. *See* also Gerald Massey, *Ancient Egypt: The Light of the World,* Volume I, (London: T. Fisher Unwin, 1907), 222-223. Gerald Massey, *Ancient Egypt: The Light of the World,* Volume II, (London: T. Fisher Unwin, 1907), 787. *See* also the terms *proximal separation* and *spiritual slumber,* in Tarík Karenga, *Review of the Kemetan Mystery System,* First Edition, (Union City: Amenism, Inc., in press).

   78. A pledge to secrecy was also part of the process of initiation. *See* George G. M. James, *Stolen Legacy,* (Trenton: African World Press, 1992), 1.

   79. The ancient Egyptian word for *day* transliterated as hru (*i.e.,* Heru) and followed by the hieroglyph for the word *sun* written with a determinative mark conceptually means newborn sun, and theologically refers to the newborn soul. This interpretation is corroborated first by the fact that ancient Egyptian priests taught that the sun was reborn daily. William J. Darby, Paul Ghalioungui and Louis Grivetti, *Food: The Gift of Osiris,* Volume 2, (London: Academic Press, 1976), 620-621.

Notes

Additional evidence: E. A. Wallis Budge, *An Egyptian Hieroglyphic Dictionary: In Two Volumes*, Volume I, (London: John Murray, 1920), 450a. Gerald Massey, *Ancient Egypt: The Light of the World*, Volume I, (London: T. Fisher Unwin, 1907), 449-450. *See* also D. M. Murdock, *Christ in Egypt: The Horus-Jesus Connection*, (Ashland: Stellar House Publishing, 2009), 83, 95, 79-116, 377, 388, 417-419. The birth of Heru is associated with the end of the three-day period of the winter solstice, which was called the "Day of the Great Coming Forth." *Ibid.*, 104-106. Osir and Heru were both symbolically represented as a "baby sun." *Ibid.*, 110. The Holy Virgin Mother Iset was quoted as saying, "The fruit which I have begotten is the sun." *Ibid.*, 111. Heru ". . . represented the new Sun which was born daily, and which was the successor of Heru-khuti or of Ra, and he was also the offspring of the dead man-god Osiris and his lawful successor." E. A. Wallis Budge, *The Gods of the Egyptians: Or, Studies in Egyptian Mythology*, Volume I, (London: Methuen & Company, 1904), 486. Author, Margaret Murray also noted the identification of Heru with the newly-born sun. *See* Margaret A. Murray, *Egyptian Religious Poetry*, (London: John Murray, 1949), 37. A title of an important religious book that was placed in the tombs of the departed has been translated: "Coming forth as the (newborn) Sun." *See* C. C. J. Baron Bunsen and Samuel Birch, *Egypt's Place in Universal History*, Volume 5, (London: Longmans, Green, and Co., 1867), 156, 164. Mine in parentheses. Many Egyptologists refer to this book as the *Book of the Dead*, because it had reportedly been found buried with the dead. *See* Maulana Karenga, *The Book of Coming Forth by Day: The Ethics of the Declarations of Innocence*, (Los Angeles: University of Sankore Press, 1990), 19-20.

  80. George G. M. James, *Stolen Legacy*, (Trenton: African World Press, 1992), 9-10, 28, 72-73, 104-105, 164. In point of fact, by the 18th Dynasty the *Book of Coming Forth as the (Newborn) Sun* was found in the tombs of ancient Egyptians of virtually all walks of life. *See* Maulana Karenga, *Maat: The Moral Ideal in Ancient Egypt*, (Los Angeles: University of Sankore Press, 2006), 137. According to the teachings of Amenism, these two requirements are preparatory to spiritual revival, union, salvation, rebirth and resurrection.

81.   See George G. M. James, *Stolen Legacy*, (Trenton: African World Press, 1992), 91. *See* also the terms *spiritual revival* and *philosophy*, in Tarík Karenga, *Review of the Kemetan Mystery System*, First Edition, (Union City: Amenism, Inc., in press).

82.   George G. M. James, *Stolen Legacy*, (Trenton: African World Press, 1992), 27-28, 104-105. According to the teachings of Amenism, spiritual union with God means union (through Christ) of the Spirit of God that dwells within us all, with our heavenly Father Amen from whom our own spirit was begotten. One attains spiritual union with God whenever he or she is "living in truth" *i.e.*, whenever his or her values, intentions, thoughts, desires and actions are congruent with the Will of God, and God's Will is for humankind to do *Maat*. See the term *spiritual union*, in Tarík Karenga, *Review of the Kemetan Mystery System*, First Edition, (Union City: Amenism, Inc., in press). An Amenist hymn that combines God's name of "Amen" with God's name of "Ra" (*e.g.*, Amen-Ra) reads: "We worship thee because thou dwell'st in us!" *See* Francis Ellingwood Abbot, William James Potter and Benjamin Franklin Underwood, eds., "Hymn to Amun-Ra," in *The Index*, (Boston: Index Association, 1879), 161. Amenism is monotheistic as evidenced by the monotheistic statement: "Amen is one." E. A. Wallis Budge, *From Fetish to God in Ancient Egypt*, (New York: Dover Publications, 1988), 18. cf. E. A. Wallis Budge, *Tutankhamen: Amenism, Atenism and Egyptian Monotheism*, (London: Martin Hopkinson, 1923), 42. *See* also, Theophile Obenga, *African Philosophy: The Pharaonic Period: 2780-330 BC*, (Paris: Per Ankh, 2004), 544. Maulana Karenga, "Restoration of the Husia: Reviving a Sacred Legacy," in *Kemet and the African Worldview*, eds. Maulana Karenga and Jacob Carruthers, (Los Angeles: University of Sankore Press, 1986), 87. It is significant to note that in the book, *The Popular Encyclopedia of Apologetics*, authors Ed Hindson and Ergun Caner write, "In Deuteronomy 6:4, Moses said, 'Hear, O Israel! The Lord is our God, the Lord is one!' This statement became Judaism's basic statement of faith (known as the *Shema*). It is a statement that grounds Judaism as monotheistic (belief in one God)." Ed Hindson and Ergun Caner, *The Popular Encyclopedia of Apologetics: Surveying the Evidence for the Truth of*

Notes

Christianity, (Eugene: Harvest House Publishers, 2008), 474. *See also* E. A. Wallis Budge, *Egyptian Religion*, (Secaucus: Citadel Press, 1987), 131-133. The king attained spiritual union with God, which simultaneously liberated the king's soul ". . . from its bodily fetters." George G. M. James, *Stolen Legacy*, (Trenton: African World Press, 1992), 27-28, 104-105. According to the teachings of Amenism, spiritual union (*i.e.*, Christhood) is brought about by the acceptance of God's gift of *true life* through Christ and as founded on doing *Maat*. The phrase "through Christ" denotes two levels of acceptance: 1) through Osir the Christ and first person of the Holy Trinity by believing in his life, ". . . divinity, death and resurrection, and absolute control of the destinies of the bodies and souls of men. The central point of each Osirian's Religion was his hope of resurrection in a transformed body and of immortality, which could only be realized by him through the (life,) death and resurrection of [[Osir]]." *See* E. A. Wallis Budge, *Osiris and the Egyptian Resurrection*, Volume I, (New York: G. P. Putnam's Sons, 1911), a2. Mine in parentheses. [[ ]] Double brackets indicate word or term substitution made by the author. Here, the spelling of the name "Osir," which refers to the first person of God, is consistent with the teachings of Amenism and has therefore been substituted for the name "Osiris," which is Greek.; 2) through Christ, the <u>exclusive</u> agency of the indwelling Triune-Phase Spirit of God that spiritually fastens together and unifies the five physical and spiritual parts of man and woman to form the *Black Community of Christ*. Note well that Osir the Christ and belief in his life, ". . . divinity, death and resurrection, and absolute control of the destinies of the bodies and souls of men" correspond to and access Christ the <u>exclusive</u> agency located in ". . . the bosom of the spirit" of God that dwells within us all; of Osir it is said, "Osiris is thy name in the bosom of the spirit." *See* Charles Loring Brace, *The Unknown God: Or, Inspiration Among Pre-Christian Races*, (New York: A. C. Armstrong and Son, 1890), 20. Mine in parentheses. *See also* Budge, *op. cit.*, Volume I, 1911, p. a2. Spiritual union is to be attained alongside the cultivation of the Arts and Sciences. *See* the terms *spiritual union* and *Christ*, in Tarík Karenga, *Review of the Kemetan Mystery System*, First Edition, (Union City: Amenism, Inc., in press).

83.   George G. M. James, *Stolen Legacy*, (Trenton: African World Press, 1992), (28), 105. Mine in parentheses. *See* the term *spiritual salvation*, in Tarík Karenga, *Review of the Kemetan Mystery System*, First Edition, (Union City: Amenism, Inc., in press).

84.   Quoting the writings of C. H. Vail concerning one of the aims of the Egyptian Mystery System, George G. M. James writes, ". . . to become godlike and see the Gods in this life and attain the beatific vision and hold communion with the Immortals." George G. M. James, *Stolen Legacy*, (Trenton: African World Press, 1992), 27. In addition to regarding the human body as a prison house of the soul, Amenist theology teaches that God is spirit, life and truth, ". . . and through Him only man liveth." James, *op. cit.*, 1992, pp. 1, 104. *See* also extracts compiled by Egyptologist, Dr. Heinrich Brugsch in E. A. Wallis Budge, *The Book of the Dead: The Papyrus of Ani*, In Two Volumes, Volume I, (London: The Medici Society, Ltd., 1913), 106-107. From this it has been deduced that God is *true life* and that true life is located in the realm of spirit, and is in fact spirit itself. Concerning the eternal well-being of Pharaoh Amenhotep IV and his Queen Nefertiti, A hymn written during the 18th Dynasty addressing God reads thus: "Grant to thy son, who loves thee, *life in truth*, to the lord of the land, Khu-n-aten, that he may live united with thee in eternity. As for her, his wife, the queen Nefer-it-Thi – may she live for evermore and eternally by his side, well pleasing to thee : she admires what thou hast created day by day." Heinrich Brugsch-Bey, *Egypt Under the Pharaohs: A History Derived Entirely From the Monuments*, A New Edition, (London: John Murray, 1891), 221. Italics mine. To be granted "life in truth" (*i.e.*, true life) is a condition to eternal life united with God in heaven. For hieroglyps of the above mentioned hymn *see* F. Ll. Griffith, ed., *Archaeological Survey of Egypt: The Rock Tombs of El Amarna: Part I. - The Tomb of Meryra*, (London: Kegan Paul, Trench, Trubner & Co., 1903), Plate XXXVI. After acquiring the finest education in Egypt, Pythagoras of Samos became a philosopher and mathematician, and subsequently began teaching his fellow Greeks the same Amenist theology that he himself was taught in Egypt: "True life is not to be found here on earth, and what men call life is really death, and the body is the tomb of

the soul." James, *op. cit.*, 1992, pp. 1, 9, (56), 91-92, 104. *See* also Theophile Obenga, *A Lost Tradition: African Philosophy in World History*, (Philadelphia: The Source Editions, 1995), 34-36. *See* also the terms *proximal separation, spiritual slumber* and *spiritual death*, in Taŕik Karenga, *Review of the Kemetan Mystery System*, First Edition, (Union City: Amenism, Inc., in press).

  85. The King underwent a spiritual resurrection (*i.e.*, the Ba and the Ka of the king were, by secret means, reunited in the sense of being made to regain their cohesion), which simultaneously enabled the king to transfer to earth, the Kingdom of Heaven located within his or her own spirit, identifying the king with Ra in the person of Osir. Osir himself came down from heaven to transmit civilization to all nations, which was in actuality the transference to earth of the Kingdom of Heaven located within his own spirit. E. A. Wallis Budge, *Osiris and the Egyptian Resurrection*, Volume I, (New York: G. P. Putnam's Sons, 1911), 2, 16. In a body of ancient Egyptian religious and philosophical texts adapted to ancient Greek culture, Tekhi says to Imhotep, "Do you know, Asclepius (*i.e.*, Imhotep), that Egypt is an image of heaven or, to be more precise, that everything governed and moved in heaven came down to Egypt and was transferred there? If truth were told, our land is the temple of the whole world." *See* Brian P. Copenhaver, *Hermetica, The Greek Corpus Hermeticum and the Latin Asclepius in a New English Translation with Notes and Introduction*, (New York: Cambridge University Press, 1995), 81. Mine in parentheses. In Amenist theology, here, the word "heaven" has an astronomical interpretation, but also a spiritual interpretation wherein it refers to the Kingdom of Heaven located within one's own spirit and as such it is the temple of the spirit, which when transferred to earth and made manifest in the physical realm by secret means, becomes "the temple of the whole world" and the Kingdom of God on earth. *See* also D. M. Murdock, *Christ in Egypt: The Horus-Jesus Connection*, (Ashland: Stellar House Publishing, 2009), 469-478. *See* the terms *spiritual resurrection, spiritual slumber* and *Kemet*, in Taŕik Karenga, *Review of the Kemetan Mystery System*, First Edition, (Union City: Amenism, Inc., in press).

86. According to the teachings of Amenism, the king is both Osir and Heru but with one caveat. The living king is literally Heru who rules on earth, while his active role in transmitting civilization to all nations, which is the transference to earth of the Kingdom of Heaven located within his own spirit, identifies him with Osir, until at death when the king is completely assimilated to him. See Margaret A. Murray, *Egyptian Religious Poetry*, (London: John Murray, 1949), 37-38. See also Margaret A. Murray, *The Osireion at Abydos*, (London: Bernard Quaritch, 1904), 32-34. See also Charles Loring Brace, *The Unknown God: Or, Inspiration Among Pre-Christian Races*, (New York: A. C. Armstrong and Son, 1890), 27. See also D. M. Murdock, *Christ in Egypt: The Horus-Jesus Connection*, (Ashland: Stellar House Publishing, 2009), 49-51. See also Maulana Karenga, *Maat: The Moral Ideal in Ancient Egypt*, (Los Angeles: University of Sankore Press, 2006), 164-165. Amenism states that spiritual union with God is possible only upon the acceptance of God's gift of *true life* through Christ and as founded on doing *Maat*. The phrase "through Christ" denotes two levels of acceptance: 1) through Osir the Christ and first person of the Holy Trinity by believing in his life, ". . . divinity, death and resurrection, and absolute control of the destinies of the bodies and souls of men. The central point of each Osirian's Religion was his hope of resurrection in a transformed body and of immortality, which could only be realized by him through the (life,) death and resurrection of [[Osir]]." See E. A. Wallis Budge, *Osiris and the Egyptian Resurrection*, Volume I, (New York: G. P. Putnam's Sons, 1911), a2. Mine in parentheses. [[ ]] Double brackets indicate word or term substitution made by the author. Here, the spelling of the name "Osir," which refers to the first person of God, is consistent with the teachings of Amenism and has therefore been substituted for the name "Osiris," which is Greek.; 2) through Christ, the exclusive agency of the indwelling Triune-Phase Spirit of God that spiritually fastens together and unifies the five physical and spiritual parts of man and woman to form the *Black Community of Christ*. Note well that Osir the Christ and belief in his life, ". . . divinity, death and resurrection, and absolute control of the destinies of the bodies and souls of men" correspond to and access Christ the exclusive agency

Notes

located in "... the bosom of the spirit" of God that dwells within us all; of Osir it is said, "Osiris is thy name in the bosom of the spirit." See Brace, *op. cit.*, 1890, p. 20. Mine in parentheses. See also Budge, *op. cit.*, Volume I, 1911, p. a2. See the terms *spiritual union* and *Christ*, in Tarík Karenga, *Review of the Kemetan Mystery System*, First Edition, (Union City: Amenism, Inc., in press). According to the teachings of Amenism, spiritual union with God means union (through Christ) of the Spirit of God that dwells within us all, with our heavenly Father Amen from whom our own spirit was begotten. One attains spiritual union with God whenever he or she is "living in truth" *i.e.*, whenever his or her values, intentions, thoughts, desires and actions are congruent with the Will of God, and God's Will is for humankind to do *Maat*. An Amenist hymn that combines God's name of "Amen" with God's name of "Ra" (*e.g.*, Amen-Ra) reads: "We worship thee because thou dwell'st in us!" See Francis Ellingwood Abbot, William James Potter and Benjamin Franklin Underwood, eds., "Hymn to Amun-Ra," in *The Index*, (Boston: Index Association, 1879), 161. Amenism is monotheistic as evidenced by the monotheistic statement: "Amen is one." E. A. Wallis Budge, *From Fetish to God in Ancient Egypt*, (New York: Dover Publications, 1988), 18. cf. E. A. Wallis Budge, *Tutankhamen: Amenism, Atenism and Egyptian Monotheism*, (London: Martin Hopkinson, 1923), 42. See also, Theophile Obenga, *African Philosophy: The Pharaonic Period: 2780-330 BC*, (Paris: Per Ankh, 2004), 544. See also Maulana Karenga, "Restoration of the Husia: Reviving a Sacred Legacy," in *Kemet and the African Worldview*, eds. Maulana Karenga and Jacob Carruthers, (Los Angeles: University of Sankore Press, 1986), 87. It is significant to note that in the book, *The Popular Encyclopedia of Apologetics*, authors Ed Hindson and Ergun Caner write, "In Deuteronomy 6:4, Moses said, 'Hear, O Israel! The Lord is our God, the Lord is one!' This statement became Judaism's basic statement of faith (known as the *Shema*). It is a statement that grounds Judaism as monotheistic (belief in one God)." Ed Hindson and Ergun Caner, *The Popular Encyclopedia of Apologetics: Surveying the Evidence for the Truth of Christianity*, (Eugene: Harvest House Publishers, 2008), 474. See also E. A. Wallis Budge, *Egyptian Religion*, (Secaucus: Citadel Press, 1987),

131-133.

      87.   *See* Karenga, *op. cit.*, 2006, p. 348. Egypt is the Kingdom of God on earth and it is there that *Maat* is to be established, maintained and, if necessary, reestablished, and thus "... the deceased declares her virtues saying that she did *Maat* in Egypt, and lives on *Maat*." *Ibid.*, 139. Italics mine. This means that when a person turns away from doing *isfet* and commits herself to living by *Maat*, she is in effect entering the Kingdom of God on earth.

      88.   *Ibid.*, 232. *See* also E. A. Wallis Budge, *Osiris and the Egyptian Resurrection*, Volume I, (New York: G. P. Putnam's Sons, 1911), a2, 312. *See* also D. M. Murdock, *Christ in Egypt: The Horus-Jesus Connection*, (Ashland: Stellar House Publishing, 2009), 398-402. *See* also the chapter, "Become a Placemaker." This answers the question: "How are we judged?"

      89.   Albert Churchward, *The Signs and Symbols of Primordial Man: The Evolution of Religious Doctrines from the Eschatology of the Ancient Egyptians*, Second Edition, (New York: E. P. Dutton & Company, 1913), 211, 399. *See* also James Bonwick, *Egyptian Belief and Modern Thought*, (London: C. Kegan Paul & Co., 1878), 66-67. A dead spirit is ineffective as opposed to an Akhu, an effective spirit. *See* James P. Allen, *The Ancient Egyptian Pyramid Texts*, (Atlanta: Society of Biblical Literature, 2005), 7-8. The Ba can be destroyed, but if one's heart is righteous at judgment he (the Ba) joins his Ka. *See* Miriam Lichtheim, *Maat in Egyptian Autobiographies and Related Studies*, (Freiburg, Schweiz: Universitatsverlag; Gottingen: Vandenhoeck und Ruprecht, 1992), 129. The Khu, on the other hand, went to heaven upon the death of the body. E. A. Wallis Budge, *The Book of the Dead: The Papyrus of Ani*, In Two Volumes, Volume I, (London: The Medici Society, Ltd., 1913), 79.

      90.   An Amenist hymn that combines God's name of "Amen" with God's name of "Ra" (*e.g.*, Amen-Ra) reads: "We worship thee because thou dwell'st in us!" *See* Francis Ellingwood Abbot, William James Potter and Benjamin Franklin Underwood, eds., "Hymn to Amun-Ra," in *The Index*, (Boston: Index Association, 1879), 161.

      91.   *e.g.*, the papyrus at Leyden, the doctrine of Judgment

Notes

of the soul, etc...

92. According to the teachings of Amenism, the modern term *color line* is the antithesis of the heart, known in ancient Egypt as the *ib*. *See* the modern term *color line* in Webster's New World Dictionary & Thesaurus, Version 2.0, Build #25, Accent Software International, Macmillan Publishers, 1998. Mine in parentheses. Note: The definition of the *color line* has here been expanded to include spiritual and educational restrictions. *See* the terms *ib* and *spiritual death*, in Tarík Karenga, *Review of the Kemetan Mystery System*, First Edition, (Union City: Amenism, Inc., in press).

93. *i.e.*, the heart.

94. In one of the teachings of Amenism there is a prayer in which the departed states: "With the mastery of my heart I am master of my arms and legs, and I can do whatsoever my Ka pleaseth, and my soul will not be fettered at the gates of the (D)uat." E. A. Wallis Budge, *Osiris and the Egyptian Resurrection*, Volume II, (New York: G. P. Putnam's Sons, 1911), 131. Mine in parentheses. Sociologist and historian Chancellor Williams wrote that "(e)quality simply means the removal of every barrier that prevents a human being from realizing his fullest potential." Chancellor Williams, *The Destruction of Black Civilization: Great Issues of a Race from 4500 B.C. to 2000 A.D.*, Third Edition, (Chicago: Third World Press, 1987), 328. According to Dr. Tony Iton, senior vice president of healthy communities, The California Endowment, creating "conditions of opportunity" that do not already exist in one's immediate surroundings, then, speaks to investing in social benefits (which are preventative) and social services (which are responsive); Tony Iton, *Tony Iton on How to Fix California's Health Care Gap* [Audio File], NPR: KQED Forum With Michael Krasny, Aired July 5, 2018.

95. According to the teachings of Amenism.

96. *See* Gerald Massey, *Ancient Egypt: The Light of the World*, Volumes I and II, (London: T. Fisher Unwin, 1907).

97. *See* Gerald Massey, *Ancient Egypt: The Light of the World*, Volume I, (London: T. Fisher Unwin, 1907), 217-220. *See* also D. M. Murdock, *Christ in Egypt: The Horus-Jesus Connection*, (Ashland:

Stellar House Publishing, 2009), 313-318, 333.

   98. Called "The Great Collar." Alexandre Piankoff, *The Tomb of Ramesses VI*, (New York: Pantheon Books Inc., 1954), 60. Alexandre Piankoff, *The Shrines of Tut-Ankh-Amon*, (New York: Pantheon Books Inc., 1955), Plate 7. *See* illustrations in E. A. Wallis Budge, *Osiris and the Egyptian Resurrection*, Volume I, (New York: G. P. Putnam's Sons, 1911), 42, 46, 255, 263. C. G. Seligmann, and Margaret A. Murray, "Note on the "Sa" Sign," in *Man*, no. 73 (1911): 115 [#13 without appendages as in #11]. *See* image of Osir wearing the Great Collar in Tarík Karenga, *Review of the Kemetan Mystery System*, First Edition, (Union City: Amenism, Inc., in press). E. A. Wallis Budge, *An Egyptian Hieroglyphic Dictionary: In Two Volumes*, Volume II, (London: John Murray, 1920), 585b.

   99. *See* Gerald Massey, *Ancient Egypt: The Light of the World*, Volume I, (London: T. Fisher Unwin, 1907), 217-220. *See* also D. M. Murdock, *Christ in Egypt: The Horus-Jesus Connection*, (Ashland: Stellar House Publishing, 2009), 313-318, 333. It is well known that followers of the religion of Christianity routinely use the monogram X to mean "Christ," and no satisfactory reason for this practice had previously been given until Gerald Massey's research into the ancient Egyptian origin of the word "Christ" was combined with ancient Egyptian depictions of Ra in the person of Osir outfitted with the Great Collar, making the reason for this practice self-evident.

   100. Gerald Massey, *Ancient Egypt: The Light of the World*, Volume I, (London: T. Fisher Unwin, 1907), 218. *See* also D. M. Murdock, *Christ in Egypt: The Horus-Jesus Connection*, (Ashland: Stellar House Publishing, 2009), 313-318, 333.

   101. Gerald Massey, *Ancient Egypt: The Light of the World*, Volume I, (London: T. Fisher Unwin, 1907), 219.

   102. The name and titles of Roman Emperor Domitian written in Hieroglyphs on an ancient Egyptian obelisk (obelisk Piazaa Navona; also called obelisk Pamphilian) were used to arrive at the transliteration "crst" with a "c" instead of with a "k." For example, the title Autocrator and the name Caesar were both transliterated into ancient

Notes

Egyptian hieroglyphs from Latin spellings. *See* E. A. Wallis Budge, *Cleopatra's Needles and Other Egyptian Obelisks*, (London: The Religious Tract Society, 1926), 246. That is because Latin was the language of the Romans and therefore when spelling the name and titles of the Roman Emperor Domitian (*e.g.*, Autocrator Caesar Domitianus Sebastus), scribes transliterated Latin characters into corresponding ancient Egyptian hieroglyphs with matching phonetic values. *See* Matthew Bunson, *Encyclopedia of the Roman Empire*, Revised Edition, (New York: Facts on File, 2002), 301-303. When transliterating hieroglyphs into letters of the English alphabet one obtains the same results (*e.g.*, *crst*) since English is a Latin based language. For hieroglyphic inscriptions *see* Alphonsi Donini and P. Athanasius, *Romani Collegii Societas Jesu Musæum Celeberrimum*, (Amstelodami: Ex Officina Janssonio – Waesbergiana, 1678). *See* also "APPROXIMATE CORRESPONDENCES BETWEEN THE EGYPTIAN AND ENGLISH ALPHABETS," in Christian Jacq, *Fascinating Hieroglyphs: Discovering, Decoding & Understanding the Ancient Art*, (New York: Sterling Publishing Co., 1998), 36. *See* also Henry Salt, *Essay on Dr. Young's and M. Champollion's Phonetic System of Hieroglyphics*, (London: Longman, Hurst, Rees, Orme, Brown, and Green, Paternoster Row, 1825), Plate VI.

    103.   *See* D. M. Murdock, *Christ in Egypt: The Horus-Jesus Connection*, (Ashland: Stellar House Publishing, 2009), 317-321. *See* also G. Elliot Smith and Warren R. Dawson, *Egyptian Mummies*, (London: Kegan Paul International, 1991), 47, 49, 51, 58, 63-64.

    104.   *See* D. M. Murdock, *Christ in Egypt: The Horus-Jesus Connection*, (Ashland: Stellar House Publishing, 2009), 318.

    105.   The ancient Egyptians used butterfly clamps to hold blocks of stone together. *See* Rosalie David, *Handbook to Life in Ancient Egypt*, (New York: Oxford University Press, 1999), 284. James Putnam, *Pyramid*, (New York: DK Publishing, 1994), 34. Of Osir it is said, "Osiris is thy name in the bosom of the spirit." *See* Charles Loring Brace, *The Unknown God: Or, Inspiration Among Pre-Christian Races*, (New York: A. C. Armstrong and Son, 1890), 20. Mine in parentheses. *See* the term *Christ*, in Tarík Karenga, *Review of the Kemetan Mystery System*, First

Edition, (Union City: Amenism, Inc., in press).

106. *See* the term X-fastener, in Tarík Karenga, *Review of the Kemetan Mystery System*, First Edition, (Union City: Amenism, Inc., in press).

107. Not only did multidisciplinary scholar and Egyptologist Dr. Cheikh Anta Diop present eleven types of evidence that proved that the mortal founding fathers and mothers of ancient Egypt, who "came from Nubia and the "heart of Africa," were both black and native African, but he also pointed out hieroglyphs for terms that the ancient Egyptians used to designate themselves as black people. *See* Cheikh Anta Diop, "Origin of the Ancient Egyptians," in *Journal of African Civilizations* 4, no. 2 (November 1982): 9-37. Cheikh Anta Diop, *The African Origin of Civilization: Myth or Reality*, (Chicago: Lawrence Hill Books, 1974), 150. Unesco, *The Peopling of ancient Egypt and the Deciphering of Meroitic Script: Proceedings of the Symposium Held in Cairo From 28 January to 3 February 1974*, (Paris: Unesco, 1978), 73-103. Listervelt Middleton and Asa G. Hilliard, *Master Keys to Ancient Kemet (Egypt)* [Video Presentation], Waset Educational Productions, 1990. *See* also Table 7: Chronological Table, in Tarík Karenga, *Kemetan Calendar and Zodiac*, First Edition, (Union City: Amenism, Inc., 2022), 31-35. The phonetic values KMT = Kemet. *See* E. A. Wallis Budge, *An Egyptian Hieroglyphic Dictionary: In Two Volumes*, Volume II, (London: John Murray, 1920), 1045b. *See* also E. A. Wallis Budge, *First Steps in Egyptian: A Book for Beginners*, (London: Kegan Paul, Trench, Trubner & Co., Ltd., 1895), 204. (1). "the Black;" *see* E. A. Wallis Budge, *An Egyptian Hieroglyphic Dictionary: In Two Volumes*, Volume I, (London: John Murray, 1920), 105a. According to Cheikh Anta Diop, the first hieroglyph in the word Kemet represents "... a length of wood charred at the end ..." *See* Diop, *op. cit.*, 1982, p. 20. *See* also Adolf Erman and Hermann Grapow, *Worterbuch Der Aegyptischen Sprache*, Volume 5, (Berlin: Akademie -Verlag, 1971), 122. According to Ludwig Borchardt, the first hieroglyph in the word Kemet "... represents a heap of charcoal from which flames issue ..." *See* F. Ll. Griffith, *A Collection of Hieroglyphs: A Contribution to the History of Egyptian Writing*, (Boston: The Egypt Exploration Fund, 1898), 23-24.

Notes

(2). "Community of Christ;" *see* Budge, *op. cit.*, Volume 1, 1920, p. 350b. Author and anthropologist Ivan Van Sertima translates the word Kemet as the "black community." *See* Ivan Van Sertima, *Blacks in Science: Ancient and Modern*, (New Brunswick: Transaction Publishers, 1983), 128. cf. Alan Gardiner, *Egyptian Grammar: Being an Introduction to the Study of Hieroglyphs*, Third Edition, Revised, (Oxford: Griffith Institute, 1994), 57, 498. That every aspect of ancient Egyptian life, including that of naming their country, was permeated with religion is undeniable and therefore calls for a return to the original definition of the word "Kemet." In the Mysteries the word "Christ" that appears in the name of the country refers to Osir the Christ and to Christ the <u>exclusive</u> agency located in ". . . the bosom of the spirit" of God that dwells within us all; of Osir it is said, "Osiris is thy name in the bosom of the spirit." Charles Loring Brace, *The Unknown God: Or, Inspiration Among Pre-Christian Races*, (New York: A. C. Armstrong and Son, 1890), 20. Mine in parentheses. *See* "Conclusion" herein. *See* location of Osir in the bosom of the spirit and the spelling of Kemet in Tarík Karenga, *Review of the Kemetan Mystery System*, First Edition, (Union City: Amenism, Inc., in press).

108. The Egyptian Mystery System became the "Ancient World Religion" from which this custom originates. George G. M. James, *Stolen Legacy*, (Trenton: African World Press, 1992), 38. *See* also the exemplary life and mystery teachings of Osir, Iset and Heru.

109. Author Alan Bowman comments that the introduction of consanguineous marriage into Egypt was by way of the foreign Macedonian rulers. *See* Alan K. Bowman, *Egypt After the Pharaohs: 332 BC-AD 642*, (Los Angeles: University of California Press, 1986), 24.

110. The Spirit of God dwells within us all. An Amenist hymn that combines God's name of "Amen" with God's name of "Ra" (*e.g.*, Amen-Ra) reads: "We worship thee because thou dwell'st in us!" *See* Francis Ellingwood Abbot, William James Potter and Benjamin Franklin Underwood, eds., "Hymn to Amun-Ra," in *The Index*, (Boston: Index Association, 1879), 161.

111. Additionally, from the inscription of Antef we learn that even a philosopher is one "…who asks for advice and sees to it that

he is asked advice." *See* Kwasi Wiredu, ed., *A Companion to African Philosophy*, (Malden: Blackwell Publishing, 2004), 35-36.

Chapter 3

1. Maulana Karenga, *Selections from the Husia*, (Los Angeles: University Of Sankore Press, 1984), 50.
2. *Ibid*. Italics mine.
3. Miriam Lichtheim, *Ancient Egyptian Literature*, Volume I, (Los Angeles: University of California Press, 1973), 137.
4. James Henry Breasted, *The Dawn of Conscience*, (New York: Charles Scribner's Sons, 1935), 155.
5. *Ibid.*, 155.
6. James Henry Breasted, *Ancient Records of Egypt*, Volume II, (Chicago: The University of Chicago Press, 1906), 274.
7. James Henry Breasted, *Development of Religion and Thought in Ancient Egypt*, (New York: Charles Scribner's Sons, 1912), 239.
8. *Ibid.*, 240.
9. Joel Kotkin, *Tribes*, (New York: Random House, Inc., 1992), 4-5.
10. Thomas E. Ludwig, "Helplessly Hoping," PsychSim 5: *Interactive Graphic Simulation and Demonstration Activities for Psychology* [CD-ROM], Worth Publishers, 2004.
11. Siegfried Morenz, *Egyptian Religion*, (Ithaca: Cornell University Press, 1973), 37-38, 44-45.
12. E. Raymond Capt, *The Great Pyramid Decoded*, (Thousand Oaks: Artisan Sales, 1971), 11.

*Richard M. Hodgetts, *Effective Supervision: A Practical Approach*, (New York: McGraw-Hill, 1987).

Chapter 4

1. Amen in his name of Ptah is called *Placemaker*, because he creates "conditions of opportunity" in which needs can be met, starting with his own needs. "The Creator in his name of Ptah is a place-maker–*ir st.f*–who of necessity is an 'active one who came forth active." Maulana Karenga, *Maat: The Moral Ideal in Ancient Egypt*, (Los Angeles: University of Sankore Press, 2006), 182. In mortuary texts dis-

Notes

covered inscribed on the inside walls of coffins and that are now known as the *Ancient Egyptian Coffin Texts,* Amen in his name of Ra and in his role of *Placemaker* states that he created everyone equal in opportunity, and equal in the sense of human equality. See James B. Pritchard, *Ancient Near Eastern Texts Relating to the Old Testament,* (London: Princeton University Press, 1950), 7-8. See also Karenga, *op. cit.*, 2006, p. 247. The religion of Amenism clearly teaches that humankind is meant to live and interact as a world community and in this way an appropriate amount of resources can be sent from areas of abundance to those of deficiency for the purpose of creating "conditions of opportunity" throughout the entire world community. See excerpt from the *Ancient Egyptian Coffin Texts* in Pritchard, *op. cit.*, 1950, pp. 7-8. The principle of reciprocity applies here; see Robert B. Cialdini, *The Power of Persuasion* [Video Presentation], Stanford University, 2001. According to Dr. Tony Iton, senior vice president of healthy communities, The California Endowment, creating "conditions of opportunity" that do not already exist in one's immediate surroundings, then, speaks to investing in social benefits (which are preventative) and social services (which are responsive); Tony Iton, *Tony Iton on How to Fix California's Health Care Gap* [Audio File], NPR: KQED Forum With Michael Krasny, Aired July 5, 2018. Elaborating on the writings of Ralph Ruddock, author John Shaw states that it is the task of the caring person (in this case the social worker, who is here playing the role of *Placemaker*) ". . . to create conditions in which these needs can usually be met . . ." For example, the need ". . . to find satisfactory work and family roles" for the ". . . unemployed young person, the deserted wife, the aged person living alone, the unemployed ex-prisoner without family ties and so on." John Shaw, *The Self in Social Work,* (London: Routledge & Kegan Paul, 1974), 96. According to the teachings of Amenism, one who performs this selfless act of love is called *Placemaker*; see above. Maulana Karenga, *The African American Holiday of Kwanzaa: A Celebration of Family, Community & Culture,* (Los Angeles: University of Sankore Press, 1988), 23.

2. Helen Diner, *Mothers and Amazons: The First Feminine History of Culture,* (Garden City: Anchor Press, 1973), 169. Italics

mine. Adolf Erman, *A Handbook of Egyptian Religion*, (London: Archibald Constable & Co. Ltd., 1907), 245.

    3.   George G. M. James, *Stolen Legacy*, (Trenton: African World Press, 1992), 42. Brenda Stalcup, *Ancient Egyptian Civilization*, (San Diego: Greenhaven Press, 2001), 11. *See* also Cheikh Anta Diop, *Civilization or Barbarism: An Authentic Anthropology*, (Brooklyn: Lawrence Hill Books, 1991), 1ff. *See* also the chapter, "Express Your Gratitude."

    4.   Henri Frankfort, H. A. Frankfort, John A. Wilson, Thorkild Jacobsen and William A. Irwin, *The Intellectual Adventure of Ancient Man: An Essay on Speculative Thought in the Ancient Near East*, (Chicago: University of Chicago Press, 1977), 34. Mine in parentheses.

    5.   Stephanie Fitzgerald, *Ramses II: Egyptian Pharaoh, Warrior, and Builder*, (Mankato: Compass Point Books, 2009), 38.

    6.   *Ibid.*, 38. Philip Briggs, *Ethiopia: The Bradt Travel Guide*, Sixth Edition, (Guilford: The Globe Pequot Press Inc., 2012), 75. *See* also Marc Van De Mieroop, *A History of Ancient Egypt*, (Malden: Wiley-Blackwell, 2011), 8. Comments of Greek historian Diodorus Siculus in John G. Jackson, "Egypt and Christianity," in *Journal of African Civilizations* 4, no. 2 (November 1982): 65. Tarík Karenga, *Kemetan Calendar and Zodiac*, First Edition, (Union City: Amenism, Inc., 2022), 9, 35.

    7.   George G. M. James, *Stolen Legacy*, (Trenton: African World Press, 1992), 27-28. Maulana Karenga, *Introduction to Black Studies*, Second Edition, (Los Angeles: University of Sankore Press, 1993), 84-90. Brenda Stalcup, *Ancient Egyptian Civilization*, (San Diego: Greenhaven Press, 2001), 11. There is one known documented exception–the Greeks were actually barred from Egyptian schools for nearly 5,000 years until around 525 B.C.E. at the time of the Persian conquest. James, *op. cit.*, 1992, p. 1. *See* also Asa G. Hilliard and Listervelt Middleton, *Free Your Mind: Return to the Source African Origins* [Video Presentation], Wa'set Educational Productions, 1998. French scholar Count Volney states that the ancient Egyptians were in fact a black race and adds, "…is the very one to which we owe our arts, our sciences and even the use of spoken word…" Cheikh Anta Diop, "Origin of the Ancient Egyptians," in

Notes

Journal of African Civilizations 4, no. 2 (November 1982): 19.

8. Author Maulana Karenga writes that one of the names of God is *Placemaker*, because he makes a place for himself and others by creating "conditions of opportunity" in which needs can be met, enabling the experience of "... ever-higher levels of human life and achievement." Humans can also become *Placemakers* by imitating God in this selfless act of love; *see* Maulana Karenga, *Maat: The Moral Ideal in Ancient Egypt*, (Los Angeles: University of Sankore Press, 2006), 182-183. Maulana Karenga, *The African American Holiday of Kwanzaa: A Celebration of Family, Community & Culture*, (Los Angeles: University of Sankore Press, 1988), 23. Tony Iton, *Tony Iton on How to Fix California's Health Care Gap* [Audio File], NPR: KQED Forum With Michael Krasny, Aired July 5, 2018.

9. Psychologist Abraham Harold Maslow organized needs according to priority in his *Maslow's Hierarchy of Needs*. Maslow found that the gratification of lower level to higher level needs helps one to actualize more of his or her potentialities. The challenge with utilizing this approach alone to meeting one's needs is that until lower level needs are addressed, higher level needs are neglected. John Shaw, *The Self in Social Work*, (London: Routledge & Kegan Paul, 1974), 24-26, 73. Corresponding to the five physical and spiritual parts of man and woman that form the *Black Community of Christ*, presented here are *Kemet's Interrelated Categories of Needs*, each (category) of which can be viewed as being sufficiently or insufficiently met simultaneously, at all times, and at varying degrees. Individually, needs tend to be viewed as either being met or unmet, but in terms of broad interrelated categories, needs are viewed holistically and hence they are also widely viewed as constantly and simultaneously being met, either sufficiently or insufficiently. Thus, in terms of broad interrelated categories, the degree to which we are sufficiently or insufficiently meeting our needs for today may, because of our own personal growth and development or lack thereof, sufficiently or insufficiently meet our needs for tomorrow and beyond. *Kemet's Interrelated Categories of Needs* allow for such meeting of needs in all five categories simultaneously, notwithstanding. *See* Tarík Karenga, *Review of the*

Kemetan Mystery System, First Edition, (Union City: Amenism, Inc., in press).

    10.   Amen in his name of Ptah is called *Placemaker*, because he creates "conditions of opportunity" in which needs can be met, starting with his own needs. "The Creator in his name of Ptah is a place-maker–*ir st.f*–who of necessity is an 'active one who came forth active." Maulana Karenga, *Maat: The Moral Ideal in Ancient Egypt*, (Los Angeles: University of Sankore Press, 2006), 182. According to Dr. Tony Iton, senior vice president of healthy communities, The California Endowment, creating "conditions of opportunity" in a practical sense speaks to investing in social benefits (which are preventative) and social services (which are responsive); Tony Iton, *Tony Iton on How to Fix California's Health Care Gap* [Audio File], NPR: KQED Forum With Michael Krasny, Aired July 5, 2018. Elaborating on the writings of Ralph Ruddock, author John Shaw states that it is the task of the caring person (in this case the social worker, who is here playing the role of *Placemaker*) ". . . to create conditions in which these needs can usually be met . . ." For example, the need ". . . to find satisfactory work and family roles" for the ". . . unemployed young person, the deserted wife, the aged person living alone, the unemployed ex-prisoner without family ties and so on." John Shaw, *The Self in Social Work*, (London: Routledge & Kegan Paul, 1974), 96. In his essay, "The Fully Functioning Person," psychologist Carl Rogers sums up what he calls, "the good life" as a process of "...stretching and growing of becoming more and more of one's potentialities." *Ibid.*, 27.

    11.   Miriam Lichtheim, *Ancient Egyptian Literature*, Volume III, (Los Angeles: University of California Press, 1980), 171.

    12.   James Henry Breasted, *Ancient Records of Egypt*, Volume I, (Chicago: University of Chicago Press, 1906), 231.

    13.   Henry Brugsch-Bey, *A History of Egypt Under the Pharaohs*, Translated by Philip Smith, 2nd Edition, Volume II, (London: John Murray, 1881), 282.

    14.   Theophile Obenga, *Ancient Egypt & Black Africa: A Student's Handbook for the Study of Ancient Egypt in Philosophy, Linguistics, & Gender Relations*, (London: Karnak House, 1992), 163.

Notes

15. Maulana Karenga, *Maat: The Moral Ideal in Ancient Egypt*, (Los Angeles: University of Sankore Press, 2006), 358.

16. *Ibid.*, 358. See also Lee Jones, *Brothers of the Academy: Up and Coming Black Scholars Earning Our Way in Higher Education*, (Sterling: Stylus Publishing, 2000), 245.

17. Helen Diner, *Mothers and Amazons: The First Feminine History of Culture*, (Garden City: Anchor Press, 1973), 173. cf. James Henry Breasted, *Ancient Records of Egypt*, Volume IV, (Chicago: The University of Chicago Press, 1906), 204-205.

18. See the term *social responsibility*, in Tarík Karenga, *Review of the Kemetan Mystery System*, First Edition, (Union City: Amenism, Inc., in press).

19. Alan H. Gardiner, "The Egyptian Word for Herdsman," in *Zeitschrift Fur Agyptische Sprache Und Altertumskunde*, Volume 42, eds. Adolf Erman and Georg Steindorff, (Leipzig: J. C. Hinrichs'sche Buchhandlung, 1905), 121. Maulana Karenga, *Maat: The Moral Ideal in Ancient Egypt*, (Los Angeles: University of Sankore Press, 2006), 197-198, 224, 323. Osir is frequently depicted holding the herdsman's and shepherd's crook and flail. E. A. Wallis Budge, *Osiris and the Egyptian Resurrection*, Volume I, (New York: G. P. Putnam's Sons, 1911), 13. E. A. Wallis Budge, *An Egyptian Hieroglyphic Dictionary: In Two Volumes*, Volume I, (London: John Murray, 1920), 448b, 512b.

20. Alan H. Gardiner, *The Admonitions of an Egyptian Sage*, (Hildesheim: Georg Olms Verlag, 1969), 13.

21. Maulana Karenga, *Maat: The Moral Ideal in Ancient Egypt*, (Los Angeles: University of Sankore Press, 2006), 226. In Amenism people are sometimes referred to as "... the noble herd or cattle of God ..." *Ibid.*, 323. There are also, in Amenism, references to people as "flocks of God." See E. A. Wallis Budge, *The Teachings of Amen-Em Apt, Son of Kanekht*, (London: Martin Hopkinson and Company, Ltd., 1924), 22.

22. Webster's New World Dictionary & Thesaurus, Version 2.0, Build #25, Accent Software International, Macmillan Publishers, 1998. Asa G. Hilliard, *Re-Education of African People* [Audio Presentation], Institute of Karmic Guidance, 1990. See the term *socialization*,

in Tarík Karenga, *Review of the Kemetan Mystery System*, First Edition, (Union City: Amenism, Inc., in press).

23. The ten virtues of the Egyptian Mystery System are as follows: truth, justice, harmony, balance, reciprocity, order, righteousness, wisdom, temperance, and courage (*i.e.*, the ten cardinal virtues of *Maat*). Asa G. Hillard, *SBA: The Reawakening of the African Mind*, (Gainesville, Makare Publishing Company, 1998), 2, 16. George G. M. James, *Stolen Legacy*, (Trenton: African World Press, 1992), 3-4, 30-31, 104-106. Philosopher and Egyptologist Gregoire Biyogo writes that *Maat* is "... the universal principle of Truth ..." Gregoire Biyogo, *Aux Sources Egyptiennes Du Savoir: Volume 1, Genealogie Et Enjeux De La Pensee De Cheikh Anta Diop*, (Yaounde: Editions Menaibuc, 2000), 7n4. Author Jeremy Naydler makes reference to *Maat* as "... the divine organizing principle." Jeremy Naydler, *Temple of the Cosmos: The Ancient Egyptian Experience of the Sacred*, (Rochester: Inner Traditions International, 1996), 104. Egyptologist John A. Wilson says of *Maat*: "It was the cosmic force of harmony, order, stability, and security, coming down from the first creation as the organizing quality of created phenomena ..." See John A. Wilson, *The Culture of Ancient Egypt*, (Chicago: The University of Chicago Press, 1957), 48. Professor of African American Studies Molefi Kete Asante wrote: "When you speak of it as the organizing principle of human society, the creative spirit of phenomena, and the eternal order of the universe, you come close to understanding what the ancient Kemetic civilization understood." Molefi Kete Asante, *Kemet, Afrocentricity and Knowledge*, (Trenton: African World Press, 1990), 89. The ancient Egyptians depicted *Maat* as the daughter of God and held that maintaining the principle of *Maat* keeps society along with the entire universe from collapsing into chaos; hence the term *divine, universal organizing principle*. Christine El Mahdy, *Tutankhamen: The Life and Death of the Boy-King*, (New York: St. Martin's, 1999), 183. "Adherence to Maat created the good order of society, while abandoning Maat plunged society into chaos." Miriam Lichtheim, *Maat in Egyptian Autobiographies and Related Studies*, (Freiburg, Schweiz: Universitatsverlag; Gottingen: Vandenhoeck und Ruprecht, 1992), "English Summary." See also Emily Teeter, "Maat,"

Notes

in *The Oxford Encyclopedia of Ancient Egypt*, Volume 2, ed. Donald B. Redford, (New York: Oxford University Press, 2001), 319-321. According to Webster's New World Dictionary, "chaos implies total and apparently irremediable lack of organization." This is the opposite of *Maat*. See "chaos" under synonyms for "confusion" in Webster's New World Dictionary & Thesaurus, Version 2.0, Build #25, Accent Software International, Macmillan Publishers, 1998. Henri Frankfort, *Ancient Egyptian Religion*, (New York: Harper Torchbooks, 1961), 54, 63. Amen in his name of Ra said: "I laid the foundation [of things] by *Maat*." E. A. Wallis Budge, *Legends of the Egyptian Gods*, (London: Kegan Paul, Trench, Trubner & Co., Ltd., 1912), 3. Italics mine. Here, *Maat* is to be understood in the sense of "truth," which is indicated through the use of the ancient Egyptian word *Maa* (mah-**AH**). *See* E. A. Wallis Budge, *The Gods of the Egyptians: Or, Studies in Egyptian Mythology*, Volume I, (London: Methuen & Company, 1904), 295-296, (309). Maulana Karenga, *Maat: The Moral Ideal in Ancient Egypt*, (Los Angeles: University of Sankore Press, 2006), 166, 307. Italics mine. *See* the term *Divine Law*, in Tarík Karenga, *Review of the Kemetan Mystery System*, First Edition, (Union City: Amenism, Inc., in press). *See* also the chapter, "Seek Wise Counsel."

  24. Maulana Karenga, *Maat: The Moral Ideal in Ancient Egypt*, (Los Angeles: University of Sankore Press, 2006), 264. Miriam Lichtheim, *Maat in Egyptian Autobiographies and Related Studies*, (Freiburg, Schweiz: Universitatsverlag; Gottingen: Vandenhoeck und Ruprecht, 1992), 67. "Adherence to Maat created the good order of society, while abandoning Maat plunged society into chaos. Man's knowledge of right, and his ability to do it, were defined as originating in his heart and in his nature: virtue was innate and inner-directed." *Ibid.*, "English Summary." *See* also Neely Fuller, Jr., *The United Independent Compensatory Code/System/Concept: A Textbook/Workbook for Thought, Speech and/or Action for Victims of Racism (White Supremacy)*, Revised, (1984), 20-21.

  25. Miriam Lichtheim, *Maat in Egyptian Autobiographies and Related Studies*, (Freiburg, Schweiz: Universitatsverlag; Gottingen: Vandenhoeck und Ruprecht, 1992), 67. Italics mine.

26. Maulana Karenga, *Maat: The Moral Ideal in Ancient Egypt*, (Los Angeles: University of Sankore Press, 2006), 233.

27. John Tait, *Never Had the Like Occurred: Egypt's View of Its Past*, (London: UCL Press, 2003), 178. *Isfet* is the universal chaos principle and according to Webster's New World Dictionary, "chaos implies total and apparently irremediable lack of organization." This is the opposite of *Maat*. "chaos" under synonyms for "confusion" in Webster's New World Dictionary & Thesaurus, Version 2.0, Build #25, Accent Software International, Macmillan Publishers, 1998. George G. M. James, *Stolen Legacy*, (Trenton: African World Press, 1992), 91, 104-106. *See* the terms *Maat* and *Isfet*, in Tarík Karenga, *Review of the Kemetan Mystery System*, First Edition, (Union City: Amenism, Inc., in press).

28. Maulana Karenga, *Maat: The Moral Ideal in Ancient Egypt*, (Los Angeles: University of Sankore Press, 2006), 203-207, (248).

29. The revered ancient Egyptian peasant Khuwenanpu delivered a brilliant discourse on *Maat* in which he stated that ". . . doing *Maat* is not only doing good, it is *increasing good and lessening evil in the world*." *Ibid.*, 184. Italics mine.

30. After having made his *Declaration of Maat*, the soul of the departed was recorded as saying that he propitiated God by doing his will. Thus God's Will is for humankind to do *Maat*. E. A. Wallis Budge, *The Book of the Dead: The Papyrus of Ani*, In Two Volumes, Volume II, (London: The Medici Society, Ltd., 1913), 587. *See* also Maulana Karenga, *Maat: The Moral Ideal in Ancient Egypt*, (Los Angeles: University of Sankore Press, 2006), 21ff.

31. Our hearts are made righteous by doing *Maat*; see Jeremy Naydler, *Temple of the Cosmos: The Ancient Egyptian Experience of the Sacred*, (Rochester: Inner Traditions International, 1996), 96. Mine in parentheses. Capitalization mine. Italics mine. Heaven was figuratively referred to as the West. *See* E. A. Wallis Budge, *From Fetish to God in Ancient Egypt*, (New York: Dover Publications, 1988), 338. *See* also Miriam Lichtheim, *Maat in Egyptian Autobiographies and Related Studies*, (Freiburg, Schweiz: Universitatsverlag; Gottingen: Vandenhoeck und Ruprecht, 1992), 97.

Notes

32. Jeremy Naydler, *Temple of the Cosmos: The Ancient Egyptian Experience of the Sacred*, (Rochester: Inner Traditions International, 1996), 97. Italics mine.

33. Alexandre Piankoff, *The Tomb of Ramesses VI*, (New York: Pantheon Books Inc., 1954), 145.

34. George G. M. James, *Stolen Legacy*, (Trenton: African World Press, 1992), 1ff. *See* also the chapter, "Seek Wise Counsel." D. M. Murdock, *Christ in Egypt: The Horus-Jesus Connection*, (Ashland: Stellar House Publishing, 2009), 2. Theophile Obenga, *African Philosophy: The Pharaonic Period: 2780-330 BC*, (Paris: Per Ankh, 2004), 125-126. *See* also the terms *Amenism, Kemetan Mystery System*, and *religion*, in Tarík Karenga, *Review of the Kemetan Mystery System*, First Edition, (Union City: Amenism, Inc., in press). According to Amenism, spiritual union with God means union (through Christ) of the Spirit of God that dwells within us all, with our heavenly Father Amen from whom our own spirit was begotten. One attains spiritual union with God whenever he or she is "living in truth" *i.e.*, whenever his or her values, intentions, thoughts, desires and actions are congruent with the Will of God, and God's Will is for humankind to do *Maat*. *See* the term *spiritual union*, in Tarík Karenga, *Review of the Kemetan Mystery System*, First Edition, (Union City: Amenism, Inc., in press). An Amenist hymn that combines God's name of "Amen" with God's name of "Ra" (*e.g.*, Amen-Ra) reads: "We worship thee because thou dwell'st in us!" *See* Francis Ellingwood Abbot, William James Potter and Benjamin Franklin Underwood, eds., "Hymn to Amun-Ra," in *The Index*, (Boston: Index Association, 1879), 161. Amenism is monotheistic as evidenced by the monotheistic statement: "Amen is one." *See* E. A. Wallis Budge, *From Fetish to God in Ancient Egypt*, (New York: Dover Publications, 1988), 18. cf. E. A. Wallis Budge, *Tutankhamen: Amenism, Atenism and Egyptian Monotheism*, (London: Martin Hopkinson, 1923), 42. *See* also, Obenga, *op. cit.*, 2004, p. 544. Maulana Karenga, "Restoration of the Husia: Reviving a Sacred Legacy," in *Kemet and the African Worldview*, eds. Maulana Karenga and Jacob Carruthers, (Los Angeles: University of Sankore Press, 1986), 87. Furthermore, it is very significant to note that in the book, *The Popular Encyclopedia*

of Apologetics, authors Ed Hindson and Ergun Caner write, "In Deuteronomy 6:4, Moses said, 'Hear, O Israel! The Lord is our God, the Lord is one!' This statement became Judaism's basic statement of faith (known as the *Shema*). It is a statement that grounds Judaism as monotheistic (belief in one God)." Ed Hindson and Ergun Caner, *The Popular Encyclopedia of Apologetics: Surveying the Evidence for the Truth of Christianity*, (Eugene: Harvest House Publishers, 2008), 474. See also E. A. Wallis Budge, *Egyptian Religion*, (Secaucus: Citadel Press, 1987), 131-133. See also the term *spiritual salvation* in Tarík Karenga, *Review of the Kemetan Mystery System*, First Edition, (Union City: Amenism, Inc., in press). This answers the question: "How are we saved?" Answer: By accepting God's gift of *true life* through Christ and as founded on doing *Maat*. **Rationale: First**, self-development was available to Initiates of the Egyptian Mystery System by way of education (*e.g.*, through the cultivation of the Arts and Sciences), and the practice of virtue (*e.g.*, by doing *Maat*). James, *op. cit.*, 1992, pp. 28, 72-73, 164. **Second**, the Arts and Sciences were organized into a curriculum that offered a vast array of courses. James, *op. cit.*, 1992, pp. 135-137. **Third**, in addition to regarding the human body as a prison house of the soul, "(i)n the Egyptian Mysteries . . . the concept of the Supreme Good is expressed as the purpose of virtue (*i.e.*, the purpose of *Maat*), and that is the salvation of the Soul, by liberating it from the ten bodily fetters . . . This process transformed man and made him godlike, and fitted him for union with God." James, *op. cit.*, 1992, pp. 1, 104, 91. Mine in parentheses. *i.e.*, it facilitated being engaged in a personal relationship and spiritual union with God, which simultaneously liberated the soul ". . . from its bodily fetters;" James, *op. cit.*, 1992, pp. 27-28, 104-105. **Fourth**, Amenist theology teaches that God is spirit, life and truth, ". . . and through Him only man liveth." See extracts compiled by Egyptologist, Dr. Heinrich Brugsch in E. A. Wallis Budge, *The Book of the Dead: The Papyrus of Ani*, In Two Volumes, Volume I, (London: The Medici Society, Ltd., 1913), 106-107. From this it has been deduced that God is *true life* and that true life is located in the realm of spirit, and is in fact spirit itself. Furthermore, to accept God's gift of *true life* through Christ is to at the same time, accept God himself, since God

Notes

is life. Concerning the eternal well-being of Pharaoh Amenhotep IV and his Queen Nefertiti, A hymn written during the 18th Dynasty addressing God reads thus: "Grant to thy son, who loves thee, *life in truth*, to the lord of the land, Khu-n-aten, that he may live united with thee in eternity. As for her, his wife, the queen Nefer-it-Thi – may she live for evermore and eternally by his side, well pleasing to thee : she admires what thou hast created day by day." Heinrich Brugsch-Bey, *Egypt Under the Pharaohs: A History Derived Entirely From the Monuments*, A New Edition, (London: John Murray, 1891), 221. Italics mine. To be granted "life in truth" (*i.e.*, true life) is a condition to eternal life united with God in heaven. For hieroglyps of the above mentioned hymn *see* F. Ll. Griffith, ed., *Archaeological Survey of Egypt: The Rock Tombs of El Amarna: Part I. – The Tomb of Meryra*, (London: Kegan Paul, Trench, Trubner & Co., 1903), Plate XXXVI. After acquiring the finest education in Egypt, Pythagoras of Samos became a philosopher and mathematician, and subsequently began teaching his fellow Greeks the same Amenist theology that he himself was taught in Egypt: "True life is not to be found here on earth, and what men call life is really death, and the body is the tomb of the soul." James, *op. cit.*, 1992, pp. 1, 9, (56), 91-92, 104. *See* also Theophile Obenga, *A Lost Tradition: African Philosophy in World History*, (Philadelphia: The Source Editions, 1995), 34-36. **Fifth**, the Egyptian Mystery System became the "Ancient World Religion." George G. M. James, *Stolen Legacy*, (Trenton: African World Press, 1992), 38. Amenism teaches that Amen, who is a single God, <u>exists</u> as spirit, is triune in phases (*e.g.*, Amen (spirit), Ra (soul) and Ptah (mind)), triune in persons (*e.g.*, Ra in the persons of Osir, Iset and Heru) and "manifold in [spiritual] forms." [ ] Brackets indicate interpolation to clarify the meaning. *See* also Budge, *op. cit.*, Volume 1, 1913, pp. 106-107. Additionally, to found one's acceptance of God's gift of *true life* through Christ on *Maat* is to conduct one's relationship with God, one's self, others, and nature in a manner that bespeaks truth, justice, harmony, balance, reciprocity, order, righteousness, wisdom, temperance, and courage (*i.e.*, in accordance with the ten cardinal virtues of *Maat*), for *Maat* is the bread on which God subsists. *See* Henri Frankfort, *Ancient Egyptian Religion*, (New York: Harper Torchbooks, 1961), 55.

THE PHARAOHS' 5 LAWS OF SUCCESS

The phrase "through Christ" denotes two levels of acceptance: 1) through Osir the Christ and first person of the Holy Trinity by believing in his life, "... divinity, death and resurrection, and absolute control of the destinies of the bodies and souls of men. The central point of each Osirian's Religion was his hope of resurrection in a transformed body and of immortality, which could only be realized by him through the (life,) death and resurrection of [[Osir]]." *See* E. A. Wallis Budge, *Osiris and the Egyptian Resurrection*, Volume I, (New York: G. P. Putnam's Sons, 1911), a2. Mine in parentheses. [[ ]] Double brackets indicate word or term substitution made by the author. Here, the spelling of the name "Osir," which refers to the first person of God, is consistent with the teachings of Amenism and has therefore been substituted for the name "Osiris," which is Greek.; 2) through Christ, the exclusive agency of the indwelling Triune-Phase Spirit of God that spiritually fastens together and unifies the five physical and spiritual parts of man and woman to form the *Black Community of Christ*. Note well that Osir the Christ and belief in his life, "... divinity, death and resurrection, and absolute control of the destinies of the bodies and souls of men" correspond to and access Christ the exclusive agency located in "... the bosom of the spirit" of God that dwells within us all; of Osir it is said, "Osiris is thy name in the bosom of the spirit." *See* Charles Loring Brace, *The Unknown God: Or, Inspiration Among Pre-Christian Races*, (New York: A. C. Armstrong and Son, 1890), 20. Mine in parentheses. *See* also Budge, *op. cit.*, Volume I, 1911, p. a2. *See* the term *Christ*, in Tarík Karenga, *Review of the Kemetan Mystery System*, First Edition, (Union City: Amenism, Inc., in press). *See* also "Conclusion" herein. Note: The three persons of the Holy Trinity in the religion of Christianity is a plagiarized, adapted and reconfigured version of the three persons of the Holy Trinity of Osir, Iset and Heru in the religion of Amenism. Anthony T. Browder, *Nile Valley Contributions to Civilization: Exploding the Myths*, Volume 1, (Washington: The Institute of Karmic Guidance, 1992), 68. E. A. Wallis Budge, *From Fetish to God in Ancient Egypt*, (New York: Dover Publications, Inc., 1988), 18. D. M. Murdock, *Christ in Egypt: The Horus-Jesus Connection*, (Ashland: Stellar House Publishing, 2009), 53-54, 67.

Notes

35.   Amen in his form of Atum (a name for Ra) is reported to have said that *Maat* was present before creation. *See* David Leeming, *The Oxford Companion to World Mythology*, (New York: Oxford University Press, 2005), 243. cf. Lucie Lamy, *Egyptian Mysteries: New Light on Ancient Knowledge*, (New York: Thames and Hudson, 1981), 17. *See* also Molefi Kete Asante, *The Egyptian Philosophers: Ancient African Voices from Imhotep to Akhenaten*, (Chicago: African American Images, 2000), 114-115. Henri Frankfort, *Ancient Egyptian Religion*, (New York: Harper Torchbooks, 1961), 63. Hence, the term *divine, universal organizing principle*. *See* Christine El Mahdy, *Tutankhamen: The Life and Death of the Boy-King*, (New York: St. Martin's, 1999), 183. "Adherence to Maat created the good order of society, while abandoning Maat plunged society into chaos." Miriam Lichtheim, *Maat in Egyptian Autobiographies and Related Studies*, (Freiburg, Schweiz: Universitatsverlag; Gottingen: Vandenhoeck und Ruprecht, 1992), "English Summary." *See* also Emily Teeter, "Maat," in *The Oxford Encyclopedia of Ancient Egypt*, Volume 2, ed. Donald B. Redford, (New York: Oxford University Press, 2001), 319-321. According to Webster's New World Dictionary, "chaos implies total and apparently irremediable lack of organization." This is the opposite of *Maat*. *See* "chaos" under synonyms for "confusion" in Webster's New World Dictionary & Thesaurus, Version 2.0, Build #25, Accent Software International, Macmillan Publishers, 1998.

36.   *Maat* is to be established and maintained within and around us. Enter the words of Amen in his form of the self-created Atum: "When the heavens were sleeping . . . , I lived with my daughter *Maat*, one within me, the other around me." *See* Lucie Lamy, *Egyptian Mysteries: New Light on Ancient Knowledge*, (New York: Thames and Hudson, 1981), 17. Italics mine. Maulana Karenga, *Maat: The Moral Ideal in Ancient Egypt*, (Los Angeles: University of Sankore Press, 2006), 264. The opposite of *Maat* is *isfet* and, like *Maat*, *isfet* can be engaged in all areas of moral concern and human activity, but instead with adverse effects to society. Racism is one form of *isfet* that author Neely Fuller contends adversely affects people in nine major areas of people activities to which I have added but one. Fuller refers to the opposite of racism as justice and

correctness, which is in fact *Maat*. *See* Neely Fuller, Jr., *The United Independent Compensatory Code/System/Concept: A Textbook/Workbook for Thought, Speech and/or Action for Victims of Racism (White Supremacy)*, Revised, (1984), 20-21.

37. *Maat* has been joined to our hearts at birth, which innately predisposes us to increase good in the world. This innate predisposition to increase good in the world is further enhanced by embracing and doing *Maat*. Huyshery, treasury scribe of the temple of Sethi I makes this case well. *See* Miriam Lichtheim, *Maat in Egyptian Autobiographies and Related Studies*, (Freiburg, Schweiz: Universitatsverlag; Gottingen: Vandenhoeck und Ruprecht, 1992), 67. When asked to suggest ways that parents can positively influence their children to impact their long-term life, social psychologist Dr. Robert Cialdini replied, "... we arrange circumstances so that they can move in those directions in ways that aren't difficult for them to do." The objective is, of course, to facilitate their moving in the direction of doing *Maat*. Anthony Robbins, *Powertalk*, Vol. 7 [Audio Presentation], Guthy-Renker Corp., 1997. The ancient Egyptian, Lady Ta-Aset says: "Doing good is not difficult . . . just speaking good is a monument." Maulana Karenga, *Maat: The Moral Ideal in Ancient Egypt*, (Los Angeles: University of Sankore Press, 2006), 124. James B. Pritchard, *Ancient Near Eastern Texts Relating to the Old Testament*, (London: Princeton University Press, 1950), 5. Emphasis mine. E. A. Wallis Budge, *Legends of the Egyptian Gods*, (London: Kegan Paul, Trench, Trubner & Co., Ltd., 1912), 3. Italics mine. Here, *Maat* is to be understood in the sense of "truth," which is indicated through the use of the ancient Egyptian word *Maa* (mah-**AH**). *See* E. A. Wallis Budge, *The Gods of the Egyptians: Or, Studies in Egyptian Mythology*, Volume I, (London: Methuen & Company, 1904), 295-296, (309). Since doing *Maat* laid *the foundation of things*, establishing, maintaining and, if necessary, reestablishing *Maat* became the mission of life, and to increase good in the world became the purpose of life. Author George G. M. James writes: "In the Egyptian Mysteries, however, the concept of the Supreme Good is expressed as the purpose of virtue (*i.e.*, the purpose of *Maat*)." George G. M. James, *Stolen Legacy*, (Trenton: African World Press, 1992), 91. Mine

Notes

in parentheses.

38. In an account of creation found in Amenist Scriptures, Amen in his name of Ptah conceives all of creation in his heart, then creates "every good thing" by the command of his tongue; *see* James B. Pritchard, *Ancient Near Eastern Texts Relating to the Old Testament*, (London: Princeton University Press, 1950), 5. Emphasis mine. *See* also utterance 1130 of the *Ancient Egyptian Coffin Texts* wherein Amen in his name of Ra describes four acts of creation as "good deeds." *Ibid.*, 7. Emphasis mine. The Importance of doing *Maat* daily is expressed by granary chief Baki who says, "Listen to this as I say it, all you people who exist: Be content with Maat daily, it is food that does not sate, the lord god of Abydos lives on it daily!" Miriam Lichtheim, *Maat in Egyptian Autobiographies and Related Studies*, (Freiburg, Schweiz: Universitatsverlag; Gottingen: Vandenhoeck und Ruprecht, 1992), 131.

39. Jeremy Naydler, *Temple of the Cosmos: The Ancient Egyptian Experience of the Sacred*, (Rochester: Inner Traditions International, 1996), 96. Mine in parentheses. Italics mine.

40. Maulana Karenga, *Maat: The Moral Ideal in Ancient Egypt*, (Los Angeles: University of Sankore Press, 2006), 182-183.

41. Noah J. Goldstein, Steave J. Martin and Robert B. Cialdini, *Yes: 50 Scientifically Proven Ways to Be Persuasive*, (New York: Simon and Schuster, 2008), 124.

42. James Henry Breasted, *Ancient Records of Egypt*, Volume IV, (Chicago: The University of Chicago Press, 1906), 205.

43. E. A. Wallis Budge, *The Dwellers on the Nile: The Life, History, Religion and Literature of the Ancient Egyptians*, (New York: Dover Publications Inc., 1977), 34. Tony Iton, *Tony Iton on How to Fix California's Health Care Gap* [Audio File], NPR: KQED Forum With Michael Krasny, Aired July 5, 2018. Maulana Karenga, *The African American Holiday of Kwanzaa: A Celebration of Family, Community & Culture*, (Los Angeles: University of Sankore Press, 1988), 23. The realization that like Amen in his name of Ptah, you are both the *Placemaker* and the place.

THE PHARAOHS' 5 LAWS OF SUCCESS

CHAPTER 5

1.	Charles Rollin, *The Ancient History of the Egyptians, Carthaginians, Assyrians, Babylonians, Medes and Persians, Grecians, and Macedonians*, In Six Volumes, Volume 1, Eighteenth Edition, (London: William Tegg and Co., 1851), 26-27.

2.	Miriam Lichtheim, *Maat in Egyptian Autobiographies and Related Studies*, (Freiburg, Schweiz: Universitatsverlag; Gottingen: Vandenhoeck und Ruprecht, 1992), 131. Italics mine.

3.	Cheikh Anta Diop, *Civilization or Barbarism: An Authentic Anthropology*, (Brooklyn: Lawrence Hill Books, 1991), 11. The founding fathers and mothers of ancient Egypt "came from Nubia and the "heart of Africa." Cheikh Anta Diop, *The African Origin of Civilization: Myth or Reality*, (Chicago: Lawrence Hill Books, 1974), 150. Anders Breidlid, Avelino Androga Said and Astrid Kristine Breidlid, *A Concise History of South Sudan*, New and Revised Edition, (Kampala: Fountain Publishers, 2014), 17, 20-22. Maulana Karenga, *Introduction to Black Studies*, Second Edition, (Los Angeles, University of Sankore Press, 1993), 80. Bruce Williams, "The Lost Pharaohs of Nubia," in *Journal of African Civilizations* 4, no. 2 (November 1982): 44-47. John Henrik Clarke, "Ancient Civilizations in Africa: The Missing Pages in World History," in *Journal of African Civilizations* 4, no. 2 (November 1982): 113-121. E. A. Wallis Budge, *A History of Ethiopia, Nubia & Abyssinia*, Volume 1, (London: Methuen & Co. LTD., 1928), 5. For the hieroglyphic spelling of Kash see E. A. Wallis Budge, *First Steps in Egyptian: A Book for Beginners*, (London: Kegan Paul, Trench, Trubner & Co., Ltd., 1895), 107. Tarík Karenga, *Kemetan Calendar and Zodiac*, First Edition, (Union City: Amenism, Inc., 2022), 34.

4.	E. A. Wallis Budge, *A History of Ethiopia, Nubia & Abyssinia*, Volume 1, (London: Methuen & Co. LTD., 1928), 2. Anders Breidlid, Avelino Androga Said and Astrid Kristine Breidlid, *A Concise History of South Sudan*, New and Revised Edition, (Kampala: Fountain Publishers, 2014), 21-22. Maulana Karenga, *Introduction to Black Studies*, Second Edition, (Los Angeles, University of Sankore Press, 1993), 79-

Notes

80. Cheikh Anta Diop, "Origin of the Ancient Egyptians," in *Journal of African Civilizations* 4, no. 2 (November 1982): 16-20. Anthony T. Browder, *Nile Valley Contributions to Civilization: Exploding the Myths*, Volume 1, (Washington: The Institute of Karmic Guidance, 1992), 50-51. Mine in parentheses. Italics mine. See also A. H. Sayce, *The Religions of Ancient Egypt, and Babylonia*, (Edinburgh: T & T Clark, 1902), 55. E. A. Wallis Budge, *A Vocabulary in Hieroglyphic to the Theban Recension of the Book of the Dead*, (London: Kegan Paul, Trench, Trubner & Co., LTD., 1898), 232.

5. George G. M. James, *Stolen Legacy*, (Trenton: African World Press, 1992), 36-37.

6. John G. Jackson, "Egypt and Christianity," in *Journal of African Civilizations* 4, no. 2 (November 1982): 65. Maulana Karenga, *Introduction to Black Studies*, Second Edition, (Los Angeles, University of Sankore Press, 1993), 79. Annual rains in the highlands of Abyssinia ("former name for Ethiopia") in turn caused the annual inundation of the Nile River in Egypt (*i.e.*, Kemet). Tarík Karenga, *Kemetan Calendar and Zodiac*, First Edition, (Union City: Amenism, Inc., 2022), 9, 35. See also the entry for "Abyssinia" in Webster's New World Dictionary & Thesaurus, Version 2.0, Build #25, Accent Software International, Macmillan Publishers, 1998.

7. John Henrik Clarke, "Ancient Civilizations in Africa: The Missing Pages in World History," in *Journal of African Civilizations* 4, no. 2 (November 1982): 115.

8. "Diodorus Siculus declares that the Egyptians claimed to have sent out colonies over the whole world in times of the remotest antiquity." John G. Jackson, *Christianity Before Christ*, (Austin: American Atheist Press, 1985), 182-183. George G. M. James, *Stolen Legacy*, (Trenton: African World Press, 1992), 1, 4. Tarík Karenga, *Review of the Kemetan Mystery System*, First Edition, (Union City: Amenism, Inc., in press). Note: The Kemetan Mystery System and the religion of Amenism are interdependent and work in concert with each other. They are seemingly one and the same.

9. See Table 7: Chronological Table, in Tarík Karenga,

Kemetan Calendar and Zodiac, First Edition, (Union City: Amenism, Inc., 2022), 31-38. See also the terms *ethnicity* and *Kemetan*, in Tarík Karenga, *Review of the Kemetan Mystery System*, First Edition, (Union City: Amenism, Inc., in press).

10. Charles Rollin, *The Ancient History of the Egyptians, Carthaginians, Assyrians, Babylonians, Medes and Persians, Grecians, and Macedonians*, In Six Volumes, Volume 1, Eighteenth Edition, (London: William Tegg and Co., 1851), 26-27.

11. James Henry Breasted, *The Dawn of Conscience*, (New York: Charles Scribner's Sons, 1935), 221. [[ ]] Double brackets indicate word or term substitution made by the author. In this case, the substitution of the ancient Kemetan word *isfet* for the word *evil*, as the word "isfet" is found in the original hieroglyphic writings from which the translations were made. Furthermore, *isfet* is the universal chaos principle and by rendering up oneself to its "ten bodily fetters" of falsehood, injustice, discord, imbalance, exploitation, disorder, unrighteousness, folly, greed, and cowardice in one's daily life and in defiance of Divine Law, evil is increased in the world. See the chapter, "Become a Placemaker." See also George G. M. James, *Stolen Legacy*, (Trenton: African World Press, 1992), 91, 104-106. Evil is therefore the offspring of doing *isfet*; however, doing *isfet* is not responsible for the existence of evil. See Maulana Karenga, *Maat: The Moral Ideal in Ancient Egypt*, (Los Angeles: University of Sankore Press, 2006), 203-207, (248). See Raymond O. Faulkner, *The Ancient Egyptian Coffin Texts*, Volume III, Spells 788-1185 & Index, (Warminister: Aris & Phillips LTD., 1978), 167.

12. Maulana Karenga, *Maat: The Moral Ideal in Ancient Egypt*, (Los Angeles: University of Sankore Press, 2006), 37, 247. Coffin Texts 1130 also contains the concept that humans are to live as a world community, sharing and distributing resources so that from them, all humanity may benefit equally.

13. Maulana Karenga, *Maat: The Moral Ideal in Ancient Egypt*, (Los Angeles: University of Sankore Press, 2006), 247. A plagiarized, adapted and reconfigured version of the Doctrine of the Two Paths is in the writings of Greek philosopher Parmenides. George G. M.

Notes

James, *Stolen Legacy*, (Trenton: African World Press, 1992), 60. *See* "The Two Paths," in Tarík Karenga, *Review of the Kemetan Mystery System*, First Edition, (Union City: Amenism, Inc., in press).

    14.   The ancient Kemetan word for *day* transliterated as hru (*i.e.*, Heru) and followed by the hieroglyph for the word *sun* written with a determinative mark conceptually means newborn sun, and theologically refers to the newborn soul. This interpretation is corroborated first by the fact that ancient Egyptian priests taught that the sun was reborn daily. William J. Darby, Paul Ghalioungui and Louis Grivetti, *Food: The Gift of Osiris*, Volume 2, (London: Academic Press, 1976), 620-621. Additional evidence: E. A. Wallis Budge, *An Egyptian Hieroglyphic Dictionary: In Two Volumes*, Volume I, (London: John Murray, 1920), 450a. Gerald Massey, *Ancient Egypt: The Light of the World*, Volume I, (London: T. Fisher Unwin, 1907), 449-450. *See* also D. M. Murdock, Christ in Egypt: The Horus-Jesus Connection, (Ashland: Stellar House Publishing, 2009), 83, 95, 79-116, 377, 388, 417-419. The birth of Heru is associated with the end of the three-day period of the winter solstice, which was called the "Day of the Great Coming Forth." *Ibid.*, 104-106. Osir and Heru were both symbolically represented as a "baby sun." *Ibid.*, 110. The Holy Virgin Mother Iset was quoted as saying, "The fruit which I have begotten is the sun." *Ibid.*, 111. Heru ". . . represented the new Sun which was born daily, and which was the successor of Heru-khuti or of Ra, and he was also the offspring of the dead man-god Osiris and his lawful successor." E. A. Wallis Budge, *The Gods of the Egyptians: Or, Studies in Egyptian Mythology*, Volume I, (London: Methuen & Company, 1904), 486. Author, Margaret Murray also noted the identification of Heru with the newly-born sun. *See* Margaret A. Murray, *Egyptian Religious Poetry*, (London: John Murray, 1949), 37. A title of an important religious book that was placed in the tombs of the departed has been translated: "Coming forth as the (newborn) Sun." *See* C. C. J. Baron Bunsen and Samuel Birch, *Egypt's Place in Universal History*, Volume 5, (London: Longmans, Green, and Co., 1867), 156, 164. Mine in parentheses. Many Egyptologists refer to this book as the *Book of the Dead*, because it had reportedly been found buried with the dead. *See* Maulana Karenga, *The*

Book of Coming Forth by Day: The Ethics of the Declarations of Innocence, (Los Angeles: University of Sankore Press, 1990), 19-20.

15. Maulana Karenga, *Maat: The Moral Ideal in Ancient Egypt*, (Los Angeles: University of Sankore Press, 2006), 138-139. Resurrection and ascension are principal concepts in Amenist theology pertaining to the afterlife. See Maulana Karenga, "Afterlife," in *Encyclopedia of African Religion*, eds. Molefi Kete Asante and Ama Mazama, (Thousand Oaks: Sage Publications, Inc., 2009), 14-15. E. A. Wallis Budge, *Osiris and the Egyptian Resurrection*, Volume II, (New York: G. P. Putnam's Sons, 1911), 123-124.

16. Maulana Karenga, *Maat: The Moral Ideal in Ancient Egypt*, (Los Angeles: University of Sankore Press, 2006), 138-139, 235. E. A. Wallis Budge, *The Book of the Dead: The Papyrus of Ani*, In Two Volumes, Volume II, (London: The Medici Society, Ltd., 1913), 572-573. E. A. Wallis Budge, *The Book of the Dead: The Papyrus of Ani in the British Museum*, (London: Kegan Paul, Trench, Trubner & Co., 1895), 206, lines 3-4. E. A. Wallis Budge, *An Egyptian Hieroglyphic Dictionary: In Two Volumes*, Volume I, (London: John Murray, 1920), 271b. The three parts of the *Declaration of Maat*: 1) the Opening Address; 2) the Declarations of Innocence; 3) the Closing Address.

17. Sidney G. P. Coryn, *The Faith of Ancient Egypt*, (New York: Theosophical Publishing Company, 1913), 54-55. Mine in parentheses. Italics mine. [[ ]] Double brackets indicate word or term substitution made by the author. Here, the spelling of the name "Osir," which refers to the first person of God, is consistent with the teachings of Amenism and has therefore been substituted for the name "Osiris," which is Greek. See the term *Declaration of Maat*, in Tarík Karenga, *Review of the Kemetan Mystery System*, First Edition, (Union City: Amenism, Inc., in press).

18. E. A. Wallis Budge, *The Book of the Dead: The Papyrus of Ani*, In Two Volumes, Volume II, (London: The Medici Society, Ltd., 1913), 572-573. Maulana Karenga, *Maat: The Moral Ideal in Ancient Egypt*, (Los Angeles: University of Sankore Press, 2006), 142-147. According to the teachings of Amenism, Divine Law is also referred to

Notes

as the "laws of *Maat*," which are not to be confused with the virtues of *Maat*. *Ibid.*, 166, 307. Italics mine. In the instruction for the <u>new</u> king Merikara, it is said that on the Day of Judgment: "Wretched is one who is accused as one who was aware." *Ibid.*, 167. Transgressions knowingly but not willingly committed such as those committed in response to great threat or coercion may warrant forgiveness under certain circumstances. A plagiarized, adapted and reconfigured version of the Declarations of Innocence is in the religion of Christianity. *See* The Holy Bible: *Comprising the Old and New Testaments*, The King James Version, (New York: American Bible Society, 1972), [(OT) Exodus 20:1-17], 73. *See* also Anthony T. Browder, *Nile Valley Contributions to Civilization: Exploding the Myths*, Volume 1, (Washington: The Institute of Karmic Guidance, 1992), 91-94.

19.   Maulana Karenga, *Maat: The Moral Ideal in Ancient Egypt*, (Los Angeles: University of Sankore Press, 2006), 290. Mine in parentheses.

20.   *Ibid.*, 302-306.

21.   *See* the term *Divine Law*, in Tarík Karenga, *Review of the Kemetan Mystery System*, First Edition, (Union City: Amenism, Inc., in press).

22.   E. A. Wallis Budge, *The Book of the Dead: The Chapters of Coming Forth by Day, The Egyptian Text in Hieroglyphic Edited From Numerous Papyri*, (London: Kegan Paul, Trench, Trubner & Co., LTD., 1898), 252.

23.   E. A. Wallis Budge, *An Egyptian Hieroglyphic Dictionary: In Two Volumes*, Volume I, (London: John Murray, 1920), 339b, 65a, 89b. E. A. Wallis Budge, *The Book of the Dead: The Chapters of Coming Forth by Day, An English Translation with Introduction, Notes, Etc.*, (London: Kegan Paul, Trench, Trubner & Co., LTD., 1898), 193.

24.   George G. M. James, *Stolen Legacy*, (Trenton: African World Press, 1992), 91, 104-106.

25.   *See* "chaos" under synonyms for "confusion" in Webster's New World Dictionary & Thesaurus, Version 2.0, Build #25, Accent Software International, Macmillan Publishers, 1998.

26. E. A. Wallis Budge, *The Book of the Dead: The Chapters of Coming Forth by Day, The Egyptian Text in Hieroglyphic Edited From Numerous Papyri*, (London: Kegan Paul, Trench, Trubner & Co., LTD., 1898), 252.

27. E. A. Wallis Budge, *An Egyptian Hieroglyphic Dictionary: In Two Volumes*, Volume I, (London: John Murray, 1920), 339b, 114b. E. A. Wallis Budge, *The Book of the Dead: The Chapters of Coming Forth by Day, An English Translation with Introduction, Notes, Etc.*, (London: Kegan Paul, Trench, Trubner & Co., LTD., 1898), 193.

28. E. A. Wallis Budge, *The Book of the Dead: The Chapters of Coming Forth by Day, The Egyptian Text in Hieroglyphic Edited From Numerous Papyri*, (London: Kegan Paul, Trench, Trubner & Co., LTD., 1898), 253. Determinative mark mine.

29. E. A. Wallis Budge, *An Egyptian Hieroglyphic Dictionary: In Two Volumes*, Volume I, (London: John Murray, 1920), 339b, 115b. Maulana Karenga, *Maat: The Moral Ideal in Ancient Egypt*, (Los Angeles: University of Sankore Press, 2006), 145-146. cf. E. A. Wallis Budge, *The Book of the Dead: The Chapters of Coming Forth by Day, An English Translation with Introduction, Notes, Etc.*, (London: Kegan Paul, Trench, Trubner & Co., LTD., 1898), 193.

30. E. A. Wallis Budge, *The Book of the Dead: The Chapters of Coming Forth by Day, The Egyptian Text in Hieroglyphic Edited From Numerous Papyri*, (London: Kegan Paul, Trench, Trubner & Co., LTD., 1898), 253.

31. E. A. Wallis Budge, *An Egyptian Hieroglyphic Dictionary: In Two Volumes*, Volume I, (London: John Murray, 1920), 339b. E. A. Wallis Budge, *An Egyptian Hieroglyphic Dictionary: In Two Volumes*, Volume II, (London: John Murray, 1920), 849a. E. A. Wallis Budge, *The Book of the Dead: The Chapters of Coming Forth by Day, An English Translation with Introduction, Notes, Etc.*, (London: Kegan Paul, Trench, Trubner & Co., LTD., 1898), 193.

32. E. A. Wallis Budge, *The Book of the Dead: The Chapters of Coming Forth by Day, The Egyptian Text in Hieroglyphic Edited From Numerous Papyri*, (London: Kegan Paul, Trench, Trubner & Co., LTD.,

Notes

1898), 253.

33. E. A. Wallis Budge, *An Egyptian Hieroglyphic Dictionary: In Two Volumes*, Volume I, (London: John Murray, 1920), 339b, 426a. E. A. Wallis Budge, *An Egyptian Hieroglyphic Dictionary: In Two Volumes*, Volume II, (London: John Murray, 1920), 668b. E. A. Wallis Budge, *The Book of the Dead: The Chapters of Coming Forth by Day, An English Translation with Introduction, Notes, Etc.*, (London: Kegan Paul, Trench, Trubner & Co., LTD., 1898), 193.

34. E. A. Wallis Budge, *The Book of the Dead: The Chapters of Coming Forth by Day, The Egyptian Text in Hieroglyphic Edited From Numerous Papyri*, (London: Kegan Paul, Trench, Trubner & Co., LTD., 1898), 253.

35. E. A. Wallis Budge, *An Egyptian Hieroglyphic Dictionary: In Two Volumes*, Volume I, (London: John Murray, 1920), 339b, 523b. E. A. Wallis Budge, *An Egyptian Hieroglyphic Dictionary: In Two Volumes*, Volume II, (London: John Murray, 1920), 876a. cf. E. A. Wallis Budge, *The Book of the Dead: The Chapters of Coming Forth by Day, An English Translation with Introduction, Notes, Etc.*, (London: Kegan Paul, Trench, Trubner & Co., LTD., 1898), 193.

36. See "The Instruction of Amenemope" in William Kelly Simpson, *The Literature of Ancient Egypt*, Third Edition, (New Haven: Yale University Press, 2003), 236. Lowercase in parentheses mine.

37. E. A. Wallis Budge, *The Book of the Dead: The Chapters of Coming Forth by Day, The Egyptian Text in Hieroglyphic Edited From Numerous Papyri*, (London: Kegan Paul, Trench, Trubner & Co., LTD., 1898), 253.

38. E. A. Wallis Budge, *An Egyptian Hieroglyphic Dictionary: In Two Volumes*, Volume I, (London: John Murray, 1920), 339b, 65a, 572a. Maulana Karenga, *Maat: The Moral Ideal in Ancient Egypt*, (Los Angeles: University of Sankore Press, 2006), 145-146. cf. E. A. Wallis Budge, *The Book of the Dead: The Chapters of Coming Forth by Day, An English Translation with Introduction, Notes, Etc.*, (London: Kegan Paul, Trench, Trubner & Co., LTD., 1898), 193.

39. E. A. Wallis Budge, *The Book of the Dead: The Chapters

of Coming Forth by Day, The Egyptian Text in Hieroglyphic Edited From Numerous Papyri, (London: Kegan Paul, Trench, Trubner & Co., LTD., 1898), 253.

40. E. A. Wallis Budge, *An Egyptian Hieroglyphic Dictionary: In Two Volumes*, Volume I, (London: John Murray, 1920), 339b, 525b. E. A. Wallis Budge, *An Egyptian Hieroglyphic Dictionary: In Two Volumes*, Volume II, (London: John Murray, 1920), 849a. Maulana Karenga, *Maat: The Moral Ideal in Ancient Egypt*, (Los Angeles: University of Sankore Press, 2006), 145-146. cf. E. A. Wallis Budge, *The Book of the Dead: The Chapters of Coming Forth by Day, An English Translation with Introduction, Notes, Etc.*, (London: Kegan Paul, Trench, Trubner & Co., LTD., 1898), 193.

41. E. A. Wallis Budge, *The Book of the Dead: The Chapters of Coming Forth by Day, The Egyptian Text in Hieroglyphic Edited From Numerous Papyri*, (London: Kegan Paul, Trench, Trubner & Co., LTD., 1898), 253.

42. E. A. Wallis Budge, *An Egyptian Hieroglyphic Dictionary: In Two Volumes*, Volume I, (London: John Murray, 1920), 339b. E. A. Wallis Budge, *An Egyptian Hieroglyphic Dictionary: In Two Volumes*, Volume II, (London: John Murray, 1920), 913b, 812a. Maulana Karenga, *Maat: The Moral Ideal in Ancient Egypt*, (Los Angeles: University of Sankore Press, 2006), 145-146. cf. E. A. Wallis Budge, *The Book of the Dead: The Chapters of Coming Forth by Day, An English Translation with Introduction, Notes, Etc.*, (London: Kegan Paul, Trench, Trubner & Co., LTD., 1898), 194.

43. E. A. Wallis Budge, *The Book of the Dead: The Chapters of Coming Forth by Day, The Egyptian Text in Hieroglyphic Edited From Numerous Papyri*, (London: Kegan Paul, Trench, Trubner & Co., LTD., 1898), 254.

44. E. A. Wallis Budge, *An Egyptian Hieroglyphic Dictionary: In Two Volumes*, Volume I, (London: John Murray, 1920), 339b, 385a, 49a. Maulana Karenga, *Maat: The Moral Ideal in Ancient Egypt*, (Los Angeles: University of Sankore Press, 2006), 145-146. cf. E. A. Wallis Budge, *The Book of the Dead: The Chapters of Coming Forth*

Notes

by Day, An English Translation with Introduction, Notes, Etc., (London: Kegan Paul, Trench, Trubner & Co., LTD., 1898), 194.

45. E. A. Wallis Budge, *The Book of the Dead: The Chapters of Coming Forth by Day, The Egyptian Text in Hieroglyphic Edited From Numerous Papyri*, (London: Kegan Paul, Trench, Trubner & Co., LTD., 1898), 254.

46. E. A. Wallis Budge, *An Egyptian Hieroglyphic Dictionary: In Two Volumes*, Volume I, (London: John Murray, 1920), 339b. E. A. Wallis Budge, *An Egyptian Hieroglyphic Dictionary: In Two Volumes*, Volume II, (London: John Murray, 1920), 794b. James B. Pritchard, *Ancient Near Eastern Texts Relating to the Old Testament*, (London: Princeton University Press, 1950), 35, (B11). cf. Maulana Karenga, *Maat: The Moral Ideal in Ancient Egypt*, (Los Angeles: University of Sankore Press, 2006), 145-146.

47. *See* "contention" under synonyms for "conflict" in Webster's New World Dictionary & Thesaurus, Version 2.0, Build #25, Accent Software International, Macmillan Publishers, 1998.

48. E. A. Wallis Budge, *The Book of the Dead: The Chapters of Coming Forth by Day, The Egyptian Text in Hieroglyphic Edited From Numerous Papyri*, (London: Kegan Paul, Trench, Trubner & Co., LTD., 1898), 254.

49. E. A. Wallis Budge, *An Egyptian Hieroglyphic Dictionary: In Two Volumes*, Volume I, (London: John Murray, 1920), 339b. E. A. Wallis Budge, *An Egyptian Hieroglyphic Dictionary: In Two Volumes*, Volume II, (London: John Murray, 1920), 841a. Maulana Karenga, *Maat: The Moral Ideal in Ancient Egypt*, (Los Angeles: University of Sankore Press, 2006), 145-146, 290. According to the teachings of Amenism, Divine Law is also referred to as the "laws of *Maat*," which are not to be confused with the virtues of *Maat*. *Ibid.*, 166, 307. Italics mine. To transgress Divine Law is a sin *i.e.*, moral offense.

50. E. A. Wallis Budge, *The Book of the Dead: The Chapters of Coming Forth by Day, The Egyptian Text in Hieroglyphic Edited From Numerous Papyri*, (London: Kegan Paul, Trench, Trubner & Co., LTD., 1898), 254.

51.	E. A. Wallis Budge, *An Egyptian Hieroglyphic Dictionary: In Two Volumes*, Volume I, (London: John Murray, 1920), 339b, 401b. E. A. Wallis Budge, *An Egyptian Hieroglyphic Dictionary: In Two Volumes*, Volume II, (London: John Murray, 1920), 668b, 784a. Maulana Karenga, *Maat: The Moral Ideal in Ancient Egypt*, (Los Angeles: University of Sankore Press, 2006), 145-146. cf. E. A. Wallis Budge, *The Book of the Dead: The Chapters of Coming Forth by Day, An English Translation with Introduction, Notes, Etc.*, (London: Kegan Paul, Trench, Trubner & Co., LTD., 1898), 194.

52.	E. A. Wallis Budge, *The Book of the Dead: The Chapters of Coming Forth by Day, The Egyptian Text in Hieroglyphic Edited From Numerous Papyri*, (London: Kegan Paul, Trench, Trubner & Co., LTD., 1898), 254.

53.	E. A. Wallis Budge, *An Egyptian Hieroglyphic Dictionary: In Two Volumes*, Volume I, (London: John Murray, 1920), 339b, 65a, 488b. E. A. Wallis Budge, *The Book of the Dead: The Chapters of Coming Forth by Day, An English Translation with Introduction, Notes, Etc.*, (London: Kegan Paul, Trench, Trubner & Co., LTD., 1898), 194. [ ] Brackets indicate interpolation to clarify the meaning.

54.	E. A. Wallis Budge, *The Book of the Dead: The Chapters of Coming Forth by Day, The Egyptian Text in Hieroglyphic Edited From Numerous Papyri*, (London: Kegan Paul, Trench, Trubner & Co., LTD., 1898), 254.

55.	E. A. Wallis Budge, *An Egyptian Hieroglyphic Dictionary: In Two Volumes*, Volume I, (London: John Murray, 1920), 339b, 114b, 490a. Maulana Karenga, *Maat: The Moral Ideal in Ancient Egypt*, (Los Angeles: University of Sankore Press, 2006), 145-146.

56.	E. A. Wallis Budge, *The Book of the Dead: The Chapters of Coming Forth by Day, The Egyptian Text in Hieroglyphic Edited From Numerous Papyri*, (London: Kegan Paul, Trench, Trubner & Co., LTD., 1898), 254.

57.	E. A. Wallis Budge, *An Egyptian Hieroglyphic Dictionary: In Two Volumes*, Volume I, (London: John Murray, 1920), 339b. E. A. Wallis Budge, *An Egyptian Hieroglyphic Dictionary: In Two*

Notes

Volumes, Volume II, (London: John Murray, 1920), 672b. Maulana Karenga, *Maat: The Moral Ideal in Ancient Egypt*, (Los Angeles: University of Sankore Press, 2006), 145-146. cf. E. A. Wallis Budge, *The Book of the Dead: The Chapters of Coming Forth by Day, An English Translation with Introduction, Notes, Etc.*, (London: Kegan Paul, Trench, Trubner & Co., LTD., 1898), 194.

58. E. A. Wallis Budge, *The Book of the Dead: The Chapters of Coming Forth by Day, The Egyptian Text in Hieroglyphic Edited From Numerous Papyri*, (London: Kegan Paul, Trench, Trubner & Co., LTD., 1898), 255.

59. E. A. Wallis Budge, *An Egyptian Hieroglyphic Dictionary: In Two Volumes*, Volume I, (London: John Murray, 1920), 339b, 416a. E. A. Wallis Budge, *An Egyptian Hieroglyphic Dictionary: In Two Volumes*, Volume II, (London: John Murray, 1920), 739b. Raymond O. Faulkner, *A Concise Dictionary of Middle Egyptian*, (Oxford: Griffith Institute, 1962), 266. cf. Maulana Karenga, *Maat: The Moral Ideal in Ancient Egypt*, (Los Angeles: University of Sankore Press, 2006), 145-146.

60. E. A. Wallis Budge, *The Book of the Dead: The Chapters of Coming Forth by Day, The Egyptian Text in Hieroglyphic Edited From Numerous Papyri*, (London: Kegan Paul, Trench, Trubner & Co., LTD., 1898), 255.

61. E. A. Wallis Budge, *An Egyptian Hieroglyphic Dictionary: In Two Volumes*, Volume I, (London: John Murray, 1920), 339b, 340a, 492b, 525a. E. A. Wallis Budge, *An Egyptian Hieroglyphic Dictionary: In Two Volumes*, Volume II, (London: John Murray, 1920), 689b. Maulana Karenga, *Maat: The Moral Ideal in Ancient Egypt*, (Los Angeles: University of Sankore Press, 2006), 145-146. Raymond O. Faulkner, *A Concise Dictionary of Middle Egyptian*, (Oxford: Griffith Institute, 1962), 240.

62. See "dispute" under synonyms for "discuss" in Webster's New World Dictionary & Thesaurus, Version 2.0, Build #25, Accent Software International, Macmillan Publishers, 1998.

63. E. A. Wallis Budge, *The Book of the Dead: The Chapters of Coming Forth by Day, The Egyptian Text in Hieroglyphic Edited From

Numerous Papyri, (London: Kegan Paul, Trench, Trubner & Co., LTD., 1898), 255.

    64.   E. A. Wallis Budge, *An Egyptian Hieroglyphic Dictionary: In Two Volumes*, Volume I, (London: John Murray, 1920), 339b, 396b, 481a. E. A. Wallis Budge, *An Egyptian Hieroglyphic Dictionary: In Two Volumes*, Volume II, (London: John Murray, 1920), 848a. E. A. Wallis Budge, *The Book of the Dead: The Chapters of Coming Forth by Day, An English Translation with Introduction, Notes, Etc.*, (London: Kegan Paul, Trench, Trubner & Co., LTD., 1898), 194. Maulana Karenga, *Maat: The Moral Ideal in Ancient Egypt*, (Los Angeles: University of Sankore Press, 2006), 145-146. [ ] Brackets indicate interpolation to clarify the meaning.

    65.   E. A. Wallis Budge, *The Book of the Dead: The Chapters of Coming Forth by Day, The Egyptian Text in Hieroglyphic Edited From Numerous Papyri*, (London: Kegan Paul, Trench, Trubner & Co., LTD., 1898), 255.

    66.   E. A. Wallis Budge, *An Egyptian Hieroglyphic Dictionary: In Two Volumes*, Volume I, (London: John Murray, 1920), 339b. E. A. Wallis Budge, *An Egyptian Hieroglyphic Dictionary: In Two Volumes*, Volume II, (London: John Murray, 1920), 864b. Maulana Karenga, *Maat: The Moral Ideal in Ancient Egypt*, (Los Angeles: University of Sankore Press, 2006), 145-146. cf. E. A. Wallis Budge, *The Book of the Dead: The Chapters of Coming Forth by Day, An English Translation with Introduction, Notes, Etc.*, (London: Kegan Paul, Trench, Trubner & Co., LTD., 1898), 194.

    67.   E. A. Wallis Budge, *The Book of the Dead: The Chapters of Coming Forth by Day, The Egyptian Text in Hieroglyphic Edited From Numerous Papyri*, (London: Kegan Paul, Trench, Trubner & Co., LTD., 1898), 255.

    68.   E. A. Wallis Budge, *An Egyptian Hieroglyphic Dictionary: In Two Volumes*, Volume I, (London: John Murray, 1920), 339b, 65a, 499a. Maulana Karenga, *Maat: The Moral Ideal in Ancient Egypt*, (Los Angeles: University of Sankore Press, 2006), 145-146. cf. E. A. Wallis Budge, *The Book of the Dead: The Chapters of Coming Forth*

Notes

by Day, An English Translation with Introduction, Notes, Etc., (London: Kegan Paul, Trench, Trubner & Co., LTD., 1898), 194. [ ] Brackets indicate interpolation to clarify the meaning.

69. E. A. Wallis Budge, *The Book of the Dead: The Chapters of Coming Forth by Day, The Egyptian Text in Hieroglyphic Edited From Numerous Papyri*, (London: Kegan Paul, Trench, Trubner & Co., LTD., 1898), 255.

70. E. A. Wallis Budge, *An Egyptian Hieroglyphic Dictionary: In Two Volumes*, Volume I, (London: John Murray, 1920), 339b. E. A. Wallis Budge, *An Egyptian Hieroglyphic Dictionary: In Two Volumes*, Volume II, (London: John Murray, 1920), 841a. cf. E. A. Wallis Budge, *The Book of the Dead: The Chapters of Coming Forth by Day, An English Translation with Introduction, Notes, Etc.*, (London: Kegan Paul, Trench, Trubner & Co., LTD., 1898), 195.

71. E. A. Wallis Budge, *The Book of the Dead: The Chapters of Coming Forth by Day, The Egyptian Text in Hieroglyphic Edited From Numerous Papyri*, (London: Kegan Paul, Trench, Trubner & Co., LTD., 1898), 256.

72. E. A. Wallis Budge, *An Egyptian Hieroglyphic Dictionary: In Two Volumes*, Volume I, (London: John Murray, 1920), 339b. E. A. Wallis Budge, *An Egyptian Hieroglyphic Dictionary: In Two Volumes*, Volume II, (London: John Murray, 1920), 817b. Maulana Karenga, *Maat: The Moral Ideal in Ancient Egypt*, (Los Angeles: University of Sankore Press, 2006), 145-146. cf. E. A. Wallis Budge, *The Book of the Dead: The Chapters of Coming Forth by Day, An English Translation with Introduction, Notes, Etc.*, (London: Kegan Paul, Trench, Trubner & Co., LTD., 1898), 195.

73. E. A. Wallis Budge, *The Book of the Dead: The Chapters of Coming Forth by Day, The Egyptian Text in Hieroglyphic Edited From Numerous Papyri*, (London: Kegan Paul, Trench, Trubner & Co., LTD., 1898), 256.

74. E. A. Wallis Budge, *An Egyptian Hieroglyphic Dictionary: In Two Volumes*, Volume I, (London: John Murray, 1920), 339b, 492b, 335a, 408a, 270b. E. A. Wallis Budge, *An Egyptian Hieroglyphic*

Dictionary: In Two Volumes, Volume II, (London: John Murray, 1920), 615a. Maulana Karenga, *Maat: The Moral Ideal in Ancient Egypt*, (Los Angeles: University of Sankore Press, 2006), 145-146. cf. E. A. Wallis Budge, *The Book of the Dead: The Chapters of Coming Forth by Day, An English Translation with Introduction, Notes, Etc.*, (London: Kegan Paul, Trench, Trubner & Co., LTD., 1898), 195.

75. E. A. Wallis Budge, *The Book of the Dead: The Chapters of Coming Forth by Day, The Egyptian Text in Hieroglyphic Edited From Numerous Papyri*, (London: Kegan Paul, Trench, Trubner & Co., LTD., 1898), 256.

76. E. A. Wallis Budge, *An Egyptian Hieroglyphic Dictionary: In Two Volumes*, Volume I, (London: John Murray, 1920), 339b, 577a. E. A. Wallis Budge, *The Book of the Dead: The Chapters of Coming Forth by Day, An English Translation with Introduction, Notes, Etc.*, (London: Kegan Paul, Trench, Trubner & Co., LTD., 1898), 195.

77. E. A. Wallis Budge, *The Book of the Dead: The Chapters of Coming Forth by Day, The Egyptian Text in Hieroglyphic Edited From Numerous Papyri*, (London: Kegan Paul, Trench, Trubner & Co., LTD., 1898), 256.

78. E. A. Wallis Budge, *An Egyptian Hieroglyphic Dictionary: In Two Volumes*, Volume I, (London: John Murray, 1920), 339b. Raymond O. Faulkner, *A Concise Dictionary of Middle Egyptian*, (Oxford: Griffith Institute, 1962), 306. [ ] Brackets indicate interpolation to clarify the meaning.

79. E. A. Wallis Budge, *The Book of the Dead: The Chapters of Coming Forth by Day, The Egyptian Text in Hieroglyphic Edited From Numerous Papyri*, (London: Kegan Paul, Trench, Trubner & Co., LTD., 1898), 256.

80. E. A. Wallis Budge, *An Egyptian Hieroglyphic Dictionary: In Two Volumes*, Volume I, (London: John Murray, 1920), 339b, 355b, 396b. cf. E. A. Wallis Budge, *The Book of the Dead: The Chapters of Coming Forth by Day, An English Translation with Introduction, Notes, Etc.*, (London: Kegan Paul, Trench, Trubner & Co., LTD., 1898), 195. cf. James B. Pritchard, *Ancient Near Eastern Texts Relating to the*

Notes

Old Testament, (London: Princeton University Press, 1950), 35, (B27). cf. Maulana Karenga, *Maat: The Moral Ideal in Ancient Egypt*, (Los Angeles: University of Sankore Press, 2006), 145-146. *See* also "sodomy" in Webster's New World Dictionary & Thesaurus, Version 2.0, Build #25, Accent Software International, Macmillan Publishers, 1998.

81. E. A. Wallis Budge, *The Book of the Dead: The Chapters of Coming Forth by Day, The Egyptian Text in Hieroglyphic Edited From Numerous Papyri*, (London: Kegan Paul, Trench, Trubner & Co., LTD., 1898), 256.

82. E. A. Wallis Budge, *An Egyptian Hieroglyphic Dictionary: In Two Volumes*, Volume I, (London: John Murray, 1920), 339b, 37b. E. A. Wallis Budge, *An Egyptian Hieroglyphic Dictionary: In Two Volumes*, Volume II, (London: John Murray, 1920), 645a. E. A. Wallis Budge, *The Book of the Dead: The Chapters of Coming Forth by Day, An English Translation with Introduction, Notes, Etc.*, (London: Kegan Paul, Trench, Trubner & Co., LTD., 1898), 195.

83. E. A. Wallis Budge, *The Book of the Dead: The Chapters of Coming Forth by Day, The Egyptian Text in Hieroglyphic Edited From Numerous Papyri*, (London: Kegan Paul, Trench, Trubner & Co., LTD., 1898), 257.

84. E. A. Wallis Budge, *An Egyptian Hieroglyphic Dictionary: In Two Volumes*, Volume I, (London: John Murray, 1920), 339b. E. A. Wallis Budge, *An Egyptian Hieroglyphic Dictionary: In Two Volumes*, Volume II, (London: John Murray, 1920), 748b. Raymond O. Faulkner, *A Concise Dictionary of Middle Egyptian*, (Oxford: Griffith Institute, 1962), 268. [ ] Brackets indicate interpolation to clarify the meaning.

85. E. A. Wallis Budge, *The Book of the Dead: The Chapters of Coming Forth by Day, The Egyptian Text in Hieroglyphic Edited From Numerous Papyri*, (London: Kegan Paul, Trench, Trubner & Co., LTD., 1898), 257.

86. E. A. Wallis Budge, *An Egyptian Hieroglyphic Dictionary: In Two Volumes*, Volume I, (London: John Murray, 1920), 339b, 240a, 105a. Raymond O. Faulkner, *A Concise Dictionary of Middle*

Egyptian, (Oxford: Griffith Institute, 1962), 91. [ ] Brackets indicate interpolation to clarify the meaning.

      87.   E. A. Wallis Budge, *The Book of the Dead: The Chapters of Coming Forth by Day, The Egyptian Text in Hieroglyphic Edited From Numerous Papyri*, (London: Kegan Paul, Trench, Trubner & Co., LTD., 1898), 257.

      88.   E. A. Wallis Budge, *An Egyptian Hieroglyphic Dictionary: In Two Volumes*, Volume I, (London: John Murray, 1920), 339b, 9b, 37b.

      89.   E. A. Wallis Budge, *The Book of the Dead: The Chapters of Coming Forth by Day, The Egyptian Text in Hieroglyphic Edited From Numerous Papyri*, (London: Kegan Paul, Trench, Trubner & Co., LTD., 1898), 257.

      90.   E. A. Wallis Budge, *An Egyptian Hieroglyphic Dictionary: In Two Volumes*, Volume I, (London: John Murray, 1920), 339b, 34b, 27b, 401a. E. A. Wallis Budge, *An Egyptian Hieroglyphic Dictionary: In Two Volumes*, Volume II, (London: John Murray, 1920), 841a. James B. Pritchard, *Ancient Near Eastern Texts Relating to the Old Testament*, (London: Princeton University Press, 1950), 35, (B32). cf. Maulana Karenga, *Maat: The Moral Ideal in Ancient Egypt*, (Los Angeles: University of Sankore Press, 2006), 146-147. Richard King, *Melanin: A Key to Freedom*, (Hampton: U. B. & U. S. Communications Systems, 1994), 71, 78. [ ] Brackets indicate interpolation to clarify the meaning.

      91.   *Ibid.*, 78. *See* also Richard King, "Neuromelanin: A Black Gate Threshold; The I33 Tissue of Heru," in *Why Darkness Matters: The Power of Melanin in the Brain*, ed. Edward Bruce Bynum, (Chicago: African American Images, 2005), 134-137. God's divine, manifest black pigment (melanin) referred to as the *Flesh of Ra* is also present in human "organs, nervous systems and glands." *See* Carol Barnes, *Melanin: The Chemical Key to Black Greatness: The Harmful Effects of Toxic Drugs on Melanin Centers Within the Black Community*, Volume 1, (Houston: C. B. Publishers, 1988), 3-5. Conclusion: The *Flesh of Ra i.e.*, the flesh of the soul, is the brown to black pigment in the skin, which is activated by the sun: melanin.

Notes

92.   Maulana Karenga, *Maat: The Moral Ideal in Ancient Egypt*, (Los Angeles: University of Sankore Press, 2006), 226, 318.

93.   E. A. Wallis Budge, *The Book of the Dead: The Chapters of Coming Forth by Day, The Egyptian Text in Hieroglyphic Edited From Numerous Papyri*, (London: Kegan Paul, Trench, Trubner & Co., LTD., 1898), 257.

94.   E. A. Wallis Budge, *An Egyptian Hieroglyphic Dictionary: In Two Volumes*, Volume I, (London: John Murray, 1920), 339b, 137b, 560a, 492b, 335a. Maulana Karenga, *Maat: The Moral Ideal in Ancient Egypt*, (Los Angeles: University of Sankore Press, 2006), 146-147. cf. E. A. Wallis Budge, *The Book of the Dead: The Chapters of Coming Forth by Day, An English Translation with Introduction, Notes, Etc.*, (London: Kegan Paul, Trench, Trubner & Co., LTD., 1898), 195.

95.   E. A. Wallis Budge, *The Book of the Dead: The Chapters of Coming Forth by Day, The Egyptian Text in Hieroglyphic Edited From Numerous Papyri*, (London: Kegan Paul, Trench, Trubner & Co., LTD., 1898), 257.

96.   E. A. Wallis Budge, *An Egyptian Hieroglyphic Dictionary: In Two Volumes*, Volume I, (London: John Murray, 1920), 339b, 31b, 65a, 211a. James B. Pritchard, *Ancient Near Eastern Texts Relating to the Old Testament*, (London: Princeton University Press, 1950), 35, (B34). Sin is to be construed as moral offense as well as the transgression of Divine Law, because in ancient Kemet there was no concept of sin nor an ontological stain or concept of original sin; but rather, there was the concept of moral offense that had the real possibility of leading to moral failure, both of which stemmed from correctable flaws, usually related to ignorance. *See* Maulana Karenga, *Maat: The Moral Ideal in Ancient Egypt*, (Los Angeles: University of Sankore Press, 2006), 204, 233-235, 248.

97.   E. A. Wallis Budge, *The Book of the Dead: The Chapters of Coming Forth by Day, The Egyptian Text in Hieroglyphic Edited From Numerous Papyri*, (London: Kegan Paul, Trench, Trubner & Co., LTD., 1898), 258.

98.   E. A. Wallis Budge, *An Egyptian Hieroglyphic*

Dictionary: In Two Volumes, Volume I, (London: John Murray, 1920), 339b, 65a, 492b, 391a. E. A. Wallis Budge, *An Egyptian Hieroglyphic Dictionary: In Two Volumes*, Volume II, (London: John Murray, 1920), 748b. E. A. Wallis Budge, *The Book of the Dead: The Chapters of Coming Forth by Day, An English Translation with Introduction, Notes, Etc.*, (London: Kegan Paul, Trench, Trubner & Co., LTD., 1898), 195. [ ] Brackets indicate interpolation to clarify the meaning.

99. E. A. Wallis Budge, *The Book of the Dead: The Chapters of Coming Forth by Day, The Egyptian Text in Hieroglyphic Edited From Numerous Papyri*, (London: Kegan Paul, Trench, Trubner & Co., LTD., 1898), 258.

100. E. A. Wallis Budge, *An Egyptian Hieroglyphic Dictionary: In Two Volumes*, Volume I, (London: John Murray, 1920), 339b, 429a, 492b, 400a. Raymond O. Faulkner, *A Concise Dictionary of Middle Egyptian*, (Oxford: Griffith Institute, 1962), 151. Maulana Karenga, *Maat: The Moral Ideal in Ancient Egypt*, (Los Angeles: University of Sankore Press, 2006), 146-147. E. A. Wallis Budge, *The Book of the Dead: The Chapters of Coming Forth by Day, An English Translation with Introduction, Notes, Etc.*, (London: Kegan Paul, Trench, Trubner & Co., LTD., 1898), 196.

101. E. A. Wallis Budge, *The Book of the Dead: The Chapters of Coming Forth by Day, The Egyptian Text in Hieroglyphic Edited From Numerous Papyri*, (London: Kegan Paul, Trench, Trubner & Co., LTD., 1898), 258.

102. E. A. Wallis Budge, *An Egyptian Hieroglyphic Dictionary: In Two Volumes*, Volume I, (London: John Murray, 1920), 339b. E. A. Wallis Budge, *An Egyptian Hieroglyphic Dictionary: In Two Volumes*, Volume II, (London: John Murray, 1920), 760a. E. A. Wallis Budge, *The Book of the Dead: The Chapters of Coming Forth by Day, An English Translation with Introduction, Notes, Etc.*, (London: Kegan Paul, Trench, Trubner & Co., LTD., 1898), 196.

103. E. A. Wallis Budge, *The Book of the Dead: The Chapters of Coming Forth by Day, The Egyptian Text in Hieroglyphic Edited From Numerous Papyri*, (London: Kegan Paul, Trench, Trubner & Co., LTD.,

1898), 258.

104. E. A. Wallis Budge, *An Egyptian Hieroglyphic Dictionary: In Two Volumes*, Volume I, (London: John Murray, 1920), 339b, 401a. E. A. Wallis Budge, *An Egyptian Hieroglyphic Dictionary: In Two Volumes*, Volume II, (London: John Murray, 1920), 748b. E. A. Wallis Budge, *The Book of the Dead: The Chapters of Coming Forth by Day, An English Translation with Introduction, Notes, Etc.*, (London: Kegan Paul, Trench, Trubner & Co., LTD., 1898), 196.

105. E. A. Wallis Budge, *The Book of the Dead: The Chapters of Coming Forth by Day, The Egyptian Text in Hieroglyphic Edited From Numerous Papyri*, (London: Kegan Paul, Trench, Trubner & Co., LTD., 1898), 258.

106. E. A. Wallis Budge, *An Egyptian Hieroglyphic Dictionary: In Two Volumes*, Volume I, (London: John Murray, 1920), 339b, 65a. E. A. Wallis Budge, *An Egyptian Hieroglyphic Dictionary: In Two Volumes*, Volume II, (London: John Murray, 1920), 738b. James B. Pritchard, *Ancient Near Eastern Texts Relating to the Old Testament*, (London: Princeton University Press, 1950), 35, (B39). cf. E. A. Wallis Budge, *The Book of the Dead: The Chapters of Coming Forth by Day, An English Translation with Introduction, Notes, Etc.*, (London: Kegan Paul, Trench, Trubner & Co., LTD., 1898), 196.

107. E. A. Wallis Budge, *The Book of the Dead: The Chapters of Coming Forth by Day, The Egyptian Text in Hieroglyphic Edited From Numerous Papyri*, (London: Kegan Paul, Trench, Trubner & Co., LTD., 1898), 258.

108. E. A. Wallis Budge, *An Egyptian Hieroglyphic Dictionary: In Two Volumes*, Volume I, (London: John Murray, 1920), 339b, 65a, 415b. E. A. Wallis Budge, *An Egyptian Hieroglyphic Dictionary: In Two Volumes*, Volume II, (London: John Murray, 1920), 630a. E. A. Wallis Budge, *The Book of the Dead: The Chapters of Coming Forth by Day, An English Translation with Introduction, Notes, Etc.*, (London: Kegan Paul, Trench, Trubner & Co., LTD., 1898), 196. Maulana Karenga, *Maat: The Moral Ideal in Ancient Egypt*, (Los Angeles: University of Sankore Press, 2006), 146-147. *See* "distinction" in Webster's New

World Dictionary & Thesaurus, Version 2.0, Build #25, Accent Software International, Macmillan Publishers, 1998.

109. E. A. Wallis Budge, *The Book of the Dead: The Chapters of Coming Forth by Day, The Egyptian Text in Hieroglyphic Edited From Numerous Papyri*, (London: Kegan Paul, Trench, Trubner & Co., LTD., 1898), 259.

110. E. A. Wallis Budge, *An Egyptian Hieroglyphic Dictionary: In Two Volumes*, Volume I, (London: John Murray, 1920), 339b, 170b, 580b, 340a, 264a, 525a. James B. Pritchard, *Ancient Near Eastern Texts Relating to the Old Testament*, (London: Princeton University Press, 1950), 35, (B41). [[ ]] Double brackets indicate word or term substitution made by the author. Here, the word "with" has been substituted for the word "in." See also James P. Allen, *Middle Egyptian: An Introduction to the Language and Culture of Hieroglyphs*, (New York: Cambridge University Press, 2001), 126. See "greedy" in Webster's New World Dictionary & Thesaurus, Version 2.0, Build #25, Accent Software International, Macmillan Publishers, 1998.

111. E. A. Wallis Budge, *The Book of the Dead: The Chapters of Coming Forth by Day, The Egyptian Text in Hieroglyphic Edited From Numerous Papyri*, (London: Kegan Paul, Trench, Trubner & Co., LTD., 1898), 259.

112. E. A. Wallis Budge, *An Egyptian Hieroglyphic Dictionary: In Two Volumes*, Volume I, (London: John Murray, 1920), 339b, 401a, 264a, 350b. E. A. Wallis Budge, *An Egyptian Hieroglyphic Dictionary: In Two Volumes*, Volume II, (London: John Murray, 1920), 634b. E. A. Wallis Budge, *The Book of the Dead: The Chapters of Coming Forth by Day, An English Translation with Introduction, Notes, Etc.*, (London: Kegan Paul, Trench, Trubner & Co., LTD., 1898), 196. [ ] Brackets indicate interpolation to clarify the meaning.

113. Margaret A. Murray, *Egyptian Religious Poetry*, (London: John Murray, 1949), 34, 41. Amen in his name of Ra said, "I have made their hearts not forget the West . . . that they may present offerings to the district gods!" James Henry Breasted, *The Dawn of Conscience*, (New York: Charles Scribner's Sons, 1935), 221.

Notes

114. Since *Maat* is joined to our hearts at birth, Divine Law points out that which is contrary to doing *Maat*, and points to our innate predisposition to increase good in the world. See the term *Divine Law*, in Tarík Karenga, *Review of the Kemetan Mystery System*, First Edition, (Union City: Amenism, Inc., in press).

115. See Maulana Karenga, *Maat: The Moral Ideal in Ancient Egypt*, (Los Angeles: University of Sankore Press, 2006), 290. See also *ibid.*, 288-294.

116. *Ibid.*, 155, 306. Maulana Karenga, "Afterlife," in *Encyclopedia of African Religion*, eds. Molefi Kete Asante and Ama Mazama, (Thousand Oaks: Sage Publications, Inc., 2009), 15. E. A. Wallis Budge, *An Egyptian Hieroglyphic Dictionary: In Two Volumes*, Volume I, (London: John Murray, 1920), 53b.

117. E. A. Wallis Budge, *Osiris and the Egyptian Resurrection*, Volume I, (New York: G. P. Putnam's Sons, 1911), 318, 327. Maulana Karenga, "Afterlife," in *Encyclopedia of African Religion*, eds. Molefi Kete Asante and Ama Mazama, (Thousand Oaks: Sage Publications, Inc., 2009), 15-16. Maulana Karenga, *Maat: The Moral Ideal in Ancient Egypt*, (Los Angeles: University of Sankore Press, 2006), 140. Jaroslav Cerny, *Ancient Egyptian Religion*, (New York: Hutchinson's University Library, 1952), 89. E. A. Wallis Budge, *An Egyptian Hieroglyphic Dictionary: In Two Volumes*, Volume I, (London: John Murray, 1920), 271b; *see* the term *justification*, in Tarík Karenga, *Review of the Kemetan Mystery System*, First Edition, (Union City: Amenism, Inc., in press).

118. Maulana Karenga, *Maat: The Moral Ideal in Ancient Egypt*, (Los Angeles: University of Sankore Press, 2006), 140. D. M. Murdock, Christ in Egypt: The Horus-Jesus Connection, (Ashland: Stellar House Publishing, 2009), 35-39. *See* also the chapter, "Seek Wise Counsel."

119. Maulana Karenga, *Maat: The Moral Ideal in Ancient Egypt*, (Los Angeles: University of Sankore Press, 2006), 140-141, 373. Francis Llewellyn Griffith, *Beni Hasan*, Part III, (London: Kegan Paul, Trench, Trubner & Co., 1896), 6. Henri Frankfort, H. A. Frankfort, John A. Wilson, Thorkild Jacobsen and William A. Irwin, *The Intellectual*

THE PHARAOHS' 5 LAWS OF SUCCESS

Adventure of Ancient Man: An Essay on Speculative Thought in the Ancient Near East, (Chicago: University of Chicago Press, 1977), 48, 98, 107. Henri Frankfort, *Kingship and the Gods*, (Chicago: The University of Chicago Press, 1978), 64-65, 90-91. E. A. Wallis Budge, *The Book of the Dead: The Papyrus of Ani*, In Two Volumes, Volume I, (London: The Medici Society, Ltd., 1913), 25, 79. "The Great Collar." *See* Alexandre Piankoff, *The Tomb of Ramesses VI*, (New York: Pantheon Books Inc., 1954), 60. The central point of each Osirian's Religion was his hope of resurrection in a transformed body and of immortality, which could only be realized by him through the (life,) death and resurrection of [[Osir]]." *See* E. A. Wallis Budge, *Osiris and the Egyptian Resurrection*, Volume I, (New York: G. P. Putnam's Sons, 1911), a2. Mine in parentheses. [[ ]] Double brackets indicate word or term substitution made by the author. Here, the spelling of the name "Osir," which refers to the first person of God, is consistent with the teachings of Amenism and has therefore been substituted for the name "Osiris," which is Greek. E. A. Wallis Budge, *An Egyptian Hieroglyphic Dictionary: In Two Volumes*, Volume I, (London: John Murray, 1920), 22b, 23b, 24a, 53b. A plagiarized, adapted and reconfigured version of these Amenist teachings is in the religion of Christianity. *See* The Holy Bible: *Comprising the Old and New Testaments*, The King James Version, (New York: American Bible Society, 1972), [(NT) John 3:15-16], 96; [1 Corinthians 15:35-38], 181; [2 Corinthians 5], 185-186. Note: Egyptologist E. A. Wallis Budge is quoted here as saying: "The exact meaning of the word Khu, or, as it is written in the Pyramid Texts *Aakhu*, is very hard to discover, and authorites have differed greatly in their translations of the word, and in their descriptions of what the Khu is." E. A. Wallis Budge, *Osiris and the Egyptian Resurrection*, Volume II, (New York: G. P. Putnam's Sons, 1911), 132. Nevertheless, Budge has provided readers with his renderings of chapters XCI, XCII and CLXXXIII of the *Book of Coming Forth as the (Newborn) Sun*, the latter chapter of which records the departed as saying, "I have come into the City of God–the region [which existed] in primeval time–with [my] soul, and with [my] double (*i.e*, my Ka), and with [my] *khu* to dwell in this land." *See* E. A. Wallis Budge, *The Book of the Dead: The Chapters of Coming Forth by Day*,

Notes

An English Translation with Introduction, Notes, Etc., (London: Kegan Paul, Trench, Trubner & Co., LTD., 1898), 345. Mine in parentheses. *See* also Budge, *op. cit.*, Volume II, 1911, 132-134. Making use of "... so-called Hermetic books, which endeavoured to translate the theology of Egypt into Greek thought" A. H. Sayce reports that the Khu is enveloped by the Ba and that "(t)he death of the body releases it from its prison-house; it once more soars to heaven and becomes a spirit . . . while the soul is carried to the hall of judgment, there to be awarded punishment or happiness in accordance with its deserts." A. H. Sayce, *The Religions of Ancient Egypt and Babylonia*, (Edinburgh: T. & T. Clark, 1902), 62-63. Lowercase in parentheses mine. The Khu is therefore present during one's biological life, and that Egyptologist James P. Allen stated that "(t)he function of the Pyramid Texts . . . was to enable the deceased to become an Akh," it becomes apparent that the Akhu, or *Aakhu* of the Pyramid Texts is in actuality a Khu that has been transfigured into a glorified spirit. James P. Allen, *The Ancient Egyptian Pyramid Texts*, (Atlanta: Society of Biblical Literature, 2005), 7. Lowercase in parentheses mine. The current hieroglyphic spelling of "Akhu" and the plural form of the word "Khu" *i.e.*, "Khuu" (**KOO**-oo) is in the Reemergent Kingdom. *See* also the terms *Khu* and *Akhu*, in Tarík Karenga, *Review of the Kemetan Mystery System*, First Edition, (Union City: Amenism, Inc., in press). **Heretofore the two terms *Khu* and *Akhu* have been conflated by Egyptologists and scholars alike; however, Amenists in the Reemergent Kingdom differentiate the term Khu from the term Akhu. They teach that when in ancient texts either of the foregoing terms was written without a reed leaf, context is the principal method used to draw out which of the two terms the scribe meant.**

   120. This answers the question: "How can we be perfect?" We are perfect in Osir the Christ (*i.e.*, perfect by being assimilated to Osir the Christ). In the Mysteries, perfection is also made to apply to one's biological life by way of *spiritual union*. *See* the term *spiritual union*, in Tarík Karenga, *Review of the Kemetan Mystery System*, First Edition, (Union City: Amenism, Inc., in press). Charles Loring Brace, *The Unknown God: Or, Inspiration Among Pre-Christian Races*, (New

York: A. C. Armstrong and Son, 1890), 20. Mine in parentheses. C. C. J. Baron Bunsen and Samuel Birch, *Egypt's Place in Universal History*, Volume 5, (London: Longmans, Green, and Co., 1867), 156, 164. Mine in parentheses. Alexandre Piankoff, *The Tomb of Ramesses VI*, (New York: Pantheon Books Inc., 1954), 145. E. A. Wallis Budge, *The Book of the Dead: The Papyrus of Ani*, In Two Volumes, Volume I, (London: The Medici Society, Ltd., 1913), 156. E. A. Wallis Budge, *The Egyptian Heaven and Hell*, Volume II, (London: Kegan Paul, Trench, Trubner & Co., Ltd., 1905), 186. E. A. Wallis Budge, *The Egyptian Heaven and Hell*, Volume III, (London: Kegan Paul, Trench, Trubner & Co., Ltd., 1906), xi, 164-165. Maulana Karenga, *Maat: The Moral Ideal in Ancient Egypt*, (Los Angeles: University of Sankore Press, 2006), 160. Mine in parentheses. Tarík Karenga, *Kemetan Calendar and Zodiac*, First Edition, (Union City: Amenism, Inc., 2022), 28. *See* also Tarík Karenga, *Review of the Kemetan Mystery System*, First Edition, (Union City: Amenism, Inc., in press). A plagiarized, adapted and reconfigured version of this Amenist teaching is in the religion of Christianity. *See* The Holy Bible: *Comprising the Old and New Testaments*, The King James Version, (New York: American Bible Society, 1972), [(NT) Matthew 5:48], 5.

      121.   Jac. J. Janssen, "Gift-Giving in Ancient Egypt as an Economic Feature," *The Journal of Egyptian Archaeology* 68, (1982): 256. Tarík Karenga, *Kemetan Calendar and Zodiac*, First Edition, (Union City: Amenism, Inc., 2022), 10, 49.

      122.   Jac. J. Janssen, "Gift-Giving in Ancient Egypt as an Economic Feature," *The Journal of Egyptian Archaeology* 68, (1982): 256. Arthur C. Mace, *The Metropolitan Museum of Art: The Murch Collection of Egyptian Antiquities*, (New York: The Metropolitan Museum of Art, 1912), 16, 26. [[ ]] Double brackets indicate word or term substitution made by the author. Here, the spelling of the name "Osir," which refers to the first person of God, is consistent with the teachings of Amenism and has therefore been substituted for the name "Osiris," which is Greek. Author Edward Bleiberg has translated the word *añew* as "official gifts" that were ". . . always part of a redistributive process" and that were transactions that expressed ". . . a socioeconomic relationship between

the king and others," but for contemporary purposes, in what present-day Amenists recognize as Kemet's Reemergent Kingdom, the word *añew* [*sing./plur.*] represents any gift(s) exchanged between two or more persons. See Edward Bleiberg, *The Official Gift in Ancient Egypt*, (Norman: University of Oklahoma Press, 1996), 27-28, 35, 114, 117. Note: In the Reemergent Kingdom ⊙ is transliterated *ny* and spelled ny and ñ (*i.e.*, the letter -*n*- with a tilde overhead, Wolof form), and is pronounced "ny" as in the Wolof language of the West African country of Senegal. The genetic relationship of modern African languages such as Wolof to the ancient Kemetan language has been well documented; furthermore, scholar and author Rekhety Wimby states: "... the languages of Africa all derive, by evolutionary processes, from an original parent, to which I give the name, suggested by C. A. Diop in *Parente genetique*, Paleo-African." Rekhety Wimby, "The Unity of African Languages," in *Kemet and the African Worldview*, eds. Maulana Karenga and Jacob Carruthers, (Los Angeles: University of Sankore Press, 1986), 151-166. See also Cheikh Anta Diop, *The Cultural Unity of Black Africa*, (London: Karnak House, 1989), 168-169. Transliterations pertaining to the object (*i.e.*, ñu vase) that the above hieroglyph represents are as follows: *nyu* and *nyw*, spelled ñu and pronounced "nyoo." See E. A. Wallis Budge, *An Egyptian Hieroglyphic Dictionary: In Two Volumes*, Volume I, (London: John Murray, 1920), 56b, 349a-b. Alan Gardiner, *Egyptian Grammar: Being an Introduction to the Study of Hieroglyphs*, Third Edition, Revised, (Oxford: Griffith Institute, 1994), 137, 530.

    123.   Eid Abdel-Aziz, "A New Year's Flask," in *The Horizon Studies in Egyptology: In Honour of M.A. Nur El-Din (10-12 April 2007)*, Volume 3, ed. Basem El-Sharkaway, (Cairo: American University in Cairo Press, 2010), 24. E. A. Wallis Budge, *Some Account of the Collection of Egyptian Antiquities in the Possession of Lady Meux*, Second Edition, (London: Harrison & Sons, 1896), 219. Arthur C. Mace, *The Metropolitan Museum of Art: The Murch Collection of Egyptian Antiquities*, (New York: The Metropolitan Museum of Art, 1912), 16, 26. Sir P. Le Page Renouf and Prof. E. Naville, *The Egyptian Book of the Dead: Translation and Commentary*, (London: The Society of Biblical Archaeology, 1904), 10.

Capitalization mine. Celebrations begin on New Year's Eve and extend into the New Year. Albert Barnes, *Notes, Critical, Explanatory, and Practical on the Book of the Prophet Isaiah*, Volume II, (New York: Leavitt & Allen, 1853), 427. Capitalization mine.

124.   Professor Migliarini, "Account of the Unrolling of a Mummy at Florence, Belonging to the Duke of Tuscany," in *Archaeologia: Or, Miscellaneous Tracts Relating to Antiquity*, Volume 36, (London: Society of Antiquaries of London, 1855), 170. Mine in parentheses. Mine in bold. Capitalization mine. Sir P. Le Page Renouf and Prof. E. Naville, *The Egyptian Book of the Dead: Translation and Commentary*, (London: The Society of Biblical Archaeology, 1904), 10. Gerald Massey, *Ancient Egypt: The Light of the World*, Volume I, (London: T. Fisher Unwin, 1907), 381-382. The Feast of the New Year is held at the beginning of the year. See P. Le Page Renouf, *The Origin and Growth of Religion as Illustrated by the Religion of Ancient Egypt*, (New York: Charles Scribner's Sons, 1880), 140.

125.   According to present-day Amenists, the Reemergent Kingdom began on 10/1/52580 Z.T.E. or 3/22/2020 C.E. See Table 7: Chronological Table, and Plate 5, in Tarík Karenga, *Kemetan Calendar and Zodiac*, First Edition, (Union City: Amenism, Inc., 2022), 31, 49. The term *Reemergent Kingdom* and the abbreviation *Z.T.E.* are in Tarík Karenga, *Review of the Kemetan Mystery System*, First Edition, (Union City: Amenism, Inc., in press). Offering tables were commonly outfitted with at least one rectangular depression for pouring libations. Andrey O. Bolshakov, "Offering Tables," in *The Oxford Encyclopedia of Ancient Egypt*, Volume 2, ed. Donald B. Redford, (New York: Oxford University Press, 2001), 574-575. The offering cup at the Feast of the New Year and the Unity Cup at the African American holiday of Kwanzaa essentially serve the same functions. Maulana Karenga, *The African American Holiday of Kwanzaa: A Celebration of Family, Community & Culture*, (Los Angeles: University of Sankore Press, 1988), 89-91. Initiates of the ancient Kemetan Mystery System who reached the highest degree were said to have been "... given a drink, called oimellas (probably consisting of wine and honey), and told that now all trials were over." Charles William

Notes

Heckethorn, *The Secret Societies of All Ages and Countries*, Volume 1, (London: George Redway, 1897), 55-56.

126.   James Bonwick, *Egyptian Belief and Modern Thought*, (London: C. Kegan Paul & Co., 1878), 128-129. Italics mine.

127.   The name of God Amen at the end of prayers; *see* Anthony T. Browder, *Nile Valley Contributions to Civilization: Exploding the Myths*, Volume 1, (Washington: The Institute of Karmic Guidance, 1992), 85. *See* also Charles W. Leadbeater, *The Science of the Sacraments*, (Los Angeles: The St. Alban Press, 1920), 41-42. Note: Amen is hidden, Ra makes manifest, so ending one's prayer with the name of God Amen-Ra esoterically means may the hidden (*e.g.*, one's prayer) be made manifest.

128.   James Henry Breasted, *Ancient Records of Egypt*, Volume III, (Chicago: The University of Chicago Press, 1906), 102-117.

129.   Pierre Montet, *Eternal Egypt*, (New York: The New American Library of World Literature, Inc., 1964), 38.

130.   In the words of Rameses II: "... to provide for them that have passed away ..." *See* James Henry Breasted, *Ancient Records of Egypt*, Volume III, (Chicago: The University of Chicago Press, 1906), 108-109. *See* also Joann Fletcher, *Exploring the Life, Myth, and Art of Ancient Egypt*, (New York: The Rosen Publishing Group, 2009), 21. The ancient Kemetan, Padisobek, says: "...the deceased is revived when his name is pronounced..." *See* Miriam Lichtheim, *Maat in Egyptian Autobiographies and Related Studies*, (Freiburg, Schweiz: Universitatsverlag; Gottingen: Vandenhoeck und Ruprecht, 1992), 198.

Conclusion

1.   *See* F. Ll. Griffith, "The Teachings of Amenophis the Son of Kanakht. Papyrus B.M. 10474," in *The Journal of Egyptian Archaeology* 12, Parts 3 & 4, (1926): 216. Italics mine.

2.   Osir himself came down from heaven to transmit civilization to all nations, which was in actuality the transference to earth of the Kingdom of Heaven located within his own spirit. E. A. Wallis Budge, *Osiris and the Egyptian Resurrection*, Volume I, (New York: G. P. Putnam's Sons, 1911), 2, 16. *See* also, Felix Guirand, *Larousse Encyclopedia of Mythology*, (New York: Prometheus Press, 1960), 16. In

a body of ancient Kemetan religious and philosophical texts adapted to ancient Greek culture, Tekhi says to Imhotep, "Do you know, Asclepius (*i.e.*, Imhotep), that Egypt is an image of heaven or, to be more precise, that everything governed and moved in heaven came down to Egypt and was transferred there? If truth were told, our land is the temple of the whole world." *See* Brian P. Copenhaver, *Hermetica, The Greek Corpus Hermeticum and the Latin Asclepius in a New English Translation with Notes and Introduction*, (New York: Cambridge University Press, 1995), 81. Mine in parentheses. In Amenist theology, here, the word "heaven" has an astronomical interpretation, but also a spiritual interpretation wherein it refers to the Kingdom of Heaven located within one's own spirit and as such it is the temple of the spirit, which when transferred to earth and made manifest in the physical realm by secret means, becomes "the temple of the whole world" and the Kingdom of God on earth. *See* also D. M. Murdock, Christ in Egypt: The Horus-Jesus Connection, (Ashland: Stellar House Publishing, 2009), 469-478. "Two temples" illustrated; *see* Tarík Karenga, *Review of the Kemetan Mystery System*, First Edition, (Union City: Amenism, Inc., in press). ". . . religious, philosophical and scientific (teachings of the Kemetan Mystery System were transmitted orally and) spread to other lands through student Initiates." George G. M. James, *Stolen Legacy*, (Trenton: African World Press, 1992), 1, 9-10, (12), 69, 154. Mine in parentheses. A plagiarized, adapted and reconfigured version of this Amenist teaching is in the religion of Christianity. *See* The Holy Bible: *Comprising the Old and New Testaments*, The King James Version, (New York: American Bible Society, 1972), [(NT) Matthew 28:16-20], 34. According to author Elmer Towns, in the so-called "Great Commission" of the mythical Christian God Jesus, there are exactly two imperatives; namely, evangelism and education carried out by disciples. Elmer Towns, *Core Christianity: What is Christianity All About?* (Chattanooga: AMG Publishers, 2007), 139. ". . . . Egypt was the greatest education centre of the ancient world . . ." and when the Greeks came in contact with Egypt, it ". . . resulted in the genesis of their enlightenment." *See* George G. M. James, *Stolen Legacy*, (Trenton: African World Press, 1992), 41-42.

Notes

3. Cheikh Anta Diop, *The African Origin of Civilization: Myth or Reality*, (Chicago: Lawrence Hill Books, 1974), 10. *See* also Table 7: Chronological Table, in Tarík Karenga, *Kemetan Calendar and Zodiac*, First Edition, (Union City: Amenism, Inc., 2022), 32-33.

4. The religious reason for the fall of Kemet from the perspective of the foreign invaders is that Amenism was supplanted by Christianity and Islam, but from the perspective of the Kemetans, it was because Kemet turned away from doing God's Will. God in his name of Ra said: "I have made *every man like his brother*, and I have forbidden that they do *isfet*, (but) it was their hearts which undid that which I had said." Thus both perspectives are correct. *See* the chapter, "Express Your Gratitude." George G. M. James, *Stolen Legacy*, (Trenton: African World Press, 1992), 37-39. *See* also James P. Allen, *Middle Egyptian: An Introduction to the Language and Culture of Hieroglyphs*, (New York: Cambridge University Press, 2001), 11. Listervelt Middleton and Asa G. Hilliard, *Master Keys to Ancient Kemet (Egypt)* [Video Presentation], Waset Educational Productions, 1990. Cheikh Anta Diop, *The African Origin of Civilization: Myth or Reality*, (Chicago: Lawrence Hill Books, 1974), 10. The first migratory wave has been dated at the time of the Persian conquest, and the last migratory wave, around the time of the arrival of the Arabs. Aboubacry Moussa Lam, *Les Chemins Du Nil: Les Relations Entre l'Egypte Ancienne et l'Afrique Noire*, (Paris: Presence Africaine, 1997), 52-54, 155-198. Charles Finch, "From the Nile to the Niger: The Evolution of African Spiritual Concepts," in *Companion to African-American Studies*, eds. Lewis R. Gordon and Jane Anna Gordon, (Malden: Blackwell Publishing, 2006), 463-464. *See* also Table 7: Chronological Table, in Tarík Karenga, *Kemetan Calendar and Zodiac*, First Edition, (Union City: Amenism, Inc., 2022), 32-33.

5. Tarík Karenga, *Kemetan Calendar and Zodiac*, First Edition, (Union City: Amenism, Inc., 2022), 1; Table 7: Chronological Table, 32.

6. Benjamin Tetteh, "2019: Year of Return for African Diaspora," *African Renewal: Dec. 2018 – Mar. 2019*, https://www.un.org/africarenewal/magazine/december-2018-march-2019/2019-year-

return-african-diaspora, Accessed 8 October 2020. *See* also Table 7: Chronological Table, in Tarík Karenga, *Kemetan Calendar and Zodiac*, First Edition, (Union City: Amenism, Inc., 2022), 31. "Note: There has never been, nor will there ever be a single book alone that contains the whole of Amenist teachings, because the very act of writing and/or identifying Scripture is facilitated through constantly engaging in a personal relationship and spiritual union with God alongside the cultivation of the Arts and Sciences, which allows for an ever-expanding written record of God Amen's Holy Word." *See* the term *Amenism*, in Tarík Karenga, *Review of the Kemetan Mystery System*, First Edition, (Union City: Amenism, Inc., in press).

7. Cheikh Anta Diop, *The African Origin of Civilization: Myth or Reality*, (Chicago: Lawrence Hill Books, 1974), 140. Mine in parentheses.

8. *Our* culture and hence our ethnicity was created by Osir and Iset and then handed down to us from our ancestors, which explains why the ethnicity of Osir and Iset is Anu, while our ethnicity is Kemetan. *See* Cheikh Anta Diop, *The African Origin of Civilization: Myth or Reality*, (Chicago: Lawrence Hill Books, 1974), 76-78, 105, 249-250. Felix Guirand, *Larousse Encyclopedia of Mythology*, (New York: Prometheus Press, 1960), 16, 18. Note: As a consequence of the Holocaust of Enslavement many Africans in the Diaspora have found that they are of a mixed ethnicity, but may have a stronger affinity for one ethnicity over all others, and therefore choose to identify themselves accordingly. *See* also the terms *ethnicity* and *Kemetan*, in Tarík Karenga, *Review of the Kemetan Mystery System*, First Edition, (Union City: Amenism, Inc., in press).

9. *See* Cheikh Anta Diop, *Civilization or Barbarism: An Authentic Anthropology*, (Brooklyn: Lawrence Hill Books, 1991), 25-68. *See* also Rebecca L. Lamason, Manzoor-Ali P.K. Mohideen, Jason R. Mest, Andrew C. Wong, Heather L. Norton, Michele C. Aros, Michael J. Jurynec, Xianyun Mao, Vanessa R. Humphreville, Jasper E. Humbert, Soniya Sinha, Jessica L. Moore, Pudur Jagadeeswaran, Wei Zhao, Gang Ning, Izabela Makalowska, Paul M. McKeigue, David O'Donnell, Rick

Notes

Kittles, Esteban J. Parra, Nancy J. Mangini, David J. Grunwald, Mark D. Shriver, Victor A. Canfield and Keith C. Cheng, "SLC24A5, a Putative Cation Exchanger, Affects Pigmentation in Zebrafish and Humans," in *Science* 310, no. 5755 (December 16, 2005): 1782-1786. *See* also Keith C. Cheng, "Skin Color in Fish and Humans: Impacts on Science and Society," in *Zebrafish* 5, no. 4 (2008): 237-242. *See* also Cecie Star, Christine A. Evers and Lisa Starr, *Biology: Today and Tomorrow*, 3rd Edition, (Mason: Cengage Learning, 2010), 161-162.

10.   The tomb of the Osir was discovered by French archaeologist Emile Amelineau. Cheikh Anta Diop, *The African Origin of Civilization: Myth or Reality*, (Chicago: Lawrence Hill Books, 1974), 75. Of Osir it is said, "Osiris is thy name in the bosom of the spirit." *See* Charles Loring Brace, *The Unknown God: Or, Inspiration Among Pre-Christian Races*, (New York: A. C. Armstrong and Son, 1890), 20. Mine in parentheses. Concerning the Spirit of God that dwells within us, an Amenist hymn that combines God's name of "Amen" with God's name of "Ra" (*e.g.*, Amen-Ra) reads: "We worship thee because thou dwell'st in us!" *See* Francis Ellingwood Abbot, William James Potter and Benjamin Franklin Underwood, eds., "Hymn to Amun-Ra," in *The Index*, (Boston: Index Association, 1879), 161.

11.   *See* The Metropolitan Museum of Art, *Egyptian Wall Paintings: The Metropolitan Museum of Art's Collection of Facsimiles*, (New York: The Metropolitan Museum of Art, 1983), 34. The ancient Kemetans even built temples in ancient Sudan (*i.e.*, Ta-Seti). *See* Torgny Säve-Söderbergh, *Temples and Tombs of Ancient Nubia*, (London: Thames & Hudson, 1987), 152-153. Fergus Fleming and Alan Lothian, *The Way to Eternity: Egyptian Myth*, (London: Duncan Baird Publishers, 1997), 30-33. *See* also Vincent Arieh Tobin, *Theological Principles of Egyptian Religion*, (New York: Peter Lang Publishing, Inc., 1989), 59, 126. According to Egyptologist E. A. Wallis Budge, clay quarries on the east bank of the Nile at Aswan just opposite to Elephantine Island contained red and yellow clays. *See* E. A. Wallis Budge, *The Nile: Notes for Travellers in Egypt*, Eighth Edition, (London: Thos. Cook & Son (Egypt), LTD., 1902), 452. Also located on the east bank of the Nile at Aswan was a temple

showing Amen in his forms of Khnum, Satis and Anukis on a chapel wall receiving offerings from a Ptolemaic king. Richard H. Wilkinson, *The Complete Temples of Ancient Egypt*, (New York: Thames & Hudson, 2000), 212-213. Author, Yaacov Lev educates readers about a quarry near Cairo in Kemet once renowned for its yellow clay. *See* Yaacov Lev, *Saladin in Egypt, The Medieval Mediterranean: Peoples, Economies and Cultures, 400-1453*, Volume 21, (Leiden: Brill, 1999), 116. For an article that identifies red clay from Aswan in Kemet *see* G. M. Gad and L. R. Barrett, "The Constitution of Some Egyptian Clays," in *Mineralogical Magazine* 28, no. 205 (June 1949): 587-597. Ptolemy I, who clearly was both white and Greek, is shown in a relief on a wall of his tomb as being formed from ocherous red Kemetan clay, indicating his adherence to the traditional color symbolism of Amenism and his recognition of the corresponding Amenist account of creation. Additionally, the woman standing next to Ptolemy I is depicted as being formed from ocherous yellow Kemetan clay. Gay Robins, *The Art of Ancient Egypt*, Revised Edition, (Cambridge: Harvard University Press, 2008), 238. At other times the Kemetans chose to depict themselves and others with their natural skin colors, as in the Table of Nations found in the tomb of Rameses III that shows both the ancient Kemetan and Ta-Setian with black skin. Cheikh Anta Diop, *Civilization or Barbarism: An Authentic Anthropology*, (Brooklyn: Lawrence Hill Books, 1991), 17, 66. In summary, ancient Kemetan men and women depicted themselves as being formed from ocherous red and yellow Kemetan clays respectively in recognition of an Amenist account of creation, to express their strict adherence to Amenism and its color symbolism, and as a humble gesture of paying homage to the Creator: Amen. The two aforementioned colors with respect to the depiction of the ancient Kemetans are not, therefore, indicative of their natural skin colors, much less of their race, but are instead characteristic colors of the Kemetan clays from which God formed the physical bodies of Kemetan men and women. Definition of Ocher: "an earthy clay colored by iron oxide, usually yellow or reddish brown: used as a pigment in paints." Webster's New World Dictionary & Thesaurus, Version 2.0, Build #25, Accent Software International, Macmillan Publishers, 1998. *See* also the

Notes

term *ethnicity*, in Tarík Karenga, *Review of the Kemetan Mystery System*, First Edition, (Union City: Amenism, Inc., in press).

12. Miriam Lichtheim, *Ancient Egyptian Literature*, Volume II, (Los Angeles: University of California Press, 1976), 141. Mine in parentheses. Our relationship with God is reciprocal.

13. *See* Table 7: Chronological Table, in Tarík Karenga, *Kemetan Calendar and Zodiac*, First Edition, (Union City: Amenism, Inc., 2022), 31. Adolf Erman and Hermann Grapow, *Worterbuch Der Aegyptischen Sprache*, Volume 4, (Berlin: Akademie -Verlag, 1971), 85. Linguist Lilias Homburger states: "The elimination of initial *r* in modern African languages is therefore but a further extension of a tendency which existed in later forms of Egyptian." Lilias Homburger, *The Negro - African Languages*, (London: Routledge & Kegan Paul LTD., 1949), 226. *See* also E. A. Wallis Budge, *An Egyptian Hieroglyphic Dictionary: In Two Volumes*, Volume II, (London: John Murray, 1920), 655a-b. Additionally, author George G. M. James informs readers that ". . . the Egyptians developed secret systems of writing and teaching, and forbade their Initiates from writing what they had learnt." George G. M. James, *Stolen Legacy*, (Trenton: African World Press, 1992), 1. Disregarding this requirement for their spiritual advancement, Greeks and other foreigners exploited the ancient Kemetan Mystery System without clearly understanding it; therefore, clarity must be given to that which has been confounded for millennia. *Ibid.*, 154-155. That being the case, according to Amenism, in the secret writing system of the ancient Kemetans the suffix –ur, sometimes containing a hidden initial *r*, forms adjectives and nouns. *See* Alan Gardiner, *Egyptian Grammar: Being an Introduction to the Study of Hieroglyphs*, Third Edition, Revised, (Oxford: Griffith Institute, 1994), 270-278. For example, the verb *Seba* (**SAY**-bah) is pronounced with the accent on the first syllable and means teach, educate, instruct. However, when used as a designation or title, the word *Seba* becomes *Seba-ur* (say-bah-**OOR**), a common noun meaning teacher, educator, instructor. On "conditions of opportunity" *see* Tony Iton, *Tony Iton on How to Fix California's Health Care Gap* [Audio File], NPR: KQED Forum With Michael Krasny, Aired July 5, 2018.

14.	James Henry Breasted, *Ancient Records of Egypt*, Volume I, (Chicago: University of Chicago Press, 1906), 244. To write a person's name is to preserve their life, and to pronounce a person's name is to cause them to live again. *See* Joann Fletcher, *Exploring the Life, Myth, and Art of Ancient Egypt*, (New York: The Rosen Publishing Group, 2009), 21.

15.	Pharaoh Queen Hatshepsut teaches us to restore what has been ruined and raise up what has been dismembered. *See* Maulana Karenga, *Maat: The Moral Ideal in Ancient Egypt*, (Los Angeles: University of Sankore Press, 2006), 398. The Mystery System of ancient Kemet had as its five chief aims 1) the revival of the spirit, which simultaneously brings about a flourishing of the spirit through philosophical enlightenment in truth; 2) spiritual union with God, which simultaneously liberates the soul ". . . from its bodily fetters;" 3) salvation of the soul, which simultaneously brings one's ". . . life into harmony with God, (humankind and nature) . . . ;" 4) spiritual rebirth, which is the birth of the soul, and which simultaneously lifts the soul from its bodily prison in which it lies spiritually unborn, in sleeping repose, and in proximal separation from *true life*; and 5) spiritual resurrection of the soul, which simultaneously awakens and raises the soul from a sleeplike state that resembles spiritual death, to renewed activity that enables the transference to earth of the Kingdom of Heaven located within one's own spirit. These five chief aims that the religion of Amenism teaches, are directly linked to the continuous process of conceiving and actualizing ever-higher levels of our infinite potentiality (*e.g.*, our Christhood), that is, the uniting of our human self with our divine self. For detailed references *see* notes for the chapter, "Seek Wise Counsel."

16.	For the ancient Kemetan aphorism "live in truth" *see* the terms *spiritual union* and *Kingdom of Heaven*, in Tarík Karenga, *Review of the Kemetan Mystery System*, First Edition, (Union City: Amenism, Inc., in press).

BIBLIOGRAPHY

Abbot, Francis Ellingwood, William James Potter and Benjamin Franklin Underwood, (Eds.). "Hymn to Amun-Ra." In *The Index*. Boston: Index Association, 1879.

Abdel-Aziz, Eid. "A New Year's Flask." In *The Horizon Studies in Egyptology: In Honour of M.A. Nur El-Din (10-12 April 2007)*. Volume 3. Edited by Basem El-Sharkaway. Cairo: American University in Cairo Press, 2010.

Akbar, Na'im. *Restoration of African Consciousness* [Audio Presentation]. Institute of Karmic Guidance, 1990.

Allen, James P. *Middle Egyptian: An Introduction to the Language and Culture of Hieroglyphs*. New York: Cambridge University Press, 2001.

Allen, James P. *The Ancient Egyptian Pyramid Texts*. Atlanta: Society of Biblical Literature, 2005.

Asante, Molefi Kete. *Kemet, Afrocentricity and Knowledge*. Trenton: African World Press, 1990.

Asante, Molefi Kete. *The Egyptian Philosophers: Ancient African Voices from Imhotep to Akhenaten*. Chicago: African American Images, 2000.

Assman, Jan. *Egyptian Solar Religion in the New Kingdom: Re, Amun and the Crisis of Polytheism*. New York: Routledge, 2009.

Babcock, Michael A. *The Humanities: A Christian Approach*. Sixth Edition. Lynchburg: HPS Publishing, 2003.

Barnes, Albert. *Notes, Critical, Explanatory, and Practical on the Book of the Prophet Isaiah.* Volume II. New York: Leavitt & Allen, 1853.

Barnes, Carol. *Melanin: The Chemical Key to Black Greatness: The Harmful Effects of Toxic Drugs on Melanin Centers Within the Black Community.* Volume 1. Houston: C. B. Publishers, 1988.

Biyogo, Gregoire. *Aux Sources Egyptiennes Du Savoir: Volume 1, Genealogie Et Enjeux De La Pensee De Cheikh Anta Diop.* Yaounde: Editions Menaibuc, 2000, 7n4.

Bleiberg, Edward. *The Official Gift in Ancient Egypt.* Norman: University of Oklahoma Press, 1996.

Bolshakov, Andrey O. "Offering Tables." In *The Oxford Encyclopedia of Ancient Egypt.* Volume 2. Edited by Donald B. Redford. New York: Oxford University Press, 2001.

Bonwick, James. *Egyptian Belief and Modern Thought.* London: C. Kegan Paul & Co., 1878.

Bowman, Alan K. *Egypt After the Pharaohs: 332 BC-AD 642.* Los Angeles: University of California Press, 1986.

Boylan, Patrick. *Thoth, the Hermes of Egypt: A Study of Some Aspects of Theological Thought in Ancient Egypt.* London: Oxford University Press, 1922.

Brace, Charles Loring. *The Unknown God: Or, Inspiration Among Pre-Christian Races.* New York: A. C. Armstrong and Son, 1890.

Breasted, James Henry. *Ancient Records of Egypt.* Volume I. Chicago: University of Chicago Press, 1906.

Breasted, James Henry. *Ancient Records of Egypt.* Volume II. Chicago: The University of Chicago Press, 1906.

Breasted, James Henry. *Ancient Records of Egypt.* Volume III. Chicago: The University of Chicago Press, 1906.

Breasted, James Henry. *Ancient Records of Egypt.* Volume IV. Chicago: The University of Chicago Press, 1906.

Bibliography

Breasted, James Henry. *Development of Religion and Thought in Ancient Egypt*. New York: Charles Scribner's Sons, 1912.

Breasted, James Henry. *The Dawn of Conscience*. New York: Charles Scribner's Sons, 1935.

Breasted, James Henry. "The Philosophy of a Memphite Priest: Hierzu Tafel I und II." In *Zeitschrift Fur Agyptische Sprache Und Altertumskunde*. Volume 39. Edited by A. Erman and G. Steindorff. Leipzig: J. C. Hinrichs'sche Buchhandlung, 1901.

Breidlid, Anders, Avelino Androga Said and Astrid Kristine Breidlid. *A Concise History of South Sudan*, New and Revised Edition. Kampala: Fountain Publishers, 2014.

Brier, Bob and Hoyt Hobbs, *Daily Life of the Ancient Egyptians*. Second Edition. Westport: Greenwood Press, 2008.

Briggs, Philip. *Ethiopia: The Bradt Travel Guide*. Sixth Edition. Guilford: The Globe Pequot Press Inc., 2012.

Browder, Anthony T. *From the Browder File: 22 Essays on the African American Experience*. Revised and Expanded. Washington: The Institute of Karmic Guidance, 2000.

Browder, Anthony T. *Nile Valley Contributions to Civilization: Exploding the Myths*. Volume 1. Washington: The Institute of Karmic Guidance, 1992.

Brugsch-Bey, Heinrich. *Egypt Under the Pharaohs: A History Derived Entirely From the Monuments*. A New Edition. London: John Murray, 1891.

Brugsch-Bey, Henry. *A History of Egypt Under the Pharaohs*. Translated by Philip Smith. 2nd Edition. Volume II. London: John Murray, 1881.

Budge, E. A. Wallis. *A History of Ethiopia, Nubia & Abyssinia*. Volume 1. London: Methuen & Co. LTD., 1928.

Budge, E. A. Wallis. *A Short History of the Egyptian People: With Chapters on Their Religion, Daily Life, Etc.* London: J. M. Dent & Sons Limited, 1914.

Budge, E. A. Wallis. *A Vocabulary in Hieroglyphic to the Theban Recension of the Book of the Dead.* London: Kegan Paul, Trench, Trubner & Co., LTD., 1898.

Budge, E. A. Wallis. *An Egyptian Hieroglyphic Dictionary: In Two Volumes.* Volume I. London: John Murray, 1920.

Budge, E. A. Wallis. *An Egyptian Hieroglyphic Dictionary: In Two Volumes.* Volume II. London: John Murray, 1920.

Budge, E. A. Wallis. *British Museum: A Guide to the Third and Fourth Egyptian Rooms.* London: British Museum, 1904.

Budge, E. A. Wallis. *Cleopatra's Needles and Other Egyptian Obelisks.* London: The Religious Tract Society, 1926.

Budge, E. A. Wallis. *Egyptian Religion.* Secaucus: Citadel Press, 1987.

Budge, E. A. Wallis. *First Steps in Egyptian: A Book for Beginners.* London: Kegan Paul, Trench, Trubner & Co., Ltd., 1895.

Budge, E. A. Wallis. *From Fetish to God in Ancient Egypt.* New York: Dover Publications, Inc., 1988.

Budge, E. A. Wallis. *Legends of Our Lady Mary the Perpetual Virgin and Her Mother Hanna.* London: The Medici Society, 1922.

Budge, E. A. Wallis. *Legends of the Egyptian Gods.* London: Kegan Paul, Trench, Trubner & Co., Ltd., 1912.

Budge, E. A. Wallis. *Osiris and the Egyptian Resurrection.* Volume I. New York: G. P. Putnam's Sons, 1911.

Budge, E. A. Wallis. *Osiris and the Egyptian Resurrection.* Volume II. New York: G. P. Putnam's Sons, 1911.

Budge, E. A. Wallis. *Some Account of the Collection of Egyptian Antiquities in the Possession of Lady Meux.* Second Edition. London: Harrison & Sons, 1896.

Budge, E. A. Wallis. *The Book of the Dead: An English Translation of the Chapters, Hymns, Etc. of the Theban Recension, with Introduction, Notes, Etc.* Second Edition, Revised and Enlarged. Books on Egypt and Chaldaea. New

York: E. P. Dutton & Co., 1938.

Budge, E. A. Wallis. *The Book of the Dead: The Chapters of Coming Forth by Day. An English Translation with Introduction, Notes, Etc.* London: Kegan Paul, Trench, Trubner & Co., LTD., 1898.

Budge, E. A. Wallis. *The Book of the Dead: The Chapters of Coming Forth by Day. The Egyptian Text in Hieroglyphic Edited From Numerous Papyri.* London: Kegan Paul, Trench, Trubner & Co., LTD., 1898.

Budge, E. A. Wallis. *The Book of the Dead: The Papyrus of Ani.* In Two Volumes. Volume I. London: The Medici Society, Ltd., 1913.

Budge, E. A. Wallis. *The Book of the Dead: The Papyrus of Ani.* In Two Volumes. Volume II. London: The Medici Society, Ltd., 1913.

Budge, E. A. Wallis. *The Book of the Dead: The Papyrus of Ani in the British Museum.* London: Kegan Paul, Trench, Trubner & Co., 1895.

Budge, E. A. Wallis. *The Egyptian Heaven and Hell.* Volume II. London: Kegan Paul, Trench, Trubner & Co., Ltd., 1905.

Budge, E. A. Wallis. *The Egyptian Heaven and Hell.* Volume III. London: Kegan Paul, Trench, Trubner & Co., Ltd., 1906.

Budge, E. A. Wallis. *The Dwellers on the Nile: The Life, History, Religion and Literature of the Ancient Egyptians.* New York: Dover Publications Inc., 1977.

Budge, E. A. Wallis. *The Gods of the Egyptians: Or, Studies in Egyptian Mythology.* Volume I. London: Methuen & Company, 1904.

Budge, E. A. Wallis. *The Gods of the Egyptians: Or, Studies in Egyptian Mythology.* Volume II. London: Methuen & Company, 1904.

Budge, E. A. Wallis. *The Literature of the Ancient Egyptians.* London: J. M. Dent & Sons Limited, 1914.

Budge, E. A. Wallis. *The Nile: Notes for Travellers in Egypt.* Eighth Edition. London: Thos. Cook & Son (Egypt), LTD., 1902.

Budge, E. A. Wallis. *The Teachings of Amen-Em Apt, Son of Kanekht.* London: Martin Hopkinson and Company, Ltd., 1924.

Budge, E. A. Wallis. *Tutankhamen: Amenism, Atenism and Egyptian Monotheism.* London: Martin Hopkinson, 1923.

Bunsen, C. C. J. Baron and Samuel Birch. *Egypt's Place in Universal History.* Volume 5. London: Longmans, Green, and Co., 1867.

Bunson, Matthew. *Encyclopedia of the Roman Empire.* Revised Edition. New York: Facts on File, 2002.

Capt, E. Raymond. *The Great Pyramid Decoded.* Thousand Oaks: Artisan Sales, 1971.

Cerny, Jaroslav. *Ancient Egyptian Religion.* New York: Hutchinson's University Library, 1952.

Cheng, Keith C. "Skin Color in Fish and Humans: Impacts on Science and Society." In *Zebrafish* 5, no. 4 (2008): 237-242.

Churchward, Albert. *The Origin and Evolution of Religion.* George Allen & Unwin LTD., 1924.

Churchward, Albert. *The Signs and Symbols of Primordial Man: The Evolution of Religious Doctrines from the Eschatology of the Ancient Egyptians.* Second Edition. New York: E. P. Dutton & Company, 1913.

Cialdini, Robert B. *The Power of Persuasion* [Video Presentation]. Stanford University, 2001.

Clarke, John Henrik. "Ancient Civilizations in Africa: The Missing Pages in World History." In *Journal of African Civilizations* 4, no. 2 (November 1982): 113-121.

Collier, Walter V. *Why Racism Persists: An Uncomfortable Truth.* Indianapolis: Dog Ear Publishing, 2017.

Bibliography

Cooke, Harold P. *Osiris: A Study in Myths, Mysteries and Religion.* Boston: Bruce Humphries, Inc. Publishers, 1931.

Copenhaver, Brian P. *Hermetica, The Greek Corpus Hermeticum and the Latin Asclepius in a New English Translation with Notes and Introduction.* New York: Cambridge University Press, 1995.

Coryn, Sidney G. P. *The Faith of Ancient Egypt.* New York: Theosophical Publishing Company, 1913.

Darby, William J., Paul Ghalioungui and Louis Grivetti. *Food: The Gift of Osiris.* Volume 2. London: Academic Press, 1976.

David, Rosalie. *Handbook to Life in Ancient Egypt.* New York: Oxford University Press.

Diner, Helen. *Mothers and Amazons: The First Feminine History of Culture.* Garden City: Anchor Press, 1973.

Diop, Cheikh Anta. *Civilization or Barbarism: An Authentic Anthropology.* Brooklyn: Lawrence Hill Books, 1991.

Diop, Cheikh Anta. "Origin of the Ancient Egyptians." In *Journal of African Civilizations* 4, no. 2 (1982): 9-37.

Diop, Cheikh Anta. *The African Origin of Civilization: Myth or Reality.* Chicago: Lawrence Hill Books, 1974.

Diop, Cheikh Anta. *The Cultural Unity of Black Africa.* London: Karnak House, 1989.

Donini, Alphonsi and P. Athanasius. *Romani Collegii Societas Jesu Musæum Celeberrimum.* Amstelodami: Ex Officina Janssonio – Waesbergiana, 1678.

Durant, Will. *The Story of Civilization, Part 1: Our Oriental Heritage.* New York: Simon and Schuster, 1954.

Elliott, Jane. "An Unforgettable Lesson." In *New Scientist* 192, no. 2581 (Dec 9-Dec 15, 2006): 52.

El Mahdy, Christine. *Tutankhamen: The Life and Death of the Boy-King.* New York: St. Martin's, 1999.

Erman, Adolf. *A Handbook of Egyptian Religion*. London: Archibald Constable & Co. Ltd., 1907.

Erman, Adolf. *The Literature of the Ancient Egyptians*. London: Methuen & Co. LTD, 1927.

Erman, Adolf and Hermann Grapow. *Worterbuch Der Aegyptischen Sprache*. Volume 4. Berlin: Akademie-Verlag, 1971.

Erman, Adolf and Hermann Grapow, *Worterbuch Der Aegyptischen Sprache*. Volume 5. Berlin: Akademie-Verlag, 1971.

Faulkner, Raymond O. *A Concise Dictionary of Middle Egyptian*. Oxford: Griffith Institute, 1962.

Faulkner, Raymond O. *The Ancient Egyptian Coffin Texts*. Volume III. Spells 788-1185 & Index. Warminister: Aris & Phillips LTD., 1978.

Finch, Charles. "From the Nile to the Niger: The Evolution of African Spiritual Concepts." In *Companion to African-American Studies*. Edited by Lewis R. Gordon and Jane Anna Gordon. Malden: Blackwell Publishing, 2006.

Fitzgerald, Stephanie. *Ramses II: Egyptian Pharaoh, Warrior, and Builder*. Mankato: Compass Point Books, 2009.

Fleras, Augie. "An Optical Delusion: 'Racializing Eye Colour.'" In *The Politics of Race in Canada*. Edited by Maria Wallis and Augie Fleras. Ontario: Oxford University Press, 2009.

Fleming, Fergus and Alan Lothian. *The Way to Eternity: Egyptian Myth*. London: Duncan Baird Publishers, 1997.

Foster, John L. and Susan T. Hollis. *Hymns, Prayers, and Songs: An Anthology of Ancient Egyptian Lyric Poetry*. Atlanta: Scholars Press, 1995.

Frankfort, Henri. *Ancient Egyptian Religion*. New York: Harper Torchbooks, 1961.

Bibliography

Frankfort, Henri. *Kingship and the Gods*. Chicago: The University of Chicago Press, 1978.

Frankfort, Henri, H. A. Frankfort, John A. Wilson, Thorkild Jacobsen and William A. Irwin. *The Intellectual Adventure of Ancient Man: An Essay on Speculative Thought in the Ancient Near East*. Chicago: University of Chicago Press, 1977.

Frazer, J. G. *Pausanias's Description of Greece*. Volume V. London: Macmillan and Co., Limited, 1913.

Fletcher, Joann. *Exploring the Life, Myth, and Art of Ancient Egypt*. New York: The Rosen Publishing Group, 2009.

Fuller, Jr., Neely. *The United Independent Compensatory Code/System/Concept: A Textbook/Workbook for Thought, Speech and/or Action for Victims of Racism (White Supremacy)*. Revised. 1984.

Gad, G. M. and L. R. Barrett. "The Constitution of Some Egyptian Clays." In *Mineralogical Magazine* 28, no. 205 (June 1949): 587-597.

Gardiner, Alan. *Egyptian Grammar: Being an Introduction to the Study of Hieroglyphs*. Third Edition, Revised. Oxford: Griffith Institute, 1994.

Gardiner, Alan H. *The Admonitions of an Egyptian Sage*. Hildesheim: Georg Olms Verlag, 1969.

Gardiner, Alan H. "The Egyptian Word for Herdsman." In *Zeitschrift Fur Agyptische Sprache Und Altertumskunde*. Volume 42. Edited by Adolf Erman and Georg Steindorff. Leipzig: J. C. Hinrichs'sche Buchhandlung, 1905.

Goldstein, Noah J., Steave J. Martin and Robert B. Cialdini. *Yes: 50 Scientifically Proven Ways to Be Persuasive*. New York: Simon and Schuster, 2008.

Griffith, F. Ll. *A Collection of Hieroglyphs: A Contribution to the History of Egyptian Writing*. Boston: The Egypt Exploration Fund, 1898.

Griffith, F. Ll. (Ed.). *Archaeological Survey of Egypt: The Rock Tombs of El Amarna: Part I. - The Tomb of Meryra.* London: Kegan Paul, Trench, Trubner & Co., 1903.

Griffith, F. Ll. "The Teachings of Amenophis the Son of Kanakht. Papyrus B.M. 10474." In *The Journal of Egyptian Archaeology* 12, Parts 3 & 4, (1926): 191-231.

Griffith, Francis Llewellyn. *Beni Hasan.* Part III. London: Kegan Paul, Trench, Trubner & Co., 1896.

Guirand, Felix. *Larousse Encyclopedia of Mythology.* New York: Prometheus Press, 1960.

Haviland, William A., Harald E. L. Prins, Dana Walrath and Bunny McBride, *Anthropology: The Human Challenge.* 13th Edition. Belmont: Wadsworth, Cengage Learning, 2010.

Heckethorn, Charles William. *The Secret Societies of All Ages and Countries.* Volume 1. London: George Redway, 1897.

Henslin, James M. *Sociology: A Down-To-Earth Approach*, Tenth Edition. Boston: Allyn & Bacon, 2010.

Herodotus. *The History of Herodotus.* Book II. Translated by George Rawlinson. Edited by Manuel Komroff. New York: Tudor Publishing Company, 1934.

Hilliard, Asa G. *Re-Education of African People* [Audio Presentation]. Institute of Karmic Guidance, 1990.

Hillard, Asa G. *SBA: The Reawakening of the African Mind.* Gainesville, Makare Publishing Company, 1998.

Hilliard, Asa G., and Listervelt Middleton. *Free Your Mind: Return to the Source African Origins* [Video Presentation]. Wa'set Educational Productions, 1998.

Hilliard, Asa G., Larry Williams and Nia Damali. *The Teachings of Ptahhotep: The Oldest Book in the World.* Atlanta: Blackwood Press, 1987.

Hindson, Ed and Ergun Caner. *The Popular Encyclopedia of Apologetics: Surveying the Evidence for the Truth of Christianity.* Eugene: Harvest House Publishers, 2008.

Bibliography

Homburger, Lilias. *The Negro - African Languages*. London: Routledge & Kegan Paul LTD., 1949.

Iton, Tony. *Tony Iton on How to Fix California's Health Care Gap* [Audio File]. NPR: KQED Forum With Michael Krasny. Aired July 5, 2018.

Jackson, John G. *Christianity Before Christ*. Austin: American Atheist Press, 1985.

Jackson, John G. "Egypt and Christianity." In *Journal of African Civilizations* 4, no. 2 (November 1982): 65-80.

Jacq, Christian. *Fascinating Hieroglyphs: Discovering, Decoding & Understanding the Ancient Art*. New York: Sterling Publishing Co., 1998.

James, George G. M. *Stolen Legacy*. Trenton: African World Press, 1992.

Janssen, Jac. J. "Gift-Giving in Ancient Egypt as an Economic Feature." *The Journal of Egyptian Archaeology* 68, (1982): 253-258.

Jowett, Benjamin. *The Dialogs of Plato*. Volume 3. London: Clarendon Press, 1871.

Karenga, Maulana. "Afterlife." In *Encyclopedia of African Religion*. Edited by Molefi Kete Asante and Ama Mazama. Thousand Oaks: Sage Publications, Inc., 2009.

Karenga, Maulana. *Introduction to Black Studies*. Second Edition. Los Angeles: University of Sankore Press, 1993.

Karenga, Maulana. *Kawaida: An African Way of Being Man in the World* [Audio Presentation]. University of Sankore Press, 1995.

Karenga, Maulana. *Kwanzaa: A Celebration of Family Community and Culture*. Commemorative Edition. Los Angeles: University of Sankore Press, 1998.

Karenga, Maulana. *Maat: The Moral Ideal in Ancient Egypt*. Los Angeles: University of Sankore Press, 2006.

Karenga, Maulana. "Restoration of the Husia: Reviving a Sacred Legacy." In *Kemet and the African Worldview*. Edited by

Maulana Karenga and Jacob Carruthers. Los Angeles: University of Sankore Press, 1986.

Karenga, Maulana. *Selections from the Husia*. Los Angeles: University Of Sankore Press, 1984.

Karenga, Maulana. *The African American Holiday of Kwanzaa: A Celebration of Family, Community & Culture*. Los Angeles: University of Sankore Press, 1988.

Karenga, Maulana. *The Book of Coming Forth by Day: The Ethics of the Declarations of Innocence*. Los Angeles: University of Sankore Press, 1990.

Karenga, Tarík. *Kemetan Calendar and Zodiac*. First Edtion. Union City: Amenism, Inc., 2022.

Karenga, Tarík. *Review of the Kemetan Mystery System*. First Edition. Union City: Amenism, Inc., In Press.

King, Richard *Melanin: A Key to Freedom*. Hampton: U. B. & U. S. Communications Systems, 1994.

King, Richard. "Neuromelanin: A Black Gate Threshold; The I33 Tissue of Heru." In *Why Darkness Matters: The Power of Melanin in the Brain*. Edited by Edward Bruce Bynum. Chicago: African American Images, 2005.

King, Richard. "The Symbolism of the Crown in Ancient Egypt." In *Egypt: Child of Africa*. Edited by Ivan Van Sertima. New Brunswick: Transaction Publishers, 1994.

Lam, Aboubacry Moussa. *Les Chemins Du Nil: Les Relations Entre l'Egypte Ancienne et l'Afrique Noire*. Paris: Presence Africaine, 1997.

Lamason, Rebecca L., Manzoor-Ali P.K. Mohideen, Jason R. Mest, Andrew C. Wong, Heather L. Norton, Michele C. Aros, Michael J. Jurynec, Xianyun Mao, Vanessa R. Humphreville, Jasper E. Humbert, Soniya Sinha, Jessica L. Moore, Pudur Jagadeeswaran, Wei Zhao, Gang Ning, Izabela Makalowska, Paul M. McKeigue, David O'Donnell, Rick Kittles, Esteban J. Parra, Nancy J. Mangini, David J. Grunwald, Mark D. Shriver, Victor

Bibliography

A. Canfield and Keith C. Cheng. "SLC24A5, a Putative Cation Exchanger, Affects Pigmentation in Zebrafish and Humans." In *Science* 310, no. 5755 (December 16, 2005): 1782-1786.

Lamy, Lucie. *Egyptian Mysteries: New Light on Ancient Knowledge*. New York: Thames and Hudson, 1981.

Leadbeater, Charles W. *The Science of the Sacraments*. Los Angeles: The St. Alban Press, 1920.

Leeming, David. *The Oxford Companion to World Mythology*. New York: Oxford University Press, 2005.

Lev, Yaacov. *Saladin in Egypt, The Medieval Mediterranean: Peoples, Economies and Cultures, 400-1453*. Volume 21. Leiden: Brill, 1999.

Levy, Janey. *Great Pyramid of Giza: Measuring Length, Area, Volume, and Angles*. New York: The Rosen Publishing Group, 2006.

Lichtheim, Miriam. *Ancient Egyptian Literature*. Volume I. Los Angeles: University of California Press, 1975.

Lichtheim, Miriam. *Ancient Egyptian Literature*. Volume II. Los Angeles: University of California Press, 1976.

Lichtheim, Miriam. *Ancient Egyptian Literature*. Volume III. Los Angeles: University of California Press, 1980.

Lichtheim, Miriam. *Maat in Egyptian Autobiographies and Related Studies*. Freiburg, Schweiz: Universitatsverlag; Gottingen: Vandenhoeck und Ruprecht, 1992.

Lipton, Bruce H. *The Biology of Belief: Unleashing the Power of Consciousness, Matter and Miracles*. Santa Rosa: Mountain of Love / Elite Books, 2005.

Ludwig, Thomas E. "Helplessly Hoping." PsychSim 5: *Interactive Graphic Simulation and Demonstration Activities for Psychology* [CD-ROM]. Worth Publishers, 2004.

MacArthur, John. *Found: God's Will*. Colorado Springs: David C. Cook, 1977.

Mace, Arthur C. *The Metropolitan Museum of Art: The Murch Collection of Egyptian Antiquities*. New York: The Metropolitan Museum of Art, 1912.

Massey, Gerald. *Ancient Egypt: The Light of the World*. Volume I. London: T. Fisher Unwin, 1907.

Massey, Gerald. *Ancient Egypt: The Light of the World*. Volume II. London: T. Fisher Unwin, 1907.

Middleton, Listervelt and Asa G. Hilliard, *Master Keys to Ancient Kemet (Egypt)* [Video Presentation]. Waset Educational Productions, 1990.

Migliarini, Professor. "Account of the Unrolling of a Mummy at Florence, Belonging to the Duke of Tuscany." In *Archaeologia: Or, Miscellaneous Tracts Relating to Antiquity*. Volume 36. London: Society of Antiquaries of London, 1855.

Missler, Chuck. "A Most Remarkable Book: The Book of Jude." *Personal Update News Journal*, (June 2000). Retrieved from http://www.khouse.org/articles/2000/259. Accessed 24 January 2010.

Montet, Pierre. *Eternal Egypt*. New York: The New American Library of World Literature, Inc., 1964.

Montet, Pierre. *Lives of the Pharaohs*. Cleveland: World Publishing Company, 1968.

Morenz, Siegfried. *Egyptian Religion*. Ithaca: Cornell University Press, 1973.

Murdock, D. M. *Christ in Egypt: The Horus-Jesus Connection*. Seattle: Stellar House Publishing, 2009.

Murray, Margaret A. *Egyptian Religious Poetry*. London: John Murray, 1949.

Murray, Margaret A. "Statue of Nefer-Sma-Āa." In *Ancient Egypt*, Part 4. Edited by Flinders Petrie. New York: Macmillan and CO., 1917.

Murray, Margaret A. *The Osireion at Abydos*. London: Bernard Quaritch, 1904.

Bibliography

Naydler, Jeremy. *Temple of the Cosmos: The Ancient Egyptian Experience of the Sacred*. Rochester: Inner Traditions International, 1996.

Obenga, Theophile. *A Lost Tradition: African Philosophy in World History*. Philadelphia: The Source Editions, 1995.

Obenga, Theophile. *African Origin of So-Called Greek Philosophy and Education* [Video Presentation]. IAS Film Night - 3 November 2016. Retrieved from https://www.youtube.com/watch?v=vJgd0D3sDzE. Accessed 27 June 2021.

Obenga, Theophile. *African Philosophy: The Pharaonic Period: 2780-330 BC*. Paris: Per Ankh, 2004.

Obenga, Theophile. *Ancient Egypt & Black Africa: A Student's Handbook for the Study of Ancient Egypt in Philosophy, Linguistics, & Gender Relations*. London: Karnak House, 1992.

Obenga, Theophile. *L'Egypte, la Grece et l'ecole d'Alexandrie: Histoire interculturelle dans l'antiquite – Aux sources egyptiennes de la philosophie grecque*. Paris: L'Harmattan, 2005.

Piankoff, Alexandre. *The Shrines of Tut-Ankh-Amon*. New York: Pantheon Books Inc., 1955.

Piankoff, Alexandre. *The Tomb of Ramesses VI*. New York: Pantheon Books Inc., 1954.

Pritchard, James B. *Ancient Near Eastern Texts Relating to the Old Testament*. London: Princeton University Press, 1950.

Putnam, James. *Pyramid*. New York: DK Publishing, 1994.

Remler, Pat. *Egyptian Mythology A to Z*, Third Edition. New York: Chelsea House Publishers, 2010.

Renouf, Sir P. Le Page and Prof. E. Naville. *The Egyptian Book of the Dead: Translation and Commentary*. London: The Society of Biblical Archaeology, 1904.

Renouf, P. Le Page. *The Origin and Growth of Religion as Illustrated by the Religion of Ancient Egypt*. New York: Charles Scribner's Sons, 1880.

Robbins, Anthony. *Powertalk*, Vol. 7 [Audio Presentation]. Guthy-Renker Corp., 1997.

Robins, Gay. *The Art of Ancient Egypt*. Revised Edition. Cambridge: Harvard University Press, 2008.

Rollin, Charles. *The Ancient History of the Egyptians, Carthaginians, Assyrians, Babylonians, Medes and Persians, Grecians, and Macedonians*. In Six Volumes. Volume 1. Eighteenth Edition. London: William Tegg and Co., 1851.

Salt, Henry. *Essay on Dr. Young's and M. Champollion's Phonetic System of Hieroglyphics*. London: Longman, Hurst, Rees, Orme, Brown, and Green, Paternoster Row, 1825.

Säve-Söderbergh, Torgny *Temples and Tombs of Ancient Nubia*. London: Thames & Hudson, 1987.

Sayce, A. H. *The Religions of Ancient Egypt and Babylonia*. Edinburgh: T. & T. Clark, 1902.

Seligmann, C. G. and Margaret A. Murray. "Note on the "Sa" Sign." In *Man*, no. 73 (1911): 113-117.

Scott, Walter. *Hermetica*. Boston: Shambhala Publications Inc., 1993.

Shafer, Byron E., John Baines, Leonard H. Lesko, and David P. Silverman. *Religion in Ancient Egypt: Gods, Myths, and Personal Practice*. Ithaca: Cornell University Press, 1991.

Shaw, John. *The Self in Social Work*. London: Routledge & Kegan Paul, 1974.

Simpson, William Kelly. *The Literature of Ancient Egypt*. Third Edition. New Haven: Yale University Press, 2003.

Smith, G. Elliot and Warren R. Dawson. *Egyptian Mummies*. London: Kegan Paul International, 1991.

Bibliography

Stalcup, Brenda. *Ancient Egyptian Civilization*. San Diego: Greenhaven Press, 2001.

Star, Cecie, Christine A. Evers and Lisa Starr, *Biology: Today and Tomorrow*. 3rd Edition. Mason: Cengage Learning, 2010.

Tait, John. *Never Had the Like Occurred: Egypt's View of Its Past*. London: UCL Press, 2003.

Teeter, Emily. "Maat." In *The Oxford Encyclopedia of Ancient Egypt*. Volume 2, 319-321. Edited by Donald B. Redford. New York: Oxford University Press, 2001.

Tetteh, Benjamin. "2019: Year of Return for African Diaspora." *African Renewal: Dec. 2018 – Mar. 2019*. https://www.un.org/africarenewal/magazine/december-2018-march-2019/2019-year-return-african-diaspora. Accessed 8 October 2020.

The Holy Bible: *Comprising the Old and New Testaments*. The King James Version. New York: American Bible Society, 1972.

The Metropolitan Museum of Art. *Egyptian Wall Paintings: The Metropolitan Museum of Art's Collection of Facsimiles*. New York: The Metropolitan Museum of Art, 1983.

Tobin, Vincent Arieh. *Theological Principles of Egyptian Religion*. New York: Peter Lang Publishing, Inc., 1989.

Unesco. *The Peopling of ancient Egypt and the Deciphering of Meroitic Script: Proceedings of the Symposium Held in Cairo From 28 January to 3 February 1974*. Paris: Unesco, 1978.

Van De Mieroop, Marc. *A History of Ancient Egypt*. Malden: Wiley-Blackwell, 2011.

Van Der Toorn, Karel, Bob Becking and Pieter W. Van Der Horst. *Dictionary of Deities and Demons in the Bible*. Second Edition, Extensively Revised. Grand Rapids: William B. Eerdmans Publishing, 1999.

Van Sertima, Ivan. *Black Women in Antiquity*. New Brunswick: Transaction Publishers, 1984.

Van Sertima, Ivan. *Blacks in Science: Ancient and Modern*. New Brunswick: Transaction Publishers, 1983.

Webster's New World Dictionary & Thesaurus. Version 2.0, Build #25. Accent Software International. Macmillan Publishers, 1998.

Wilkinson, Richard H. *The Complete Temples of Ancient Egypt*. New York: Thames & Hudson, 2000.

Williams, Bruce. "The Lost Pharaohs of Nubia." In *Journal of African Civilizations* 4, no. 2 (November 1982): 38-52.

Williams, Chancellor. *The Destruction of Black Civilization: Great Issues of a Race from 4500 B.C. to 2000 A.D.* Third Edition. Chicago: Third World Press, 1987.

Wilson, Epiphanius. *Egyptian Literature: Comprising Egyptian Tales, Hymns, Litanies, Invocations, the Book of the Dead, and Cuneiform Writings*. Revised Edition. New York: Colonial Press, 1901.

Wilson, John A. *The Culture of Ancient Egypt*. Chicago: The University of Chicago Press, 1957.

Wimby, Rekhety. "The Unity of African Languages." In *Kemet and the African Worldview*. Edited by Maulana Karenga and Jacob Carruthers. Los Angeles: University of Sankore Press, 1986.

Wiredu, Kwasi (Ed.). *A Companion to African Philosophy*. Malden: Blackwell Publishing, 2004.

Young, Serinity (Ed.). *Encyclopedia of Women and World Religion*. Volume 1. New York: Macmillan Reference USA, 1999.

Zandee, Jan. "Hymnical Sayings, Addressed to the Sun-God by the High-Priest of Amun Nebwenenef, from His Tomb in Thebes." In *Jaarbericht: Van Het Vooraziatisch-Egyptisch Genootschap, Ex Oriente Lux*, no. 18. Leiden: Ex Oriente Lux, 1964.

INDEX

A

Aboubacry Lam, 57
Abyssinia, 40, 41. *See* Ethiopia
Account of Creation, 37, 59
Africa, 31, 40, 41, 58
African, 25, 41, 58, 59
Afterlife, 42, 43, 44, 53
Akhu, 54
Amen, 5, 11, 12, 13, 17, 18, 19, 20, 53, 56, 59
Amenemaopet, 57
Amenemhet I, 27, 32
Amenhotep III, 1
Amenirdis, 32
Amenism, 4, 12, 14, 19, 34, 36, 39, 41, 50, 53, 57, 58, 59
Amenist, 14, 20, 22, 37, 44, 50, 53, 55, 59
Amenta, 53, 54. *See* Heaven
Ancestors, 2, 10, 41, 55, 57, 58, 59, 158
Añew, 54
Ani, 12, 59
Anthony Browder, 40
Anu [Ethnicity], 158. *See also* Kemetan [Ethnicity]
Anu (Heliopolis), 13, 56
Anup, 17
Asa Grant Hilliard, 34
Ascension, 21, 43
Assimilation, 21, 54

B

Ba, 1, 12, 21, 53, 54
Baki, 39
Baptized by Fire. *See* Born of Spirit
Begotten of Spirit, 17, 18, 20
Birth of Heru, 17, 19
Birth of Ra, 54
Birth of the Soul. *See* Spiritual Rebirth
Black, 11, 15, 22, 25, 31, 40, 58, 59
Black Community of Christ, 25, 41, 58
Book of Coming Forth as the Newborn Sun, 19, 21, 43, 54, 55
Book of Gates, 36
Born of Spirit, 17, 20
Bread [Maat], 37, 54
Breath of Life, 11
Bruce Williams, 39
Butterfly Clamps, 25
Byblos, 16

C

Caesar Domitianus Sebastus, 24

Christ, 23, 24, 25, 31, 36, 41, 53, 54, 58
Christhood, 60
Christianity, 6, 23
Christ Monogram, 23, 25, 54. *See also* X-fastener
Coffin Texts, 42, 44
Color Line, 71
Color Symbolism, 59
Coronation, 30
Crook and Flail, 33

D

Damnation, 36
Day of Great Reckoning, 53
Day of Judgment. *See* Day of Great Reckoning
Day of the Great Coming Forth, 19
Death of Osir, 16
Death of the King, 21, 22
December 25th. *See* Birth of Heru
Declaration of Maat, 43, 53
Declarations of Innocence, 43, 44
Delegate, 27, 28, 30
Delusional Sense of Superiority (DSS), 7
Desert, 31
Diodorus Siculus, 40
Divine Birth, 17, 18, 19, 20
Divine Law, 1, 13, 18, 34, 35, 42, 43, 44, 45, 46, 47, 48, 49, 50, 51, 52, 53
Divine Revelation, 13, 14, 34, 44, 53
D. M. Murdock, 24
Duat, 54. *See* Kingdom of Heaven
Duauf, 10

E

East Africa, 39

E. A. Wallis Budge, 7, 38
Erica Tree, 16
Ethiopia, 31, 39, 40, 41. *See* Abyssinia
Ethnicity, 58
Exodus, 6

F

Feast of the New Year, 55
Flesh of Ra, 50
Flocks of God, 34
Forty-Two Divine Judges, 43
Frankincense, 24
Free Will, 18, 35, 42, 53

G

Gaston Maspero, 41
Gateway, 14, 22, 59
George G. M. James, 21, 26, 40
Gerald Massey, 23
Ghana, 58
Gift-Giving, 54
Glorified Spirit, 54. *See* Akhu
God's Wife, 19
God's Will, 35, 42. *See also* Will of God
Good Herdsman, 33
Good Shepherd, 33
Great Ancestor-God, 15
Great Collar, 23, 54
Great God, 11
Great Hall of Maati, 43, 53
Great House, 7, 38
Great Lakes, 39
Great Pyramid, 4, 30
Greeks, 11, 12, 23, 39, 40, 57

H

Hall of Judgment. *See* Great Hall of Maati
Hatshepsut, 33, 37

Index

Heaven, 13, 15, 18, 21, 35, 36, 53, 54, 57. *See* Amenta
Heavenly Father, 18, 20, 26
Herdsman, 33, 34
Herodotus, 10, 40, 73
Heru, 15, 17, 18, 19, 20, 21
Heteros, 6, 69
Hetkaptah (Memphis}, 13, 40
Holocaust of Enslavement, 57
Holy Land, 40
Holy Trinity, 15, 19, 20
Hor, 3
Human Equality, 42
Huyshery, 35

I

Ib, 12
Image of God, 11, 14, 50, 77
Immortality, 21, 42, 53, 54
Infinite Potentiality, 2, 14, 22, 32, 60
Innate Predisposition, 34, 37, 42
Inspired (by God), 58
Inundation, 31, 41
Invasions, 57
Iset, 15, 16, 17, 19, 25
Isfet, 35, 42, 44
Islam, 2, 65, 157
Island of Elephantine, 59

J

Jerome, 55
Judge, 18, 21, 33
Judgment, 22, 44
June 25th. *See* Birth of Ra
Justified, 18, 36, 43, 54, 55

K

Ka, 12, 21, 40, 53, 54
Kash. *See* Kush
Kemet, 25, 41, 43, 50, 54, 55, 56, 57, 58, 59
Kemetan calendar, 54, 55
Kemetan Clays, 59
Kemetan [Ethnicity], 58. *See also* Anu [Ethnicity]
Kemetans, 42, 57, 60
Khat, 12
Kheti, 4, 9, 10, 11, 27, 34
Khnum, 59
Khu, 12, 54
Kingdom of God on Earth, 41, 57
Kingdom of Heaven, 19, 21, 54. *See* Duat
Know Thyself, 4
Kush, 39, 41. *See* Ta-Seti; *See also* Sudan

L

Laws of Maat. *See* Divine Law
Leadership of the Aggressor, 6
Leadership of the Pharaoh, 3, 7, 8, 60
Leadership of the Supremacist, 6
Libation, 55
Live in Truth, 60

M

Maa-Kheru (True of Voice), 54
Maat, 1, 2, 13, 18, 19, 21, 34, 35, 36, 37, 38, 39, 42, 43, 44, 45, 46, 47, 48, 49, 50, 51, 52, 53, 54, 60. *See also* Ten Cardinal Virtues of Maat
Makhiar, 19
Martin Seligman, 29
Maulana Karenga, 8, 37, 43
Meaning of Life, 59
Medu Netur, 11
Melanin, 50
Mena, 39
Merikara, 4

Migration, 40, 58
Migratory Waves, 57
Mission of Life, 36
Monotheistic, 11
Moral Offense, 51, 69, 145
Mummification, 14, 16, 24, 25
Mummy, 23, 24
Myrrh, 24
Mystery System, 19, 20, 21, 25, 26, 36, 41, 60

N

Na'im Akbar, 7
Nana Akufo-Addo, 58
New Year, 54, 55, 56
New Year's Greeting, 55
New Year's Wishes, 55
Nile Crab. *See* Oxyrhynchid
Nile River, 16, 31, 39
Nitocris, 33
Nubia, 39, 41. *See* Ta-Seti; *See also* Sudan

O

Oimellas, 55
Omo Valley, 39
Oral Tradition, 58
Osir, 15, 16, 17, 18, 19, 21, 23, 25, 31, 33, 34, 43, 54, 55, 58
Osirian, 23, 24
Ostrich Feather, 54
Oxyrhynchid, 16

P

Papyrus at Leyden, 11, 12, 42, 44, 75
Per-aa, 7
Perfection of Being, 54
Petosiris, 35
Piankhi, 32
Placemaker, 32, 33, 37, 38

Plutarch, 15
Potter's Wheel, 59
Prayer, 10, 11, 12, 26
Proximal Separation, 20, 21
Ptah, 11, 13, 37, 40
Ptahhotep, 1, 3, 5, 6
Purpose of Life, 37

R

Ra, 11, 12, 13, 20, 34, 36, 42, 50, 54, 55, 56
Rameses II, 56
Rameses III, 33, 38
Red, 15, 59
Reemergent Kingdom, 55, 59
Reflective Arts, 2, 60
Religion, 10
Resurrection of Osir, 17, 18, 19
Resurrection (Proper), 21, 43
Revelatory-Perception, 14, 82
Richard King, 50

S

Sahu, 23, 43
Salvation. *See* Spiritual Salvation
Scripture, 37, 50, 53, 58
Second Death, 22, 53
Sense-Perception, 79, 82
Sepdta, 19
Sesostris I, 8, 27, 60
Sesostris III, 14
Seth, 15, 16, 18, 59
Sethi I, 1, 35, 56
Seven Wonders of the World, 4
Sin. *See* Moral Offense
Sirius. *See* Sepdta
Skin Pigmentation, 50, 58
Sobekneferu, 33
Socialization, 34
Social Responsibility, 33, 34
Son of God, 19

Index

Son of Ra, 20
Son of the Sun. *See* Son of Ra
Sothis, 19, 20. *See* Sepdta
Spiritual Death, 21, 22
Spiritual Insight, 4, 5, 9, 13, 14, 26, 82
Spirituality, 10, 14
Spiritual Knowledge, 4, 5, 9, 13, 14, 26, 82
Spiritually Unborn, 20, 21
Spiritual Rebirth, 17, 20, 21, 59
Spiritual Resurrection, 19, 20, 21, 59
Spiritual Revival, 16, 17, 19, 20, 21, 59
Spiritual Salvation, 20, 21, 35, 36, 59
Spiritual Understanding, 4, 5, 9, 14, 26, 82
Spiritual Union, 10, 19, 20, 21, 22, 25, 26, 36, 59
Stela, 14
Stephanie Fitzgerald, 31
Sudan, 39. *See also* Ta-Seti
Sudanese, 31, 39

T

Table of the Sun, 55. * Table of Ra
Ta-Seti, 39, 40, 41. *See also* Sudan
Tawesret, 33
Tekhi, 12, 13, 14, 16, 17, 18
Temple of Ptah, 40
Ten Bodily Fetters, 35, 44
Ten Cardinal Virtues of Maat, 34. *See also* Maat
Theophile Obenga, 33
Three Days, 16, 19
Thutmose III, 29
Transfigured [Soul], 54
Transmute, 14
Trinity, 15, 19, 20

Triune, 11, 22, 123
Triune-Phase Spirit of God, 13, 25
True Life, 18, 20, 21, 36
True of Voice, 18, 54
Two Paths, 42

V

Virgin, 17, 18, 20
Virgin Birth. *See* Divine Birth
Vizier, 1, 3, 5, 10, 29

W

Waset (Thebes), 13, 32, 56
West Africa, 57, 58
White, 15, 23, 71, 160
Will of God, 5, 14. *See also* God's Will
Winter Solstice, 19
Wisdom, 3, 4, 5, 6, 9, 12, 14, 26, 33, 34, 36, 60
Wisdom Teachings, 27
Written in Our Heart, 13

X

X-fastener, 25. *See also* Christ Monogram

Y

Year of Return, 58
Yellow, 59

Z

Z.T.E., 55, 58

www.ingramcontent.com/pod-product-compliance
Lightning Source LLC
Chambersburg PA
CBHW071920290426
44110CB00013B/1425